0050317

DATE DUE

APR. 4 1994	
JUN. 22 1994	
MAR. 15 1995	

FOLK TREASURES OF MEXICO

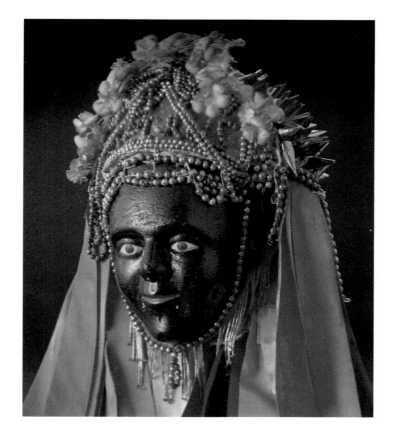

FOLK TREASURES

The Nelson A. Rockefeller Collection
in the San Antonio Museum of Art and the Mexican Museum, San Francisco

OF MEXICO

By Marion Oettinger, Jr.

Foreword by Nelson A. Rockefeller

Preface by Ann Rockefeller Roberts

Introduction by Avon Neal

Commentaries on the plates by Annie O'Neill

Plate photographs by Lee Boltin and John Dyer

HARRY N. ABRAMS, INC., PUBLISHERS, NEW YORK

Folk art has in it the pulse beat of the human hand.

—Pál Kelemen, *Vanishing Art of the Americas,* 1977

Editor: Margaret Blythe Rennolds
Designer: Dana Sloan

On page 1:
Negrito Mask. Michoacán. San Antonio Museum of Art (detail of Plate 59)

On pages 2–3:
Teodora Blanco. **Animal Band.** Oaxaca. Mexican Museum, San Francisco, and San Antonio Museum of Art (Plate 86)

Note on the plate captions:
The abbreviations MM and SAMA stand for the Mexican Museum, San Francisco, and the San Antonio Museum of Art, respectively.

Library of Congress Cataloging-in-Publication Data
Oettinger, Marion.
   Folk treasures of Mexico: the Nelson A. Rockfeller Collection/
by Marion Oettinger, Jr.; foreword by Nelson A. Rockefeller;
preface by Ann Rockefeller Roberts; introduction by Avon Neal;
commentaries on the plates by Annie O'Neill; photographs of the
plates by Lee Boltin and John Dyer.
        p.   cm.
   Includes bibliographical references.
   ISBN 0–8109–1182–5
   1. Folk art—Mexico. 2. Rockefeller, Nelson A. (Nelson Aldrich),
1908–1979—Art collections. 3. Folk art—Private collections—New
York (N.Y.)   I. Title.
NK844.035   1990
745′ .0972′ 07473—dc20   90–30088
                                                               CIP

Published in 1990 by Harry N. Abrams, Incorporated, New York
All rights reserved. No part of the contents of this book may be
reproduced without the written permission of the publisher

A Times Mirror Company

Printed and bound in Japan

Contents

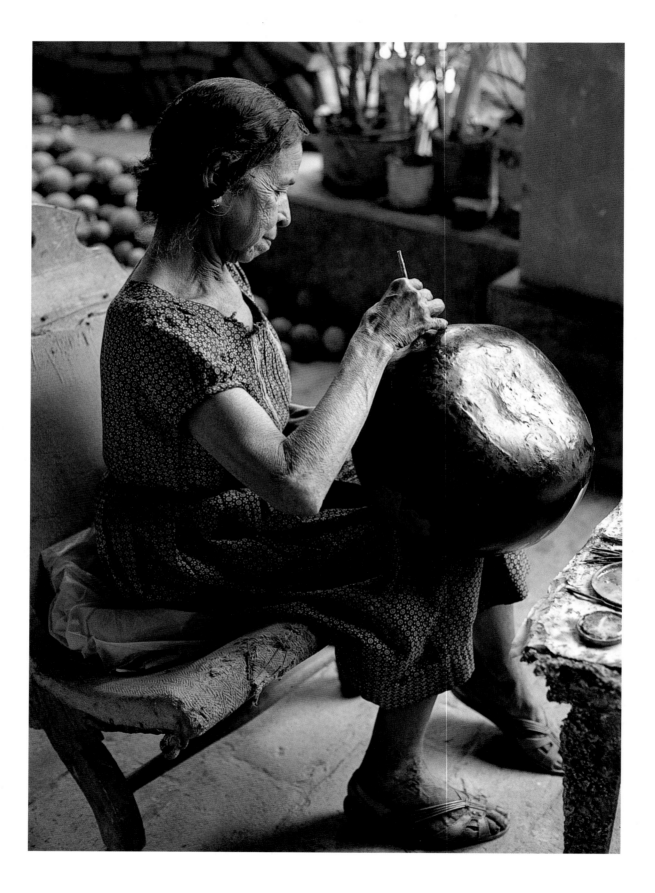

Contents

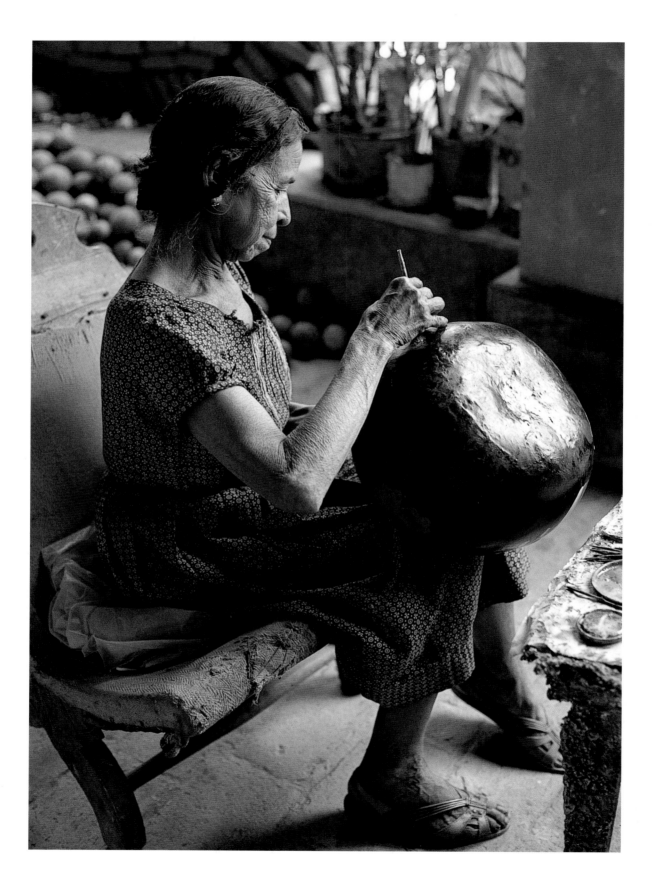

Acknowledgments

This book owes a great deal to many people. It was essentially a work of collaboration not only between author and photographers but also with others who knew Nelson Rockefeller and were able to provide valuable personal insight into his love for and commitment to Mexican folk art. Ann R. Roberts, daughter of the late Governor Rockefeller, is responsible for purchasing the collection from her father's estate and for painstakingly locating a permanent home for it, thereby assuring its preservation. She has been the catalyst for this book, and I am grateful for her vision of its necessity and importance and for her constant help, support, and encouragement throughout this entire endeavor.

Annie O'Neill, artist, folk art specialist, and former adviser to Nelson Rockefeller on his collection, has been a close friend and collaborator during this project. She worked closely with Rockefeller on his collection and traveled to Mexico with him and Ann Roberts to photograph folk artists and to make new acquisitions. She also curated the collection before it found its way to final homes in San Antonio and San Francisco. Her special sensitivity to the collection and deep respect for Nelson Rockefeller have been important to the overall success of this project.

Since an important part of understanding Mexican folk art is through visual means, it was absolutely crucial that the photographs for the book be of the highest quality. Lee Boltin, an internationally respected photographer who had collaborated with Rockefeller on two earlier art projects, began work on this material in 1978, and most of the photographs of the objects were made by him. The rest were shot by John Dyer, from San Antonio, and Steve Tucker, of New York City. They bring to this publication not only superb understanding of photographic techniques and methods but also

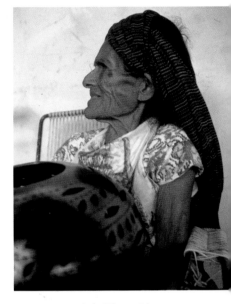

Doña Rosa Real de Nieto with one of her decorative pieces, San Bartolo Coyotepec, Oaxaca, October 1978

A lacquered gourd being carefully decorated with traditional floral motifs in Chiapa de Corzo, Chiapas, 1976

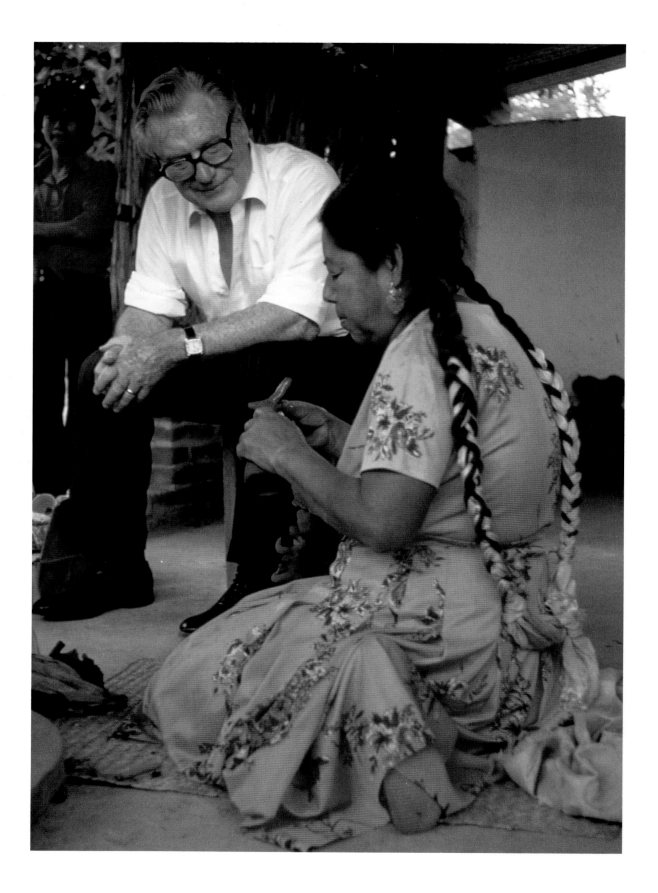

remarkable sensitivity to the objects themselves. I thank them for sharing these gifts with us.

I interviewed many people who knew Nelson Rockefeller well and who generously provided important perspectives on his great passion for art in general and his love for Mexican folk art in particular. Among those whose insights were most important to the formation of this book were Laurance Rockefeller, Mary Rockefeller, Rodman Rockefeller, Christine Roussell, Carl Fox, and Susan Herter. Their views on Rockefeller's love of Mexico, her people, and her art have added warmth and special understanding to our book, and I greatly appreciate the time and thoughts they shared with me. To properly understand Nelson Rockefeller's involvement in Mexican folk art requires a familiarity with the happenings of the 1930s and 1940s in Mexico that brought to light the existence of that country's popular arts. I interviewed dozens of people who collectively painted for me a vivid picture of the intellectual and artistic currents of that exciting time in Mexico that had held Rockefeller's attention so firmly. Among those whose thoughts were most helpful were Sarah d'Harnoncourt (Mrs. René), Mildred Constantine, and Dr. Merle Wachter.

Dr. Joseph Ernst, director emeritus of the Rockefeller Archive Center in North Tarrytown, New York, generously gave of his time, knowledge, and energy to guide me through myriad boxes of documents, and his kind assistance is greatly appreciated. Claire Collier, also of the center, graciously assisted me in locating valuable photographs in the archives, some of which are included in this book.

I also acknowledge the help of Mary Kreske and Kendall Lutkins, of the Rockefeller offices in New York City, who kindly assisted me in locating other important relevant material that had not yet found its way to the permanent family archives.

Few manuscripts make it into print without the help of good editors, and I was lucky to have several people who read and commented on mine. John Mahey, former director of the San Antonio Museum of Art, and John Olbrecht carefully read my manuscript and made valuable comments on

Rockefeller talking with Teodora Blanco, Santa María Atzompa, Oaxaca, October 1978

content and style. Patty Spencer, Gretchen Schumacher, and Didi Cowley also helped with the manuscript preparation, and I thank them for their assistance. Baker Duncan and Dr. Ronald Calgaard of Trinity University in San Antonio generously arranged an office for me to escape the clutter and clatter of my normal museum work space, and I thank them for their kind hospitality. I worked closely with several key people at Abrams on the editing and production phases of this book. Margaret Rennolds, Abrams' project director for this publication, did an excellent job of sorting out inconsistencies and duplications in both form and content. She shepherded the manuscript through its many steps toward production, and I thank her for her skillful labors. Dana Sloan, who designed the book, showed that she has not only a keen eye for design but also a strong sensitivity for the text and photographs.

Finally, I thank my wife, Jill, for abiding the great amount of time I had to spend away from home and for her love and support during this entire project.

—Marion Oettinger, Jr.
Curator of Folk Art and Latin American Art,
San Antonio Museum of Art,
San Antonio, Texas

In addition to joining with my own heartfelt thanks in acknowledging the many people recognized by Marion Oettinger, Jr., I would like to make a few acknowledgments of my own.

This book had a firm base in the splendid photographs taken by Lee Boltin, which made all the difference in putting it together after Father's death. The delight Father had in Lee's company and their banter as they worked was a pleasure to see and reflected the spirit of both men. Annie O'Neill has been a wonderful friend and collaborator throughout this entire process. From the initial search for a home for the collection, to the selection of photographs, the writing of the commentaries on the plates, and almost every other phase of the book, she has lent her untiring support and considerable skills. Before the collection was released to its final homes, the inventory was done meticulously by David Fawcett; he also organized the packing and shipping of the fragile objects with tender care and attention to every detail.

The staff, trustees, and friends of both the San Antonio Museum of Art (SAMA) and the Mexican Museum (MM), in San Francisco, were wonderfully efficient and attentive to the collection during the transition. I am particularly grateful to John Mahey, the former director of the SAMA, and David de la Torre, the former director of the MM, for their guidance and the enjoyment of working with them. I am most appreciative of the generosity of the SAMA in allowing Marion Oettinger to take a leave of absence in order to research and write the text for this book. His fine work as an anthropologist, a researcher, and a writer speaks for itself in the quality of his text, and it has also been a real pleasure to work with him. His unflagging enthusiasm for this project and his devotion to Mexican folk art inform every part of his contribution. Avon Neal's willingness to take time out from his own folk art work to write the introduction is very much appreciated and brings an important dimension to the book as well.

In addition to the editors already mentioned, my thanks go to Jon Swan for his substantial assistance with the organization of the text. Richard Parsons' legal skills and clearheadedness were essential in untangling the book from past commitments, and he gave willingly of his time.

Finally, my thanks go to my family for encouraging me to take on this project and see it through to completion. My uncle Laurance never waived in his support of me and his belief in this book. He and Father's widow, Happy Rockefeller, made it possible for me to acquire the collection and the rights to the book. My children and my husband T. George Harris were unquestioning in their loving support and enthusiasm.

—Ann Rockefeller Roberts

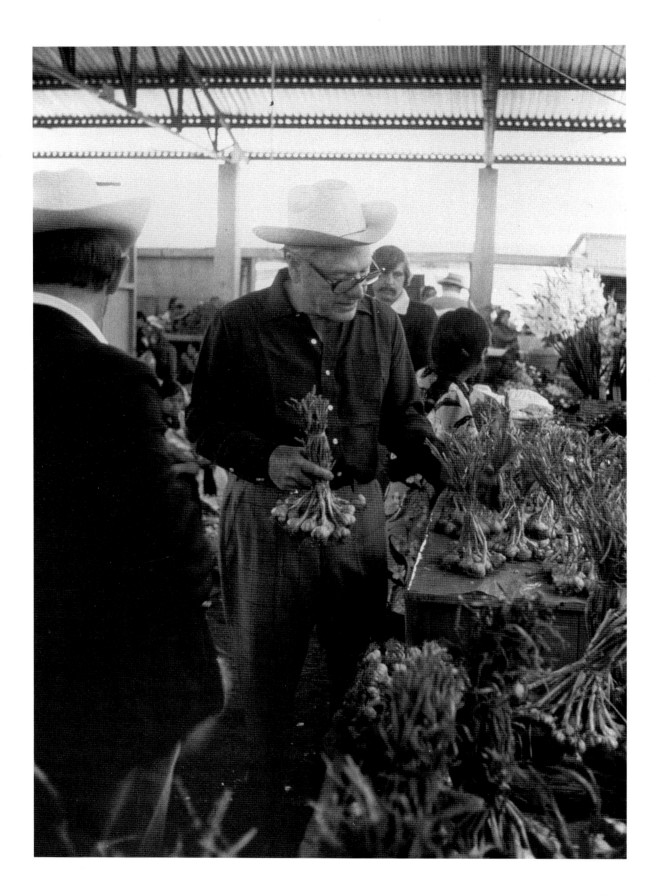

Foreword by Nelson A. Rockefeller

October/November 1978

As I start to write these words for the introduction of this book on "Arte Popular de México," I'm flying across the Gulf of Mexico, on my way to Oaxaca to participate in the celebrations of the Día de los Muertos—the Day of the Dead. In Mexico, and especially in Oaxaca, this is a day of special significance in the Indian folklore of the country. It is celebrated by an outpouring of the entire community following weeks of preparation by local craftsmen who create the original, colorful, and exotic figures, decorations, costumes, and carvings that become an integral part of the celebration. The Day of the Dead, as no other festival in Mexico, brings forth joyously the traditions of past centuries. It reveals in heightened form the unique qualities of the Mexican people, qualities that combine an inherent sense of human dignity with sensitivity and gentleness; great imagination and fantastic ability with love of family and pride in the country's rich and varied cultural heritage.

To one who loves Mexico and the Mexican people and profoundly admires the breathtaking evidences of their twenty centuries of artistic creations, this great festival day has to be one of the most thrilling experiences of one's life. The people are living and celebrating the quintessence of their heritage in a setting of unparalleled beauty—the great temples of Monte Albán reflecting the dignity and glory of the Zapotec civilization, which flourished in the sixth century B.C., and the monumental Spanish colonial cathedrals, the most beautiful of which in Oaxaca is Santo Domingo, built in the sixteenth century for the Spanish conquistadors with exquisite skill by the Indian artisans of the conquered Aztec empire.

In Oaxaca one sees the drama of this endless flow of creativity still pulsating with the vitality of a great people.

Rockefeller buying garlic in the Ocotlán market, Ocotlán de Morelos, Oaxaca, October 1978

 13

Mexican popular art is the outgrowth of this great tradition that, throughout the centuries, has been an integral part of various aspects of the daily lives of the people. It comprises objects made for utilitarian purposes, as religious symbols, and for festivals and celebrations of all kinds—but always expressing the creativity and imagination of the individual artists-craftsmen who fashioned them.

It was just forty-five years ago, in 1933, that I first went to Mexico and discovered the beauty and excitement of this unique land. By good fortune, my wife and I had planned an extensive visit to widely varied regions of the country with their distinct histories and fascinating characteristics.

We were fortunate in the friends we made—Diego Rivera, Miguel and Rosa Covarrubias, Fred Davis, Roberto Montenegro, and Frances Flynn Paine—for it was through their eyes and thanks to their great kindness that we were privileged to see and begin to appreciate the four great epic phases of Mexico's cultural history: the monumental works of the pre-Columbian civilizations, the richness of the colonial period, the unending flow of indigenous popular art, and the tremendous vitality of the modern art movement.

But perhaps the most exciting part of that trip was the time we spent in the small cities, villages, and rural areas with Frances Flynn Paine. Frances had devoted her life to studying the popular arts of the Mexican people. Her knowledge of the art and of the artists throughout the country was encyclopedic. Her love of their works was matched by the affection and respect each artist-craftsman felt for her.

It was a privilege to travel with her from marketplace to marketplace, where the colorful displays—and beautiful fascinating objects—left one breathless. My fascination and enthusiasm resulted in endless purchases of an infinite variety of pottery, wood carvings, sarapes, and handwoven rugs, ranging in price from a few cents to a few dollars. However, invariably there were one or two craftsmen in each area whose work was outstanding and to whose homes we were taken by Frances. There we came to know the gentle warmth and hospitality so typical of the Mexican people and experience the thrill of watching creation in its simplest and most genuine form. Thanks to Frances' knowledge and love of the people and their art, we gained unique insight into Mexican popular art.

I have never stopped collecting in this field since. Now, forty-five years after that first visit, I am on my way back to Oaxaca for a final visit before completing this book on one of the most exciting and colorful phases in the rich cultural history of Mexico. With me in the airplane are my daughter Ann Roberts and Lee Boltin, the photographer for the book.

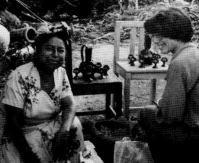

Teodora Blanco with Rockefeller's daughter Ann R. Roberts, Santa María Atzompa, Oaxaca, October 1978

Annie O'Neill and Carl Fox were at the airport to meet us, having made all the arrangements for the ensuing day's visits.

The extraordinary good fortune was that some of the greatest original artists and potters were still creating with the same vigor, insights, and sensitivities: Teodora Blanco, Doña Rosa, and members of the Aguilar family.

We went, that first afternoon, directly to Teodora Blanco's house in a small village outside of Oaxaca. She was there with her large family, including children and relatives, all living in a courtyard with lovely trees, flowers, old buildings, chickens, goats, and a little pig tied with a string to an old broken-down truck. The little pig kept up a shrill squeal until, about halfway through our visit, someone finally fed it. Teodora worked on the veranda of the house, which also served as a storage place for her pottery figures. The kiln was in the courtyard, just in front.

Our arrival was like a reunion full of warmth and enthusiasm. After the initial greetings and *abrazos,* Teodora showed us her latest, almost monumental, figures, which were more elaborately decorated than her earlier work. Later, as we watched her sculpt as she swiftly modeled an allegorical horned figure holding a child in each arm, describing what she was doing as she worked, it was easy to understand the evolution in her work. She is a person of such an active mind, so feeling and creative, that one thought leads to another and each is expressed in sculptural form through some additions to or elaboration of the piece in hand—with lightning speed and sensitivity.

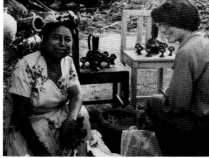

Annie O'Neill visiting the home of Doña Rosa during the October 1978 trip to Mexico

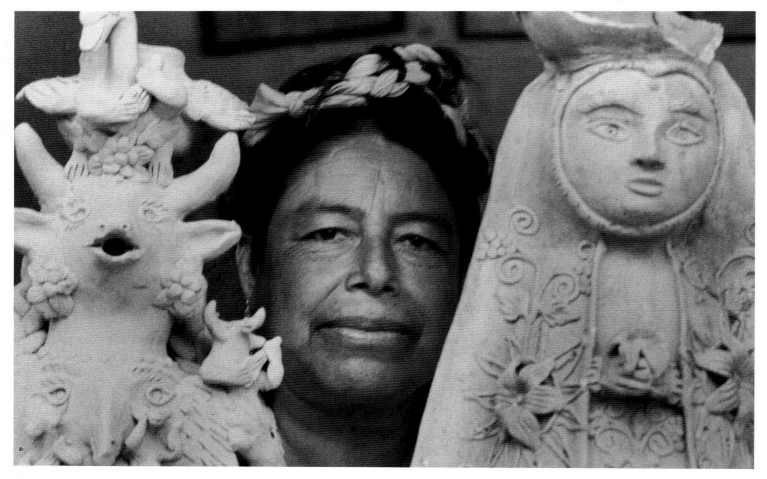

Ceramic artist Teodora Blanco, of
Santa María Atzompa, surrounded
by her pieces, reveals her stylistic
facility and typical use of abundant
surface decoration, October 1978

The result is that her compositions increasingly resemble the paintings of her environs in both their imagination and their bizarre compositions.

We spent two fascinating hours with Teodora, talking with her and selecting objects for purchase. Although they ranged in price from a few cents to less than a hundred dollars for her largest monumental piece, aesthetically they represented a subtle sophistication possessed by but few of the finest contemporary artists. Already we felt more than rewarded for the two-thousand-mile trip.

After leaving Teodora, we drove farther out into the country to a larger village with a large plaza shaded by majestic old trees. This was Ocotlán. The plaza was carpeted with the most colorful pottery, basketwork, raffia weaving, and wooden furniture. Woolen handwoven sarapes and blankets hung on ropes strung between trees. The entire area was alive with Indians, the men wearing big hats, coming and going, picking their way through the crowds, buying and selling, while the women sat quietly, weaving raffia, embroidering, feeding their babies, and enjoying the hustle and bustle of this important weekly social event.

We wove our way through the fabulous variety of objects, one more fascinating than the next, watching potters paint their wares, and all the time trying to spot the unusual and especially beautiful creations. We bought objects here and there, and as we came back to where the great displays of pottery were spread out, Annie O'Neill presented me with a large, beautifully decorated dish that she had had the artist inscribe: *"Al gobernador, un recuerdo de Ocotlán"* ("to the governor, a souvenir of Ocotlán"), which was typical of her thoughtful sensitivity and love of Mexican popular art.

From Ocotlán we drove, at sunset, up the mountain to the monumental Zapotec temples, from which one looks out over the whole valley. There the ancestors of the Oaxaca Indians of today flourished more than 2,500 years ago. The dignity and cultural vitality of the ancestors live on in a never-ending flow of creativity and in the people's respect for the honor of the individual.

The events of that first day brought back vivid memories of the very

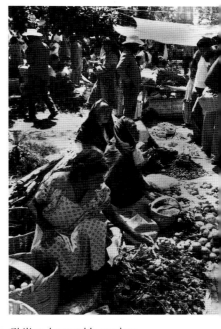

Chili and vegetable vendors, Ocotlán de Morelos, Oaxaca, October 1978

Pottery vendor at the Friday market, Ocotlán de Morelos, Oaxaca, October 1978

Woman arranging lemons at the Friday market, Ocotlán de Morelos, Oaxaca, October 1978

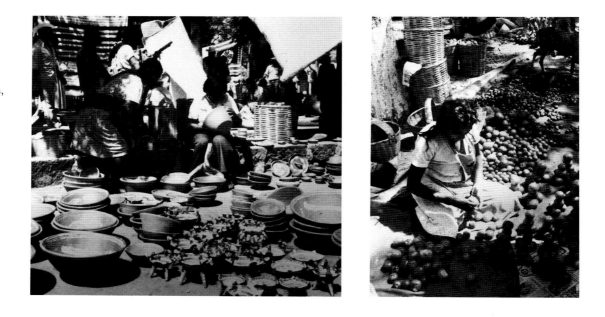

similar days we had spent with Frances Flynn Paine forty-five years before.

I remember especially two experiences—one, a visit to the last of the great sarape weavers, an elderly Indian woman whose weaving was so fine that no one of the younger generation had the patience to develop the skills required to carry it on. I was so excited by her wonderful work that I bought virtually her entire collection. Although I have continued to collect hand-woven sarapes and blankets ever since, I have never found anything to compare with the work of that beautiful and gentle little lady who was so pleased by the joy we derived from her works.

The other experience that stands out in my memory from that first visit to Mexico was my encounter with the outstanding Indian sculptor Mardonio Magaña, in Mexico City. We first saw one of his works in a square near the San Angel Inn, at which we were staying, in a Mexico City suburb. This piece of sculpture evidenced such sensitivity and humanity, as well as artistic quality, that I asked Mrs. Paine if she could make arrangements for a visit to his studio.

Mardonio Magaña was as beautiful and gentle as his sculpture. Without hesitation, I bought two of his stone pieces and two wood carvings, each of which manifested the same deep love and sensitive human understanding of the Mexican campesino that I had found in his larger piece in the square.

There was an immediate bond of sympathy between us and out of this grew a warm friendship. Magaña asked if we would like to visit the school he had started to teach children to sculpt. We said we would be delighted, and the following day we went with him to the school. It was an overwhelming experience—a few dozen children in their teens working on a wide variety of stones, carving wood, or casting in metal. The quality of their work, inspired by this extraordinary man, was unbelievably good.

I couldn't help thinking of the enormous reserves of talent that existed among the Indian people of this great country—talent that the rulers and high priests of the pre-Columbian emperors had so effectively mobilized and that the Spanish conquistadors and the clergy of the Spanish Church had again called upon to create one of the richest and most beautiful colonial periods in history.

There, in Mardonio Magaña's studio, five hundred years after the first Spanish architect-builders had retrained Indian artisans, those same talents were being awakened and redirected into modern forms of expression. It was a moving experience to see these young artists so absorbed in their work. We watched in wonder at the way Magaña—through his example and his love—inspired them to create in a totally natural and unselfconscious manner.

I asked with some hesitation whether it might be possible to purchase a few pieces. Magaña was thrilled and said the children would be delighted because we were the first people to have visited the school and none of the children's work had ever been sold. I ended up buying twenty-two pieces for a total of $220. No purchase has given me more lasting pleasure.

Since my first visit to Mexico in the 1930s, I have sensed something strong, imaginative, and beautiful about her popular arts, and I have collected it and lived with it in my house ever since.

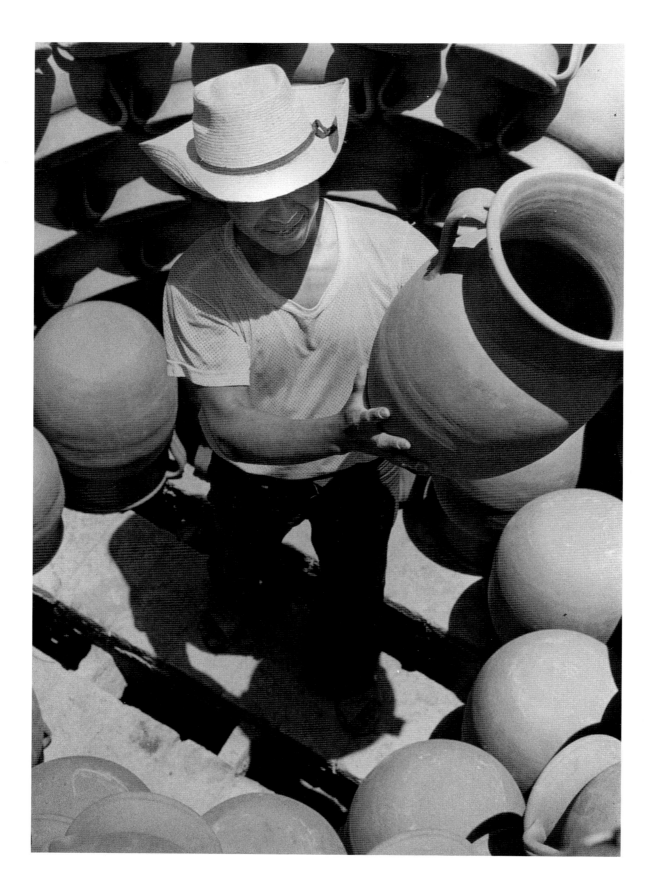

Preface

This book represents the final stage of a ten-year odyssey that began in 1979, shortly after the death of my father, Nelson Aldrich Rockefeller.

It all started with a phone call from him on a Wednesday afternoon in October of 1978. Without preamble and in his exuberant way, he asked if I would like to go to Mexico on Friday for the weekend. Somehow it was clear to me that there might not be another chance like this, so, canceling my own plans, I flew off with my father. It was an amazing weekend, both a mad buying spree and a revisiting of old times and old places. It turned out to be the last trip of this kind he was to make. He died just three months later.

As a result of the trip, I became fully aware for the first time of the extent of Father's Mexican folk art collection and its priceless quality. Even though part of it was exhibited in 1968 at the Museum of Primitive Art in New York, which he founded, most of the collection had been in storage for years, and no one in his family had ever seen it all. Father had unpacked the entire collection early in 1978 in order to have it photographed for this book. It was arrayed on shelf after shelf in a large storage area. His pleasure at seeing it again let loose a flood of stories about his love of folk art and his years of deep involvement in Latin America. It turned out there were nearly 3,000 pieces, many of them no longer being made or extremely rare.

After his death, it became apparent that no one knew exactly what to do with all these thousands of pieces of folk art created by village artists who were better understood by travelers than by museum critics. The works were in danger of being auctioned off or divided up among family members.

Neither option made sense to me. I felt the collection should be preserved and be in a place where both Anglo-Americans and people of Latin descent could see it. Only in that way could the visions that my father had

A potter loading his below-ground kiln in Amozoc, Puebla, October 1978

devoted many years working toward in the early part of his career be realized.

The Rockefeller collection is now securely and happily established in not one but two excellent museums. The major portion is at the San Antonio Museum of Art, the premier art museum in San Antonio, Texas. The other part of the collection is housed at the Mexican Museum in San Francisco, one of the only American museums founded by a Mexican-American artist. In these places, North Americans can see the richness of Mexican culture through her folk arts, and Mexican-Americans can see their own abundant Spanish and Indian folk heritage fully honored—a solution that reflects my father's respect for Latin culture and his desire for it to be represented in the United States.

Publishing this book completes a journey for me as well—the search for a deeper understanding of my father's early involvement with Mexican folk art. This is his book. It honors his unwavering love of Mexican folk art, the Mexican people, and the Mexican culture. He believed in the beauty and artistic power of these pieces, in their lasting value, and in the skill of their creators. He enjoyed many other forms of folk art—American, African, Native American, Indian, and Southeast Asian. However, Mexican folk art was a passion that endured throughout his life, resurfacing whenever there was an opening for him in time or space.

The Mexican people and their art connected father with a deep part of himself. Their exuberance, their close relation to the earth's natural processes, and their sense of the sacredness of the routines of their daily lives were in tune with Father's own inner processes. His naturally extroverted nature blossomed when surrounded by their enthusiasm. I remember, as a child, watching with delight and fascination as father greeted his Mexican friends with a hearty *abrazo*, a natural Latin greeting that would have been impossible among his acquaintances in New York. I think that his love of the Mexican marketplace had as much to do with the openness and vitality of the life there as with the chance to find new treasures.

These folk artists that father was drawn to were part of a culture in which the ordinary events of daily life were celebrated: birth, infancy, adolescence, courtship, marriage, old age, and death. An enormous amount of creative energy was showered onto the special objects that manifested the deeper meaning of these events. He and I came from a culture where the celebrations of life's passages were carefully controlled and made so tidy they were often not fully experienced. Through his folk art collection, Father could savor the Latin joy in life even when he could not be there among the artisans.

This love and understanding of the importance of the ordinary to the essential vitality of life is perhaps the most treasured of the many things I learned from my father. He knew instinctively that the mundane things made to carry out everyday acts—the containers we put things in, the clothing we wear, the religious objects we pray with, the toys we give our children—are all valuable and worthy of the greatest creative expression.

He could also see that it is the nature of the cycles of life to repeat themselves and that folk artists recreate each new birth, life, or death through their art. In this way, the folk arts allow us to renew our own experience and understand the uniqueness of each human passage.

So, reader, in these pages, come to the marketplace with the exuberant collector, my father, who taught me the beauty of the myriad colorful tools of Mexican daily living and who loved the rich flavors of Mexican life.

—Ann Rockefeller Roberts

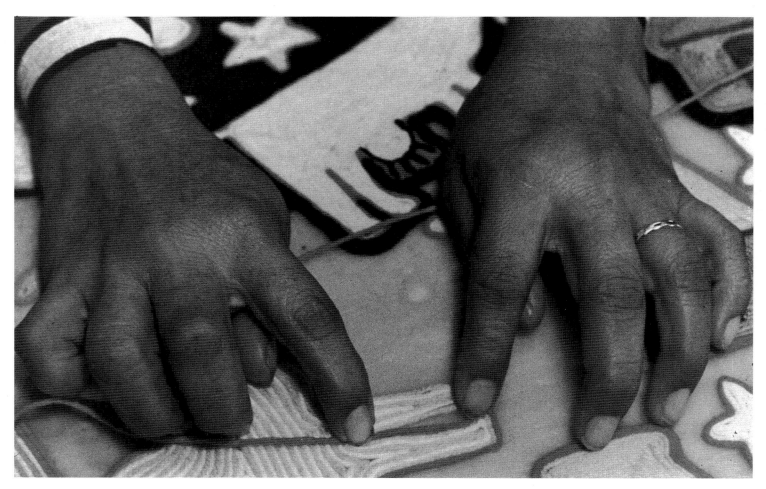

The human hand, always felt in
Mexican folk art, meant a lot to
Rockefeller. In this photograph we
see the hands of Elena Carillo
Hernández at work on a *tabla*,
pressing yarn into beeswax, Mexico
City, October 1978

Introduction

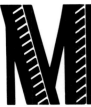exico holds a unique place in the context of modern folk art. Its artisans produce some of the world's most exciting and creative examples of art for the common man. Using whatever materials are found at hand, both organic and inorganic, they fashion a fantastic array of utilitarian and decorative objects ranging from simple toys to highly elaborate ceremonial and religious art. While most of these creations are regional, even local, in concept and design, they have in common a distinctly Mexican character that gives them a supreme sense of national identity. Many of these objects are pre-Hispanic in origin and can be traced by a continuous line through Spanish colonial times to the present day.

Since the early twentieth century, when a widespread cultural awakening inspired a lively interest in things folkloric, Mexico's popular arts have flourished, more or less, in accordance to demand. As tourism increased that demand, local craftsmen labored to meet it. The recent advent of museum shops and specialty stores dealing in ethnic arts is mainly responsible for introducing the best—and, often, the worst—of Mexican folk art to the general public and for elevating it to the exalted position it enjoys today. Well-informed buyers tirelessly scour the countryside searching out hitherto-undiscovered yet talented artists while a whole new generation of discriminating collectors is helping to keep the tradition alive. It is estimated that one person in every six of Mexico's population is involved, either full- or part-time, in the manufacture and sale of "popular art."

After the tragic upheaval of the 1910 revolution—"the wind that swept Mexico"—a wave of confidence pervaded all levels of Mexican society, and during the 1920s a bold new nationalism took hold of the land. Artists and intellectuals began to explore their country's Indian heritage, discovering untapped sources of inspiration for their creative endeavors. A handful of

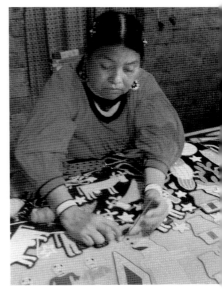

Elena Carillo Hernández, from Las Pilas, Santa Catarina, Nayarit, working on a large yarn painting (*tabla*) in Mexico City, October 1978

connoisseurs and prominent painters, already fascinated by pre-Columbian artifacts, began collecting examples of the everyday art objects that were commonplace in markets. Some of these, they were quick to proclaim, bore an uncanny resemblance to the antique pieces they admired and assiduously collected. They were convinced that these contemporary pieces—carved, molded, woven, painted; some grotesquely beautiful, others inventively decorated utilitarian objects—represented a truly indigenous art expression that sprang from the hearts of their people. They saw in these objects a connection to Mexico's archaeological past, a national heritage, to be appreciated and preserved, something to be championed in the wider world of art.

During the 1930s and 1940s, interest in Mexican folk culture increased by leaps and bounds. Writings on the subject began to appear in books and popular journals. It was not long before exhibitions were being mounted at home and abroad. Viewers liked what they saw and promptly fell into step with the inquisitive surge toward south-of-the-border civilizations that had lately occupied intellectually curious travelers. Tourism from across the northern border was developing rapidly, helping to stimulate arts and crafts production. Merchandising began in earnest, with a number of well-stocked shops such as Cervantes, Victor's Artes Populares Mexicanos, and the colorful but touristy Sanborn's House of Tiles in Mexico City supplying eager buyers with a wide variety of handcrafted objects. Souvenir hunters and serious collectors vied with one another in open-air markets as haphazard accumulations were gradually organized into rudimentary private collections. It was a heady excursion into unexplored territory for those involved with collecting indigenous arts and crafts.

Nelson Rockefeller was in this vanguard of Mexican folk art aficionados. His collecting activities had already brought him into the company of several distinguished Mexican painters, who encouraged and advised him on matters of Latin American art. These were eminent artists such as Miguel Covarrubias, Diego Rivera, Gerardo Murillo (better known as Dr. Atl), Roberto Montenegro, and others who were engaged in revealing the folkloric mysteries of their country's past. As he listened to them extolling the artistic merits of the charming handcrafted objects they were discovering almost daily in local marketplaces, Rockefeller was quick to realize the validity of this art form. It wasn't long before he found himself sharing their passion for what was then most frequently referred to as *artes populares*. He soon succumbed to temptation and started a random gathering of representative pieces on his own. From that time forward, he never stopped.

For Rockefeller, collecting was a labor of love. Luckily, he was not hampered by the conservative academic fetters that so often restrict curators. He simply purchased whatever struck his fancy. It is to his credit and our good fortune that he had the vision and energy to pursue this newfound interest—and, one might add, the means, although money was hardly a factor, since the cost of the carvings, paintings, weavings, and other handcrafted items that so excited those early connoisseurs was reckoned in favorably exchanged pesos and sometimes even in centavos. Although he limited himself to buying only those objects that pleased him, Rockefeller soon accumulated a richly diversified assortment of wonderful folk art pieces, among them some of the finest examples from that fertile period of the 1920s, 1930s, and 1940s. It is a tribute to the man that his efforts resulted in such an extensive and spectacularly varied collection.

Even before his duties as coordinator of the Office of Inter-American Affairs took him officially to Latin America, Rockefeller had acquired an intimate firsthand knowledge of Mexican folk artists and the things they produced. Whenever and wherever he could, he sought out the work of the most skilled and imaginative artisans to augment his growing collection. He visited these people in their humble dwellings, chatted with them in their own language, shared their food, and closely observed how they worked. His open, easy manner fit perfectly with their Latin nature.

The search for superior examples of folk arts and crafts was exhilarating. Dedicated collectors never knew what they might come upon in the next marketplace. One thing was certain: beautiful handwrought art objects were coming to light every day.

A few artisans achieved reputations as particularly talented craftsmen.

They often signed their work, and as competition grew among collectors, they were able to command higher prices for the things they produced. Signing handcrafted items was mostly a matter of personal pride. Once a proper evaluation of folk art was initiated, however, signatures proved important to scholars as a means of facilitating identification and helping to establish a particular piece's provenance. As is the case with most folk-produced art, the large majority of craftsmen remained anonymous. Nonetheless, from that great body of artisans issued a steady flow of vigorous folk art, some pieces every bit as beautiful and skillfully wrought as any of those bearing prestigious signatures. Aesthetic criteria were already being formulated.

In some areas, the makers of folk art seem determined to outdo themselves. An illustrative example involves the Indian's preoccupation with death. In a three-day festival ending on the second of November, Mexico celebrates its traditional Day of the Dead, the nation's most important Indian fiesta. It is famous for the multitudinous ways in which death is alternately mocked and romanticized by young and old alike. This ritual outpouring has contributed an entire genre of festive figures to the folk art repertory. The best are those made in the shape of skulls and skeletons posed in comic, everyday attitudes. Transcending any sense of morbidity, these reminders of man's foibles and mortality often find inspiration in the engravings of Mexico's turn-of-the-century satiric artist José Guadalupe Posada. In turn this great innovator had himself been influenced by graphic and sculptural interpretations of death personified in the folkloric tradition of an ancient cultural background. Workaday artisans—toy-makers, folk painters, clay modelers, woodcarvers, indeed, the whole community of craftspeople— happily devote themselves to this macabre theme. Collectors who prowl village marketplaces just prior to the Day of the Dead can still find folk art treasures strikingly similar to those that so intrigued Rockefeller and his fellow devotees half a century ago.

No dyed-in-the-wool collector will deny that half the fun of collecting is in the chase. For Mexican folk art enthusiasts that chase inevitably leads to the marketplace, whether it be in an urban center or in an isolated mountain village where Indian craftsmen gather on designated days to sell their wares. Some of the best specialized collections (such as those of Nativity tableaux, wooden animals, or lacquerware trays and boxes) have been assembled by hardy souls willing to brave intolerable weather conditions, exasperating transportation problems, and claustrophobia-inducing crowds.

The Mexican market system has been a thriving enterprise for centuries. Examples of certain handicrafts bartered there in pre-Hispanic times can still be found today. Although modernization has sharply modified some of the articles offered for sale, a zealous collector will usually come away with folk art treasures fashioned along traditional lines—pottery in its myriad forms, woven textiles, painted toys, carved gourds, plain or decorated wooden masks, or various utensils for use in field and home.

As in ancient times, today's trading centers swarm with Indians—and, more likely than not, insatiable collectors can be spotted in the crowds. Anyone who has ever visited a village market and been caught up in its stream of bustling humanity will agree that it is an unforgettable experience. Market days are festive occasions and the marketplace itself is a scene of pure exuberance. The exotic sights and riotous colors, the cacophony of sound, and the pungent and aromatic smells blend together to create a fantastic carnival atmosphere. What to an outsider appears to be utter chaos is in reality a controlled exchange of material goods. Despite visible evidence of modern encroachments, the market-day pattern remains essentially unchanged. It is almost a ritualistic performance.

Traditional market days are still observed. Many existed as highlights on the social calendar during Aztec, Toltec, and Mayan times, and were described in detail by Cortez and chroniclers of the conquest. The same kinds of handcrafted products appear in their assigned places. Members of the same families who once counted Rockefeller and his artist friends as customers continue to pursue their respective crafts and to work as regular vendors. Just as they have done from time immemorial, backcountry Indians trek for days through desert wastes or along mountainous trails, carrying heavy loads of pottery and countless other wares. Trucks and buses bring itinerant peddlers from the capital or nearby towns with factory-manufactured goods. The raucous cries of hawkers and vendors compete with the chime of cathedral bells and the blare of jukebox music from cantinas, with the honking of horns and the guttural growl of overloaded buses trying to make their way through milling crowds.

Mexico's complex network of roads and highways, with connections extending from the capital to hundreds of outlying Indian communities, has facilitated a modern-day cultural diffusion in the distribution of arts and crafts. First-, second-, and third-class buses ply the highways at all hours. Since fares are cheap, vendors often travel long distances to sell their wares, thereby perpetuating the classic textbook exchange of goods and ideas. During holidays and special celebrations, buyers join sellers to ride bus lines with such eye-catching and deceptively speed-suggestive names as "Galgos" (Greyhounds), "Estrella Blanca" (White Star), and "Flecha Roja" (Red Arrow) as they follow what are often the same routes traversed by their ancestors to traditional markets in some of the country's remotest villages.

Nelson Rockefeller loved marketplaces. Seeking and finding in exotic surroundings appealed to his spirit of adventure. Much of his Mexican folk art collection is the result of on-the-spot selections made in regional market centers. He had a keen eye for things beautiful and unusual, and he possessed, as well, the inveterate collector's joy of discovery and acquisition. His idea of great fun was to stroll through a busy marketplace, mingling with the colorful crowds that thronged cobbled streets and village plazas. He reveled in sampling local foods, trying out his Spanish, pausing at vendors' stalls and striking up conversations with them. He scrutinized their wares before making a selection. Once satisfied with an object, he made his purchase and hurried on to the next possibility. He thoroughly enjoyed these interchanges and delighted in the pieces he brought home.

The Mexico of Rockefeller's era is fondly remembered as a time when tourists could still count on one hand the traffic lights in downtown Mexico City; when ox carts and burros were common sights along the capital's broad avenues and dusty side streets; when the ubiquitous taxicabs cruised at curbside with beeping horns to solicit fares; when organ-grinders and itinerant photographers pursued their precarious livelihoods in the spacious grounds of Alameda Park; when *cargadores,* those human beasts of burden, could be seen straining against sweaty tumplines as they shuffled along under inhumanly heavy loads; when sidewalks were uncrowded and there were no skyscrapers to block the sun; when noise levels were tolerable and the city's air was unpolluted; when the residential *colonias* were still distinctly separate; when street vendors' cries broke each morning's silence; when village Indians, lately come to town, could still be recognized by their unique costumes; when Mexico City, with all its cultural ebullience and colonial grandeur, was the nation's great gathering place. That was the metropolis that charmed travelers and stimulated collectors to seek out and define the nation's essence in its popular arts and crafts.

Over the years, including a final buying trip to his old haunts in Mexico shortly before his death, Rockefeller amassed more than three thousand representative examples of Mexican folk art, some of them among the best available from that fruitful early period. As with all great collections, this one reflects a unique personal vision, as well as its creator's deep commitment to an indigenous art. The Nelson A. Rockefeller Mexican folk art collection represents a marvelous achievement by a very remarkable man.

—Avon Neal
North Brookfield, Massachusetts

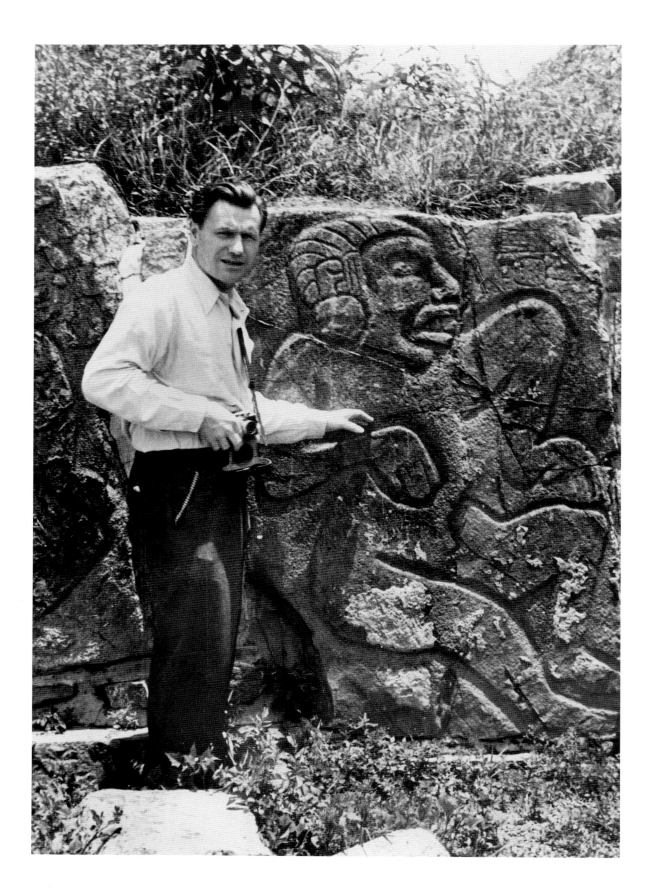

Rockefeller the Collector

*By now I was rapidly gaining a more catholic understanding of the word
"art." I saw "art" as widely varying expressions of individuals—
individuals from all parts of the world and from all ages, with strong
feelings and great creative capacities to express those feelings. No longer was
my appreciation confined to classical forms of art as taught in our schools
and shown in our great universities.*

—Nelson A. Rockefeller[1]

n the spring of 1969 the New York art world hummed with excitement
over the simultaneous openings of three important exhibitions. At the
Metropolitan Museum of Art, an exhibition of one thousand pieces of
primitive art from Oceania, Africa, and the Americas left visitors
dazzled by the intrinsic power and dramatic scale of these long-overlooked
objects. Thirty blocks away, at the Museum of Modern Art, the public was
treated to a remarkably comprehensive survey of modern art: more than two
hundred paintings and sculptures by Cubists, Futurists, Dadaists, and Abstract Expressionists. And, just around the corner, at the Museum of Primitive Art, more than seven hundred pieces of Mexican folk art reminded the
public of Mexico's rich cultural heritage. These three exhibitions represented the best of the creative work of people from all over the world, much of
which had been previously dismissed as unimportant by the Western art
establishment.

Astonishingly, all three exhibitions were drawn from the collections of
one man, Nelson A. Rockefeller, then governor of New York, later vice
president of the United States. The exhibitions provided a close look at the
collections of a man who had been given every opportunity to be at the very
center of fashionable collecting but who had, instead, chosen to go his own

Rockefeller at Monte Albán in 1948

way. While most of his peers were collecting the long-accepted works of the Old Masters and the Impressionists, and European and Oriental porcelains, Rockefeller enthusiastically embraced the aesthetic values and artistic creativity of African tribesmen, Mexican peasants, and New Guinean hunters, as well as relatively unknown contemporary painters and sculptors from the United States and abroad. At the time of his death, in 1979, Rockefeller's entire personal collection contained well over sixteen thousand objects and was recognized internationally for its superb quality and extraordinary range of vision. His activities in the world of art went far beyond mere collecting to demonstrate a strong advocacy of the art that he loved best and an unflagging support both for individual artists and for the public institutions involved in the exhibition and preservation of their work.

Nelson Rockefeller's fascination with and dedication to art in general, and folk and primitive art in particular, were the result of a number of factors. Family, environment, and schooling all contributed to opening up the artistic paths he would pursue in later years.

Being born into one of America's wealthiest families could have isolated Rockefeller in the rarified circles of the rich and famous. Owing to the concerted efforts of his parents, it did not. Instead of sending him to the elite, conservative private schools in the Northeast, his parents enrolled him in New York's Lincoln School, where more attention was given to the study of modern culture and social science than to the classics. From its beginning, Lincoln School provided scholarships for poor and minority students, and so, early on, Nelson was able, and encouraged, to mix with a wide cross section of people.

At the age of eighteen, he entered Dartmouth. During his four years there, his interest in art developed in a variety of ways. He became editor-in-chief of the *Dartmouth Pictorial,* a photographic magazine recording campus life (he took many of the photographs himself). He also became editor of *The Five Lively Arts,* a short-lived journal that featured the works of poets, musicians, and painters. In his senior year he was elected president of *The Arts,* a student club that brought to Dartmouth such distinguished speakers as Carl Sandburg, Edna St. Vincent Millay, and Thornton Wilder, as well as a number of gifted painters. During this year, too, he became interested in American country furniture and folk art, enthusiastically combing the countryside around Hanover, New Hampshire, until he had assembled an impressive collection of Americana. Much of this collection would later be used to furnish Hawes House, his residence on the family's Pocantico Hills estate in Tarrytown, New York.

Although he majored in economics at Dartmouth, Nelson was continually torn between that "logical choice" and another one in which he was becoming passionately involved: art. This conflict would remain with him for the rest of his life and become at times a source of great frustration. Throughout his years at Dartmouth he managed to slip into his schedule a course or two in art. In his senior year, he pursued the study of art, architecture, and landscape architecture. Characteristically, he attacked these subjects with great zeal. His energetic approach to life and art is clearly seen in a letter to his parents in 1930, just months before graduation:

> *Yesterday, I spent the most interesting kind of day possible. In the morning, I went to the Boston Art Museum and spent several hours in the American wing. Then I visited the Egyptian and Greek wings for an hour or so. Before lunch, I stopped at the Boston Library to see the Sargent paintings. In the afternoon, I went out to Cambridge and we made a thorough tour of the Fogg Museum. It was great. Then we stopped in at the Harvard Library to look it over and see Sargent's two murals. And finally we went to visit the exhibition of Modern Mexican painters shown by the Harvard Modern Art Society. . . . I had a minute when I got back to Boston, so I dropped into the Doll and Richards Galleries to see an exhibition of O'Hara's watercolors—he uses lovely fresh colors.[2]*

Even then, Nelson Rockefeller was approaching art as he approached most other things—with gusto and an almost superhuman energy.

In addition to Rockefeller's schooling, the family environment provided important exposure to art and the impetus to collect it. Through his father, John D. Rockefeller, Jr., Nelson was exposed to the more formal and classical art of the masters and the well-established art of Europe and Asia. As well as being a collector, his father put a great deal of his energy toward art philanthropy, most notably the restorations of the Cloisters, Versailles, and Colonial Williamsburg.

It is clear, however, that Nelson's strongest feelings about art came through his mother, Abby Aldrich Rockefeller. In his own words, "The major influence in my life as a collector was my mother. She, in turn, got this interest from her father, Senator Nelson Aldrich, and she spent her life assembling a collection that evolved with her tastes. I think she would have been classified as one of the avant-garde collectors in her day."[3] Abby Aldrich Rockefeller was willing to trust her intuitive response to works of art. She sought out new painters and sculptors who were the bold spokesmen of their era and collected, among other things, primitive art, American folk art, and Japanese prints. At home, Abby Rockefeller installed a changing gallery on the upstairs floor of their West Fifty-fourth Street town house. Later, Nelson would do likewise in his own homes. He clearly resembled his mother

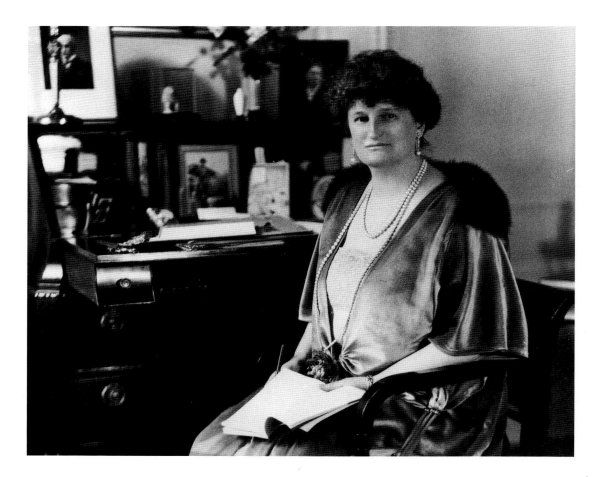

Abby Aldrich Rockefeller, mother of Nelson A. Rockefeller, ca. 1915

physically and in temperament and inherited her unbridled enthusiasm for art, particularly art that was not in the mainstream.

An energetic and creative supporter of public art institutions, Mrs. Rockefeller was the most influential of the three initial founders of the Museum of Modern Art, which opened to the public in November 1929. Her objective for the new museum was "to reduce dramatically the time lag between the artist's creation and the public's approval of great works of art."[4] She also restored Bassett Hall at Colonial Williamsburg and filled it with pieces of American folk art that she and her husband had purchased. When the Folk Art Center at Williamsburg bearing Abby Aldrich Rockefeller's name opened in 1957, it housed 424 splendid examples of American folk art that she had collected from 1929 to 1942.[5]

Abby Rockefeller took pleasure in a shared affinity for art with Nelson, reflected in several letters between them. Early in 1928, while Nelson was still at Dartmouth, he enthusiastically described a weekend he had spent with her in New York:

> *Dear Ma,*
>
> *You don't know how much I enjoyed our two trips to Mr. [Arthur B.] Davies and the visit to the Down Town Galleries. I feel as if I had been introduced to a new world of beauty, and for the first time I think I have really been able to appreciate and understand pictures even though only a little bit. I hope to continue this when I am in New York and maybe do a tiny bit of collecting myself. I feel that was the outstanding event of my vacation.[6]*

Shortly afterward, his mother replied:

> *It would be a great joy to me if you did find you had a real love for and interest in beautiful things. We could have such a good time going about together, and if you start to cultivate your taste and eye so young, you ought to be very good at it by the time you can afford to collect much. To me art is one of the great resources of my life. I feel that it enriches the spiritual life and makes one more sane and sympathetic, more observant and understanding, as well as being good for one's nerves.[7]*

Clearly, Abby Rockefeller's influence on her son's interest in art was profound. Of particular importance to the formation of Nelson Rockefeller's

Mexican folk art collection, however, is the role she played in introducing Nelson to the art of Latin America, especially that of Mexico.

Abby Rockefeller's interest in Mexican art grew out of a visit in early 1928 to an exhibition of Mexican fine and applied arts at the Art Center, a New York organization formed by the General Education Board, an entity that, in turn, had been founded in 1902 by John D. Rockefeller, Sr., to improve the quality of education in the United States. Abby Rockefeller visited the exhibition on four occasions and bought a number of pieces, primarily pottery and tiles, which she installed in one of the houses at the family's Pocantico Hills estate.

The exhibition was organized by Frances Flynn Paine, a Texas-born woman who had spent many of her formative years in Mexico and had, early on, been fascinated by the fine craftsmanship of Mexican Indians.[8] She subsequently was given $15,000 by the Rockefeller Foundation to conduct research on Mexican folk art, set up a cooperative among Mexican folk artists, and market their goods in the United States. Through Frances Paine, Abby Rockefeller continued to purchase Mexican folk art for herself and her friends. She also commissioned Paine to purchase Spanish colonial furniture and decorative pieces in Mexico for Colonial Williamsburg, feeling that including pieces similar to ones that had been brought to Williamsburg by ship in the early days from other colonies in the Americas would make the collection more authentic. And, with her, she set up the Mexican Arts Association in New York, with initial funding from John D. Rockefeller, Jr. The association's primary purpose was to "promote friendship between the people of Mexico and the United States of America by encouraging cultural relations and the interchange of fine and applied arts [folk art]."[9]

One of the first projects developed by this group was a major retrospective of the work of the Mexican painter Diego Rivera, at the newly formed Museum of Modern Art. It opened on December 23, 1931, as the second one-man show to be held at the museum (the first was of Matisse's work). The exhibition displayed 150 of Rivera's most important works, including oils, watercolors, drawings, and frescoes. Some of the frescoes were made specially for the show. Included in this enormously popular and historically important show was Rivera's notebook of Russian May Day sketches, which Abby Rockefeller had purchased for her own collection through Paine and which she later donated to the museum. It was during this period that Abby Rockefeller became a strong benefactor of Rivera and a good friend to Rivera's exotic wife, the artist Frida Kahlo—this despite Rivera's much-publicized communist sympathies.

Abby Rockefeller's involvement in Mexican art was most intense at precisely the same time young Nelson was developing his own likes and dislikes. Not only did she introduce him to Mexican art, but she also instilled in him a confidence to follow his own instincts and, by her example, taught him that there was valuable artistic expression well beyond the walls of the "safe" art fields of his time.

Nelson Rockefeller's iconoclastic trajectory in art was now set. Although no other person would influence that direction quite as much as his mother, others did assist in adding depth to his artistic commitments. Wallace K. Harrison, a brilliant architect who became a close friend of Rockefeller's, had a tremendous impact on his life in terms of "understanding the relation between the cultural creations of our times and the environment from which they spring."[10] Another such friend was René d'Harnoncourt, an Austrian who had studied pre-Columbian and folk art in Mexico during the late 1920s. D'Harnoncourt later became director of the Museum of Modern Art and a staunch ally in Rockefeller's battle to gain recognition and respect for primitive and folk art. Together, they traveled throughout Latin America and other parts of the world and spent hundreds of hours poring over exotic art from distant cultures and discussing its merits and meanings.

Finally, there were certain events that would build on the foundation laid down by Nelson Rockefeller's mother. Most notable were his early travels abroad, especially during the early 1930s. Nelson married Mary Todhunter Clark in 1930, and his parents gave the young couple a nine-month trip around the world as a wedding gift. They attended native feasts in Hawaii, rode elephants in Indochina, enjoyed folk puppets in Japan, and toured the great temples of India. Rockefeller was greatly touched by the warmth and beauty of the people he met and tremendously impressed by their performing and visual arts. It was during this trip that Nelson put into practice some of the strategies of collecting that he had learned from his mother. Among the pieces he purchased were a simple wooden poi bowl from Hawaii, a graceful lute from Sumatra, and a seated wooden figure from Bali.

Of particular interest was an introduction in Bali to Miguel Covarrubias, probably arranged through his mother, who had known Covarrubias earlier in New York. The well-known Mexican illustrator, writer, and amateur archaeologist was in Bali to write a book on Balinese culture and society—a book that has become recognized as a classic in the study of that part of the world. Covarrubias and his wife, Rosa, encouraged the Rockefellers to visit them in Mexico.

From these early experiences came a deep interest in art, which Rockefeller used personally in his private collecting, publicly in his sponsorship of artists and great museums, and diplomatically in his never-ending struggle for better international understanding. The myriad influences of those early days led him to develop not only a keen eye for art but also a personal philosophy that governed his attitude toward art. Rockefeller applied this informal philosophy to all of his great collections—modern, primitive, and folk—which he saw as tightly connected to one another.

For Nelson Rockefeller, art was a truly great pinnacle of man's achievement and the purest expression of human energy, creativity, and spirituality. He felt that art was "a source of faith and hope, of inspiration to people throughout the world,"[11] and that the power of art could be felt, captured if you will, and enjoyed by all those who partook of it. His interest was in the object of art itself, not in its contextual importance, period, or investment potential. In his own words, his interest was "not an intellectual one. It is strictly aesthetic. . . . I enjoy the form, the texture, the color, the shape."[12]

Shortly after returning from his honeymoon, Nelson became a vice president and director of Rockefeller Center, the "city within a city" being built by his father in central Manhattan. The center was to be a showplace for

American free enterprise and was designed to feature murals and sculpture of many of the world's greatest living artists. Diego Rivera had been invited to paint the central panel for Thirty Rockefeller Plaza, the center's main structure. (Picasso and Matisse had been approached; both had declined.[13])

At the time he received the commission, Rivera was working on a series of large frescoes at the Detroit Institute of Art, his Maecenas in this case being Edsel Ford.[14] Rivera worked on the project for more than a year, and when, in March 1933, the frescoes were officially unveiled, they immediately provoked tremendous controversy. As Bertram D. Wolfe, a friend of Rivera's, writes in his life of the artist: "The vaccination panel dedicated to the glorification of scientific research . . . aroused particular ire because of its reminiscence of the Holy Family; the stalwart child held by the 'halo'-crowned nurse, being vaccinated by a physician, suggested Mary, Joseph, and the Child; the horse, ox, and sheep, whence the serum is derived, carried overtones of the stable of the Nativity; the three scientists working in the background were three Magi bearing gifts."[15] The controversy in Detroit proved to be a warning of things to come.

As soon as he had finished work in Detroit, Rivera came to New York, where several young artists, including Ben Shahn, had started preparing the walls at Thirty Rockefeller Plaza. Rivera had less than two months to complete a mural that would cover more than one thousand square feet. Rockefeller Center officials had provided the artist with a theme: "Man at the Crossroads Looking with Hope and High Vision to the Choosing of a New Better Future." Rivera wrote up a detailed description of how he intended to carry out this rather vague assignment and submitted it to the center officials, who gave their approval. May 1 was set as the deadline, because, as Nelson Rockefeller explained to Rivera in a letter written in early April, ". . . the building opens the first of May and it will be tremendously effective to have your mural there to greet the people as they come in for the opening."[16]

As the mural evolved, features that had not been discussed in detail began to emerge; most notably, a central figure Rivera had described merely as "the Worker" or "the labor leader" became a portrait of Lenin. Rivera had joined the Communist Party in 1924, but by the time he came to America, he had resigned from it, been readmitted, and in 1929 been expelled. His expulsion had done nothing to lessen his revolutionary ardor and, Wolfe writes, "the fact that he was painting for a Rockefeller and that the Communist Party was attacking him as a painter for millionaires strengthened his determination to show what a Communist he was."[17]

On May 4, Rockefeller, who had repeatedly been obliged to resolve differences between the painter and the center's chief architect, wrote Rivera, urging him to "substitute the face of some unknown man where Lenin's face now appears."[18] Rivera refused to do so but offered to balance the portrait of Lenin with a similarly strong likeness of Lincoln on the other side of the mural.

Some days later, while Nelson was out of town, officials at the center stopped Rivera's work, paid him in full ($21,500), and covered the mural with cloth. There were protests and demonstrations, but both sides refused to give in. Nelson tried to make arrangements for the unfinished mural to be removed from Rockefeller Center and placed on permanent exhibition at the Museum of Modern Art, but the plan proved to be unworkable. Sadly, Rivera's mural was chipped from the wall in February 1934. It was reproduced in modified form in Mexico City's Palace of Fine Arts.

The Rivera mural episode had greatly shaken Rockefeller. He had worked hard to reach an acceptable compromise, but none had been found. Furthermore, he was upset that the mural, which he thought to be a masterpiece in spite of part of its content, had been destroyed. Forty years later, he lamented that "my mother and I lost ground on the Rivera mural."[19] The controversy had taught young Rockefeller several important lessons. First, it demonstrated the tremendous ability of art, when moved outside of studios, galleries, and museums, to become a powerful catalyst for political and social change. Clearly, the Rivera mural was as charged with social and political criticism as any of the moving speeches or printed opinions of the time. It had the power to make people rally in favor of its stance and to drive others into highly charged opposition. It could not be ignored. Second, the incident showed how much of Mexican art was integrated into the everyday life and politics of that nation. Social Art had become a solid part of the New Order in Mexico, and the art community was behind it. When the Rockefeller Plaza dispute erupted, most of the Mexican art community quickly fell in behind Rivera.

Rockefeller did not allow the painful situation to deflect him from pursuing his strong interest in Mexican art. Eventually amends were made, and the friendship with Frida and Diego was renewed. Rockefeller was determined to visit Mexico, a country in which, uniquely, art was helping to reshape the way the nation thought of itself. So, in the summer of 1933, only a few months after the covering of Rivera's mural, Nelson and Mary decided to sail from New York to Veracruz.

MEXICO: A NATION DISCOVERS ITSELF

Mexico in the 1930s was a radically different country than it had been only a decade before, and, artistically, a far more exciting one. The Mexican Revolution of 1910–1921 put an end to the stagnant, corrupt government of dictator Porfirio Díaz; thereafter, the country began looking inward, and into its own past, for symbols and ideals on which to base a new Mexican identity.

During the Díaz era, the upper classes had looked down on native art—if, indeed, they even took notice of it—regarding only European art and culture, and to a lesser extent North American art and culture, as significant. The architecture, sculpture, and painting of the era all reflected this basically anti-Mexican bias. An example of this attitude was provided on the occasion of the celebration in 1910 of the centennial of the first uprising against Spanish rule. President Díaz imported an exhibition of Spanish paintings and, in preparation for the festivities, had ordered the construction of a new museum, the Palace of Fine Arts. Amy Conger, an early admirer and collector of Mexican folk art, notes in her book on the American photographer Edward Weston: "The building was designed by Italians, the survey and foundation were carried out by North Americans, the marble statues were carved by a Catalan, the facade sculpture and dome were planned and carried out by Italians, the marble was imported from Carrara, and the crystal screen was executed by Tiffany in New York—all while the building rapidly sank into the ground. It was the embodiment of Mexico's cultural inferiority complex."[20]

Weston's tart comment was that Díaz "should have been dethroned for aesthetic reasons, not political. In such a revolution I could joyfully take part!"[21]

In 1921, the year after General Alvaro Obregón, a hero of the revolution, became president of the shaky republic, he appointed humanist and writer José Vasconcelos minister of public education. Daniel Rubín de la Borbolla, a specialist in this period, describes Vasconcelos as being "determined to fulfill part of the mandate of the Mexican Revolution by incorporating the Indian into society, partly through public education and the promotion of the aesthetic accomplishments of Mexicans in Mexico."[22]

The results of this change of attitude on the part of Mexico's leaders were made dramatically manifest in a celebration that was, in effect, a counter-celebration to the one staged by Díaz. Nineteen twenty-one marked the centennial of Mexico's independence. To celebrate this national birthday, the government asked three artists—Jorge Enciso, Roberto Montenegro, and Dr. Atl—to put together a first-class collection of popular art from all over the republic and to mount an exhibition in a building on Avenida Juárez, in the center of Mexico City. With this exhibition, officially opened by President Obregón, the government put its new face on display for the first time and declared that the future was to be built on internal strengths and traditions rather than imported ones.

Frances Toor, who became a leader in Mexican folk art research, recalls the effect this show had on her as well as others:

I had just come to Mexico City to attend the National University Summer School, when it was shown there and the beauty of it was to be one of the motivating factors in my remaining. I wanted to know more of the country in which such humble people could make such beautiful things.

The exhibition was a revelation to the Mexicans themselves. Since then, it has become quite the mode among well-to-do Mexican families, especially those connected with the government, to have a Mexican Room, decorated with Indian handy-crafts. [23]

Almost as important as the exhibition itself was the catalogue, written by Dr. Atl, titled *Las Artes Populares en México*. This publication, issued in two volumes, one of text, the other of illustrations, provided a remarkable overview of Mexican popular arts of the 1920s.

In 1922 the Mexican Secretariat of Industry, Commerce, and Labor organized another pioneering folk art exhibition—designed this time to travel to Los Angeles. Historians and artists assembled the best objects to be found in village markets and shops. Novelist Katherine Anne Porter wrote the catalogue, titled *Outline of Mexican Arts and Crafts*. It contains original insights into Mexican folk culture, but the prose is steeped in the sort of romantic sensibility that characterized much of the writing on the arts following the revolution. Its chief significance lies in its being the first catalogue on Mexican folk art published in the United States to treat that art as an integral part of Mexican culture.

Several foreigners who were living in Mexico City during the 1920s played major roles in recording, collecting, and preserving folk art. Edward Weston traveled about the country photographing folk murals, black pottery from Oaxaca, lacquerware from Michoacán, and thousands of other folk art objects. He was captivated by Mexican folk toys, which he described as "major art," "graceful," and "elegant."[24]

Another key participant in the folk art scene was Fred Davis—who, incidentally, initially sponsored René d'Harnoncourt upon his arrival in Mexico as a refugee from Austria in 1927. An American collector and folk art dealer who had moved to Mexico early in the century, Davis had set up one of the first folk art shops of quality in Mexico City. Later, he directed

Sanborn's gallery on Avenida Madero. Davis was at the center of a group of writers, collectors, folk art specialists, and painters—among them, Roberto Montenegro and Miguel Covarrubias—and, according to d'Harnoncourt's widow, Sarah, Davis belonged to a more specialized group, as well: a band of men who not only studied folk art but also scoured the countryside, looking for new and exciting examples. "They would travel together to faraway Indian villages," she recalls, "and each would try to be the first person up the next morning in order to beat the others to the market for the best pieces."[25] Weston, remembering a trip to Lake Pátzcuaro, confirms this competitive spirit: "That night we overslept, and René beat us to the market, returning in triumph with a water bottle, a fat round little duck—a gem in red clay. Leaving coffee half finished, I scurried to the plaza and bought one—the last, for myself. Later I purchased a bird—a transfigured gourd."[26]

Painter Jean Charlot, who was at the center of Mexico's artistic ferment during this period, remembers:

> In the Mexico of the 1920s, the concept of a fine arts market was still meaningless in terms of a 57th Street of velvet-lined displays. Yet art was everywhere: devotees bribed saints with ex-votos, lovers melted the hearts of their beloved with portaits, artisans and merchants hired the painter to beautify their shops with murals and thus increased business. Sculpture existed for specialized aims—dark pieces, idols of secret worship, semblances used for black magic; innocent pieces, those marvelous toys worth a few cents, beautiful as Han tomb figures. The output was so varied as to be unclassifiable, so cheap as to be despised, so close to all, so thrust under everyone's eyes as to become invisible.[27]

The year 1930 marked yet another milestone in Mexican folk art, particularly in the international arena. Dwight W. Morrow, one of the United States' most beloved and successful ambassadors to Mexico, had a deep appreciation for all forms of Mexican art. So, too, did his wife, Elizabeth, who, with Abby Aldrich Rockefeller, had been a founding member of the Mexican Arts Association in New York. An avid collector of folk art, ancient and contemporary, Morrow had personally underwritten the Rivera murals in the Cortez Palace in Cuernavaca in the late 1920s. Feeling that citizens of the United States knew far too little about the arts of

Mexico, he and silver designer William Spratling of Taxco organized a nearly encyclopedic exhibition of Mexican art that traveled to major cities in the United States between 1930 and 1932. Morrow asked d'Harnoncourt to select the objects, write a catalogue, and travel with the exhibit, taking charge of the installation at each stop. Following its inauguration in Mexico City on June 25, 1930, the exhibition opened at the Metropolitan Museum of Art in New York in October; its eight-city itinerary ended in San Antonio in September 1931.

In his introduction to the catalogue, titled *Mexican Arts*, d'Harnoncourt explained the parameters of the exhibition:

> *This is an exhibition of Mexican arts, not of arts in Mexico. Many art objects are produced within the physical limits of the Republic that are Mexican only in a geographical sense, but these unassimilated copies of foreign models must be disregarded for the purposes of this exhibition. We are concerned here with the presentation only of such works as are an expression of Mexican civilization.*[28]

The contemporary painters and sculptors whose works were included were those who called on indigenous folk forms, colors, and themes for inspiration: Rivera, Covarrubias, Abraham Angel, Julio Castellanos, Carlos Mérida, and others. The exhibition displays, all designed by d'Harnoncourt, were spectacular. Sixteenth-century feather mosaic portraits, *retablos, milagros,* early and contemporary dance masks, textiles of every color and texture, and lacquerware were included—each the finest examples available in its particular medium. Pottery from all over Mexico, old and new furniture, glassware, and dozens of other types of objects, all displayed with originality and charm, made this exhibition the talk of the art world. In addition to the scope and quality of the folk art it presented to the American public, the show was significant in that it made the strongest statement yet on the art of the Mexican Renaissance and its importance in establishing a national identity.

Mildred Constantine, a keen observer of the Mexican art movement of the 1930s, states that "art took its proper place with politics and other things. Mexico was full of ferment—part art and part politics. There was a tremendous cohesion in Mexico in those days among poets, painters, and writers."[29] They were all participants in the Mexican Renaissance; they all directed much of their energy toward achieving the goals of the Mexican Revolution — bettering the lot of the masses who had been overlooked by the previous regime. Art had been taken out of the rarified climates of galleries and museums; instead of drawing from European models, it looked inward to pre-Columbian and folk art to build a new identity. Constantine recalls, "The same people who were painting posters against illiteracy were painting murals. The *zócalo* [main plaza] was theater in action, and each day people came in from the countryside to see the great murals which chronicled their struggles."[30]

VOYAGE TO MEXICO

The Rockefellers sailed from New York for Veracruz on July 26, 1933, by way of Havana. Their itinerary had been set up by Frances Flynn Paine, who also served as their guide throughout the trips. Charles R. Richards, director of the art section of the General Education Board, described her special qualifications for dealing with folk societies:

> *Since first meeting Mrs. Paine . . . I have come to know her somewhat intimately and find that she is a woman of much quiet power and resolution, with a fine mind and a deep and abiding interest in the welfare and in the arts of the Indians of Mexico. She was born in Laredo, Texas, but spent most of her early days in Mexico, where her father was for a time Superintendent of Railways and also acted at times as American Consul. He was a man who possessed, I understand, mining and agricultural interests in various parts of Mexico and to these various places Mrs. Paine traveled when she was quite young, living in many remote parts of Mexico. It was during this period that she first conceived her interest in the crafts of the Mexican Indians. As a consequence, she possessed a knowledge of these crafts, as well as an intimate knowledge of the Indian character, that has developed steadily during her almost life-long residence in Mexico.* [31]

Paine had arranged for the Rockefellers to see some of the great collections of pre-Columbian art in Mexico, among them those belonging to Miguel and Rosa Covarrubias. Nelson recalled that, "I found myself capti-

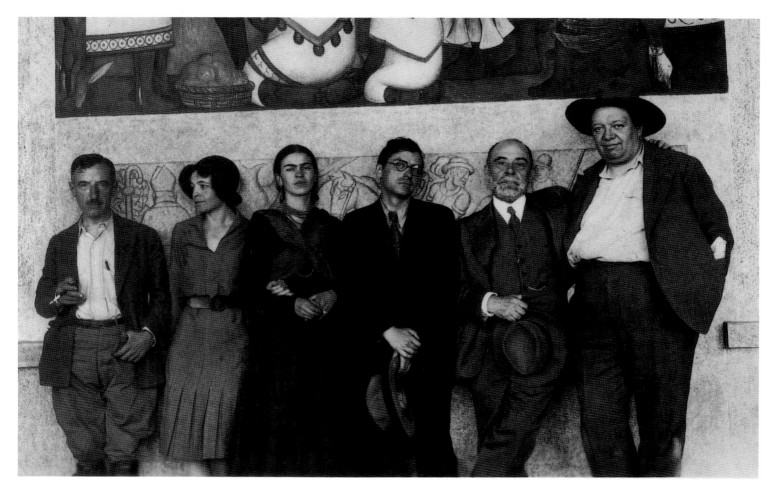

Frances Flynn Paine, second from left, who guided the Rockefellers on their first trip to Mexico. She is with, from right to left, Diego Rivera, Elie Faure, Jean Charlot, Frida Kahlo, and Dr. Leo Eloesoer. This photograph was taken in August 1931 at Cuernavaca on the portal of the Cortez Palace, where Rivera painted frescoes depicting the Conquest of Mexico. These frescoes were commissioned by Ambassador Dwight Morrow as a gift to the State of Morelos

vated by the power and exquisite refinement of these works. It was a most exciting and exhilarating experience, opening up new worlds—worlds little known and little appreciated at that time outside of Latin America and anthropological circles."[32] Many of Mexico's artists and writers lived with the art of their ancestors as well as folk art produced by contemporary Indians. For the first time, Rockefeller had the opportunity to see these objects and to talk with collectors about the availability of folk art and the context in which it was being produced and used.

While he was awed by the pre-Columbian art he saw on this trip, it was folk art—and the people who made and used it—that made the deepest impression on him. The Rockefellers traveled through the central highlands of Mexico, in and out of shops and museums in Mexico City, and into the states of Puebla and Morelos to visit old churches, many of them embellished with folk sculpture and paintings. Forty-five years later, reflecting on this trip, Nelson recalled that he and Mary were uniquely privileged to travel with Frances Paine from marketplace to marketplace.[33]

Rockefeller distinctly remembered several of the folk artists he met on that first trip to Mexico. One was an elderly Indian woman who wove sarapes in a village in the State of Tlaxcala. Her "weaving was so fine that no one of the younger generation had the patience to develop the skills required to carry it on," he recalled. "I was so excited by her wonderful work that I bought virtually her entire collection. . . . I have never found anything to compare with the work of that beautiful and gentle little lady who was so pleased by the joy we derived from her works."[34]

Another artist who made a lasting impression on Rockefeller was an Indian sculptor named Mardonio Magaña, from Mexico City. "We first saw one of his works in a square near the San Angel Inn. . . . This piece of sculpture evidenced such sensitivity and humanity, as well as artistic quality, that I asked Mrs. Paine if she could make arrangements for a visit to his studio. Magaña was as beautiful and gentle as his sculpture. Without hesitation, I bought two of his stone pieces and two wood carvings, each of which manifested the same deep love and sensitive human understanding of the Mexican campesino that I had found in his larger piece in the square."[35] In Magaña's work, Rockefeller found a combination of pre-Hispanic and folk forms redirected into modern forms of expression.

Paine also introduced Rockefeller to Roberto Montenegro, a portrait painter and muralist and an avid collector and student of folk art. Later, it would be Montenegro who would lead Rockefeller more deeply into folk art. Like many of the other great Mexican artists of that period, Montenegro looked to the folk art of his country for inspiration and was vitally interested in its recognition and preservation. In 1922 he organized Mexico's first popular arts exhibit in the United States and subsequently set up the Museo de Artes Populares in Mexico City. Rockefeller chose Montenegro to head up the folk art section of the Museum of Modern Art's pioneering 1940 exhibition of Mexican art.

Nelson and Mary returned to New York at the end of August. He had purchased Mexican art of all types, including pre-Columbian and colonial pieces and contemporary paintings and sculpture. But most of the twenty-six crates of art he shipped back were filled with folk art. Some of these pieces had been bought from collectors such as Covarrubias and Montenegro; others at Fred Davis' legendary folk art shop in Mexico City. The great majority of the pieces of the folk art had been bought directly from the artists who had created them. This human connection made these works special to Nelson.

Rockefeller made several other trips to Mexico during the 1930s. Each visit reinforced his interest in folk art. In 1939 he became president of the Museum of Modern Art and immediately set about organizing a major exhibition of Mexican art. He went to Mexico to meet with President Lázaro Cárdenas, who agreed to cosponsor the event and share in the expenses. He chose leading authorities in the field to head each of the four sections of the exhibition. Alfonso Caso, Mexico's dean of archaeology, was put in charge of the pre-Columbian section; Manuel Toussaint, of the colonial material; Miguel Covarrubias, of modern art; and Roberto Montenegro, of folk art. The show, called *20 Centuries of Mexican Art,* bringing together two thousand masterpieces from these various periods, was the most extensive survey of Mexican art ever presented outside of Mexico.

To build a great collection of Mexican popular arts for the exhibition, Rockefeller commissioned Montenegro to travel about the Mexican countryside to purchase old and new folk art. This was done with the understanding that the works would become part of Rockefeller's private collection once the show was over. Some of the rarest and most important pieces in the Rockefeller collection are those purchased by Montenegro for the *20 Centuries* exhibition.

In addition to rare and historically important pieces of folk art, everyday contemporary crafts were also purchased and used in a replica of a

Mexican marketplace that was constructed in the garden of the Museum of Modern Art for their display and sale. The exhibition was a tremendous success; after it closed, the folk art section traveled to museums throughout the United States under the auspices of the Museum of Modern Art.

Rockefeller's motivations for supporting the *20 Centuries of Mexican Art* project were twofold. First, he was attracted to the works and believed in their artistic value. Second, he saw the exhibition as an excellent opportunity to shore up relations between Mexico and the United States. Opening at about the same time that President Roosevelt appointed him to the post of Coordinator for Inter-American Affairs, the show was an initial expression of his commitment to inter-American cooperation. Because of his interest in the cultural-exchange aspect of the project, he saw it as an opportunity for the Mexican government to set up markets in the United States for Mexican folk art and crafts. Rockefeller was elated, for example, when he learned that

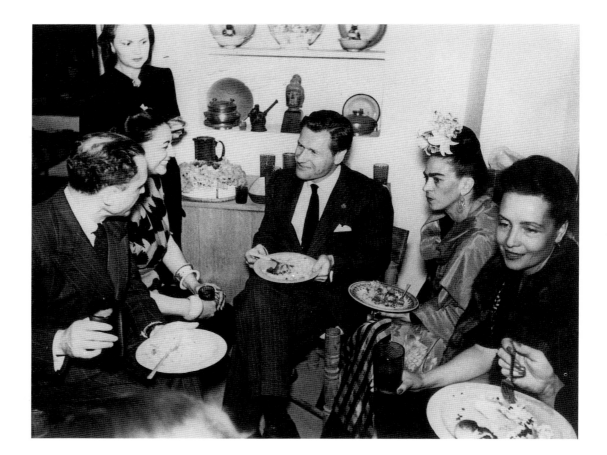

Rockefeller at a party in Mexico City, with Frida Kahlo on his left and Rosa Covarrubias on his right, mid-1940s

Kaufman's Department Store in Pittsburgh had decided to launch a major merchandising campaign featuring popular Mexican crafts and other objects, basing its decision on the publicity generated by the Museum of Modern Art's exhibit. William Spratling, who revived the silver arts in Taxco, writes that Rockefeller worked hard in the 1940s to lower United States silver tariffs, to improve trade relations between the United States and Mexico.[36] Rockefeller saw these kinds of responses as important steps in strengthening economic ties with Latin American republics at a time when such ties were tenuous at best.

During World War II, while working for the Roosevelt administration, Rockefeller continued to travel to Mexico and other parts of Latin America—and, whenever he had free time, he collected folk art. Susan Herter, who served as an assistant to Rockefeller during that period, remembers that "in 1945 in Mexico City during the Chapultepec conference to revitalize hemispheric unity, Rockefeller would often disappear at breaks and at lunchtime. He was out seeking new pieces for his growing collection and was greatly excited with his finds; he gave many wonderful pieces away when they were admired by friends and visitors."[37]

After the war, Rockefeller kept in close contact with Mexican politics, development programs, and art. In 1948, feeling that he had been away from folk art too long, he decided to take his wife and five children to Mexico for several weeks of vacation.

The Rockefeller family flew to Mexico City on June 20. They dropped in for a visit with their friends Rosa and Miguel Covarrubias, in whose home the family admired the couple's splendid collections of pre-Columbian and folk art.

Roberto Montenegro was to be the family's guide on this trip, and after much discussion and debate, Oaxaca was chosen as the destination, presumably because it would provide an ideal spot to give the Rockefeller children an overview of Mexican art in one locale. Within the Valley of Oaxaca the ruins of Monte Albán and Mitla provided constant reminders of the antiquity and early splendor of the region. Then, too, there were the Spanish colonial

Rockefeller with Miguel and Rosa Covarrubias in Mexico City, mid-1940s

From left to right: Nelson A. Rockefeller; Rosa Covarrubias; William Spratling, the designer who revived the silver industry in Taxco; and Roberto Montenegro, in Mexico City, mid-1940s

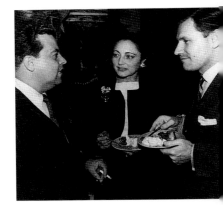

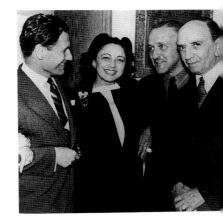

churches—two hundred years older than the earliest North American churches—richly decorated with sixteenth-century frescoes and gold-leafed walls and ceilings. And, of course, every village in the region produced folk art of some type, much of it marketed in the main square of Oaxaca City.

In those days the outdoor Oaxaca market encompassed dozens of square blocks in the center of the city. One needed only to sit for a brief time on a nearby bench in order to see hundreds of colorfully dressed Indians—Mixtecs, Zapotecs, Triques, and others from the mountains surrounding the Valley of Oaxaca—bringing their wares to market to sell or exchange for items not available in their home communities. Oaxaca was the ideal place to see many of Mexico's most dramatic elements all at once.

The Rockefellers visited dozens of villages in the Valley of Oaxaca, and his elder daughter, Ann R. Roberts, recalls "the excitement and fascination of going in and out of the homes of artisans with Father—going in empty-handed and coming out with little treasures."[38]

The family ended their Mexican trip with a visit to Tehuantepec, about 150 miles south of Oaxaca City. Miguel Covarrubias had just published a major study of the Tehuantepec region, and this influenced Rockefeller's decision to include this stop in the itinerary. Tropical and filled with exotic flowers and birds, Tehuantepec provided a vivid contrast to the semiarid Valley of Oaxaca. There they saw Zapotec and Huave Indian women skill-fully running markets offering for sale exotic regional specialties such as iguana cooked in a red sauce and eaten on a tortilla, richly lacquered bowls used in fiestas, and textiles dyed purple with the secretions from a local shellfish gathered by the nearby Chontal Indians. This southern foray also gave the family an opportunity to visit San Blas Atempa, a Zapotec village famous for its ceramics, especially large figural pieces used as water-container supports.

Montenegro was in his element and added enormously to the success of the trip. Mary Rockefeller recalls that "Roberto made an enormous impression on Nelson. Not only was he very knowledgeable about folk art, but he also enjoyed a special rapport with folk artists and delighted in being with

Roberto Montenegro with his portrait of fellow artist José Clemente Orozco in 1949

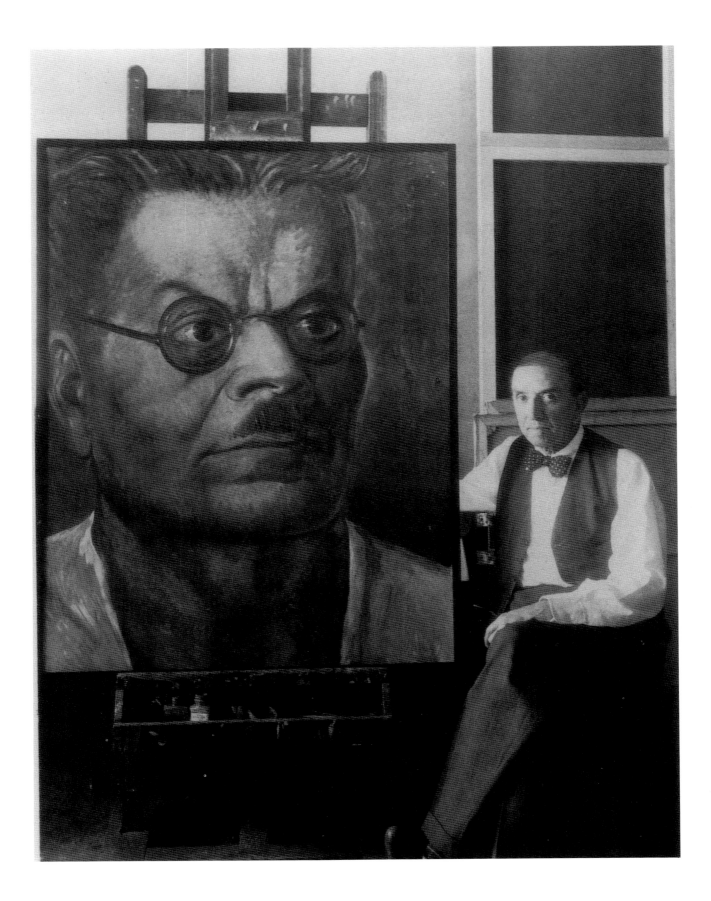

them in their homes. Nelson found Roberto's enthusiasm contagious and soon he was reacting to folk art in a similar fashion."[39] Roberto became a close family friend, and correspondence between him and Nelson continued until Montenegro's death in 1968.

As Rockefeller became more deeply involved in domestic politics, his involvement with Mexican art and culture diminished. During his long tenure as governor of New York from 1959 to 1973, he had little opportunity to visit Latin America and the Indian markets he loved so much. But in 1968 his interest in Mexican folk art was rekindled when, quite by accident, he happened upon a small and colorful folk art gallery/shop in Manhattan called the Mexican Folk Art Annex. It was owned and run by Annie O'Neill, an artist with an effervescent personality and a good eye for folk art. O'Neill recalls her first meeting with Rockefeller, who would later employ her as a folk art consultant.

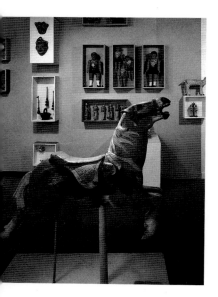

Part of the exhibition of Mexican folk art in the Museum of Primitive Art in 1969. Rockefeller often encouraged a market flavor in the installation of his folk art collection

I still clearly remember his first visit. It was after five o'clock and the shop was closed. When I looked through the peephole to decide whether or not to let one last person in, I thought that I had better let that tired-looking man come in. What a surprise to discover he was the governor! An even greater treat was to watch him voraciously assimilate everything on all the shelves and in every corner. After a few minutes he looked like a different person—he had been energized.[40]

Shortly after this chance encounter, Rockefeller started unpacking all of the old crates of folk art left over from the *20 Centuries of Mexican Art* exhibition and began planning a new folk art exhibit at the Museum of Primitive Art. O'Neill was dispatched immediately to Mexico to make additional purchases to fill in gaps in the collection. Carl Fox, a folk art specialist who had worked with the Smithsonian Institution and the Brooklyn Museum, was hired to design the exhibition and assemble a catalogue. The exhibition opened on May 21, 1969. Its success with the public pleased Rockefeller enormously.

In his foreword to the catalogue, he wrote:

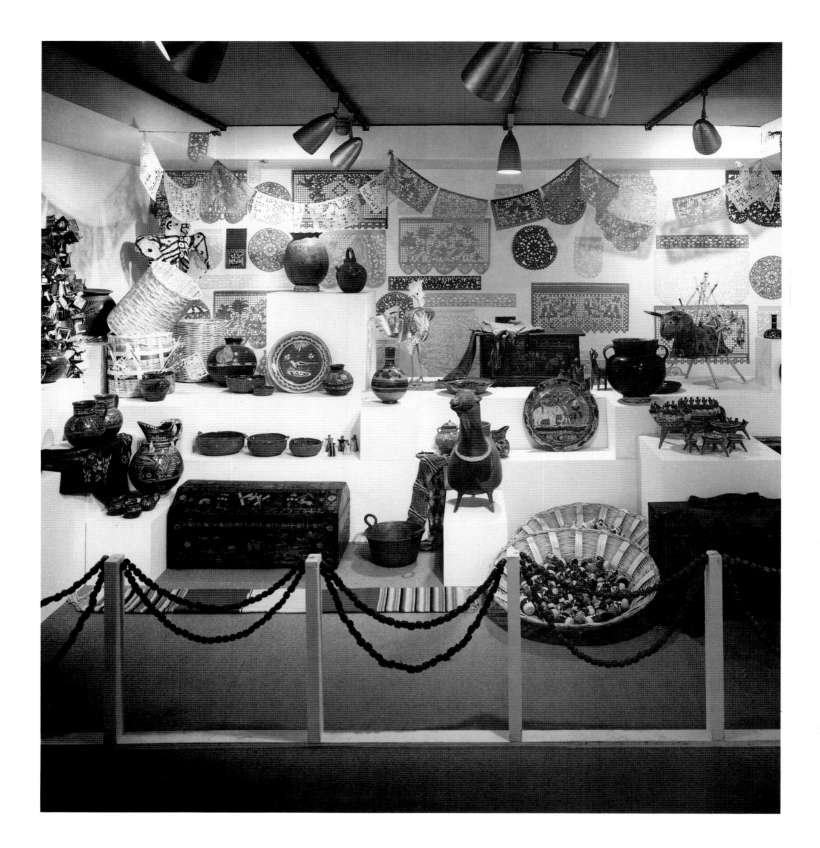

It does not matter if these [objects] are categorized as "minor" arts. Artificial categories disappear before works whose vivid color and spontaneous design reflect such pleasure in their making. They delight and fascinate us—and happily let us share in the vitality and love that went into their creation. [41]

Rockefeller continued collecting and studying Mexican folk art well into the 1970s. When he became vice president of the United States in 1974, he was again drawn away from his collections. But, in 1977, he returned to New York and the family offices, where he worked almost daily on projects related to art. A year later, he announced plans to publish a series of five books on his art collections. One of these was to concentrate on his Mexican folk art collection. As part of this project he decided to visit Mexico again, to photograph folk artists, make new purchases, and visit old haunts.

Rockefeller asked several friends to accompany him, including Carl Fox, Annie O'Neill, and art photographer Lee Boltin. Another member of this group was Rockefeller's daughter Ann, who inherited her father's love of folk art and who, after his death, arranged for his Mexican folk art collection to be preserved and placed in new and permanent homes.

In 1978 Rockefeller returned to Oaxaca, where he had spent such a pleasant time with his family thirty years before. Moreover, in what was to be the last year of his life, he arranged to be there in early November for the preparations of the Day of the Dead—a three-day religious festival lasting from October 31 to November 2, All Souls' Day. It is a time of year when folk art is most visible and abundant. In his biography of Diego Rivera, Bertram Wolfe writes of "the mordant-reckless-festive-friendly-familiar Mexican attitude toward death," [42] an attitude made fantastically manifest during this festival, when death is at once mocked and honored. In every city and village, families go out to the cemeteries, carrying flowers, sweets, food, and drink to the graves of the dead. Children make cardboard skeletons dance and amuse themselves with little figures of death made of metal foil, with chick-peas serving as heads, or with small coffins made of cardboard or clay. Death is also eaten in the form of sugar-candy skulls or figures made of sugar or marzipan.

Shortly after arriving in Oaxaca, the group set off to visit the great figural ceramist Doña Teodora Blanco in the village of Santa María Atzompa. Rockefeller was captivated by the woman, by her work, and by the way she worked. "She is a person of such an active mind," he later wrote, "so feeling and creative that one thought leads to another and each is expressed in sculptural form through some additions to or elaboration of the piece in hand—with lightning speed and sensitivity."[43]

He spent two hours with Doña Teodora, talking with her about her life, photographing her at work, and enjoying the ambience of her open-air workshop—with babies crying, animals moving about, and shade trees providing shelter from the sun. He purchased everything she was willing to sell, even old broken pieces that Doña Teodora had discarded. Her works, Rockefeller later recalled, ranged in price "from a few cents to less than a hundred dollars for her largest monumental piece, [and yet,] aesthetically, they represented a subtle sophistication possessed by but few of the greatest contemporary artists."[44]

Later, Rockefeller and his companions drove to San Bartolo Coyotepec to visit the legendary Doña Rosa Real de Nieto in her home, where he admired the black pottery for which she and her family are renowned. He bought many pieces from Doña Rosa to complement others he had bought in the 1940s. He also visited the home of the Aguilar family in Ocotlán de Morelos to watch as pottery figures were sculpted and painted. While there, he noticed an assortment of old ceramic figures, some broken, all faded, which had been stuck on the fence posts surrounding the Aguilar home to advertise their business. Noting the special charm of these forgotten pieces, Rockefeller purchased nearly all of them; today they comprise an important part of the figural ceramics in the collection.

The group also visited several large markets while in Oaxaca, including that in Ocotlán de Morelos. Rockefeller plunged right into the middle of the activity. Ocotlán, he remembered, "was alive with Indians, the men wearing big hats, coming and going, picking their way through the crowds, buying and selling, while the women sat quietly, weaving raffia, embroidering,

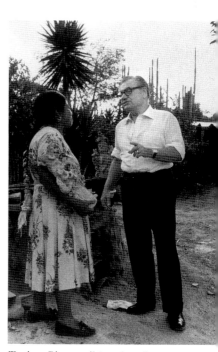

Teodora Blanco talking about her work with Rockefeller, Santa María Atzompa, Oaxaca, October 1978

Plate 1
Ceramic Dolls
Mezcala region, Guerrero
1930s
Hand-built, single-fired
earthenware, approximate heights,
18″. MM and SAMA

These stately hand-built figures,
painted in earth tones over a creamy
white wash, are disappearing from
the indigenous Mezcala region
figural repertoire. They are being
replaced by gaudily decorated ceramic dolls painted for the tourist
trade. These unusually shaped dolls,
with imploring eyes and head shapes
reminiscent of pre-Hispanic figura-
tive pieces, reflect an innovative
treatment of the mother-and-child
theme. The simple floral and animal
motifs are characteristic of the
painting in the early decades of this
century.

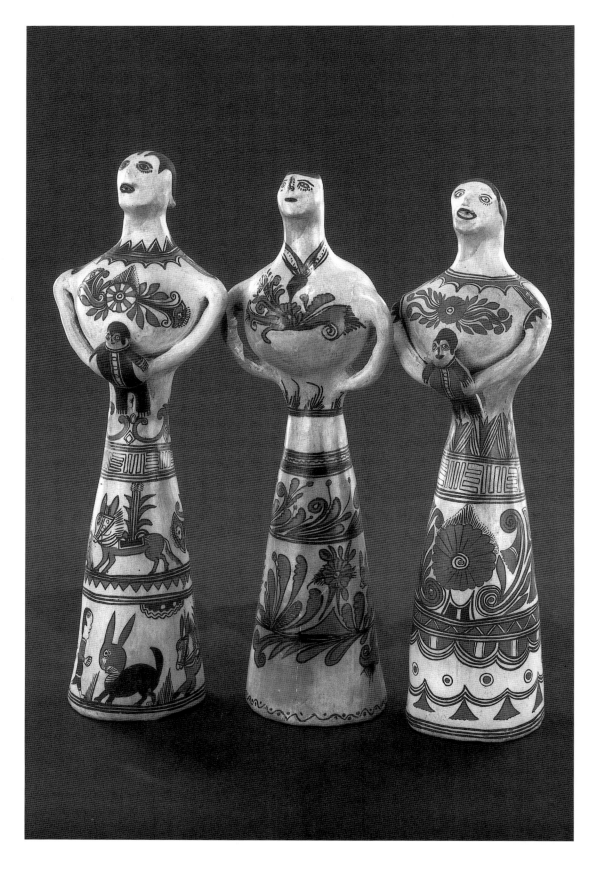

feeding their babies, and enjoying the hustle and bustle of this important weekly social event."[45]

Again, he bought whatever impressed him as beautiful and interesting. When he noticed the graceful lines of a handmade ox yoke, he struck a deal with its owner and had it lugged off to a waiting van. He bought small clay whistles, tinsel-covered candles, Day of the Dead bread, and wooden combs. He even purchased great wreaths of garlic—much to the dismay of those who were traveling with him.

A PHILOSOPHY OF COLLECTING

Rockefeller's relationship to art was very personal and, almost always, emotionally charged. He felt that "art fulfilled a spiritual need in our over-mechanized industrial age," and added that "twentieth-century man is so surrounded by mass-production, by machines and anonymous consumer goods that his eye thirsts for individuality. He turns to art to enjoy individual expression. Paintings and sculpture, artifacts created by individual hands and conceived by individual spirits, satisfy a craving for personality, for uniqueness."[46]

For the most part, Rockefeller tended to avoid highly representational art and art that gave the viewer everything at once, and only once. Instead, he proclaimed that what we are all looking for is something "that takes us out of ourselves and gives us the kind of excitement, the kind of aesthetic satisfaction and challenge that is unending and from which you constantly get new satisfaction and rewards."[47] He felt that a good piece of art, whether it be folk, modern, or primitive, would continue to give the viewer a sense of something new and exciting—a new shape, texture, or color, and that this would, in turn, be a true reflection of the artist's own evolving qualities. He was particularly drawn to pieces that he felt were direct expressions of strong emotions, pieces made by special artists to be found in every society, no

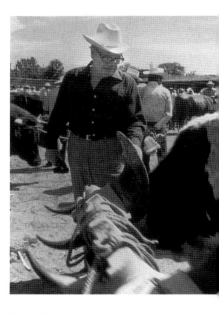

Rockefeller completing his sombrero purchase in Ocotlán, October 1978

Rockefeller considering buying an ox yoke in the crowded Ocotlán animal market, October 1978

Doña Rosa at right, working clay, and at left, at work with her son. They both use small kick wheels. San Bartolo Coyotepec, Oaxaca, October 1978

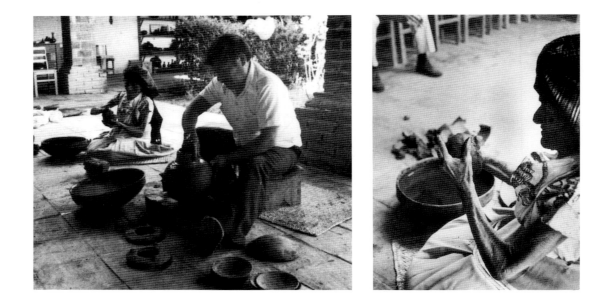

matter what its level of development. "I have always liked forms of art in which I could feel—feel the artists, feel the material."[48]

The direct expressiveness he saw in folk art and certain primitive pieces was shared by some of the great modernists, such as Pablo Picasso. Rockefeller agreed with Gertrude Stein, the author and great collector of modern art, when she wrote that before Picasso, with the exception of the creators of some African sculpture, "no one had ever tried to express things seen not as one knows them but as they are when one sees them without remembering having looked at them."[49] Rockefeller responded to this directness and used it as a guideline for his collecting.

He felt that each of the areas in which he collected was related to the others and that each had something of value to offer the other. He strongly believed that the "so-called primitive artist, in his economical and varied use of homely materials—sea shells, feathers, bark cloth, straw and bone—can still teach his modernist colleagues a good deal." And one reviewer adds, "No doubt it is Rockefeller's recognition of that fact [of closeness] that explains his interest in folk art and that sends him rummaging in foreign bazaars and second-story craft shops where collectors concerned only with the prestige of a price tag would never venture."[50]

Rockefeller's unorthodox manner of collecting reflected his attitude toward art. He always knew exactly what he liked and acted on his likes very quickly, without stopping to consider the overall significance of a purchase. According to Laurance Rockefeller, "Nelson's reaction to art was visceral," and he had great confidence in his good eye and natural feeling for art. "Collecting," he adds, "gave Nelson a sense of solace and allowed him to get out of the world of day-to-day problems into the quieter dimension of art."[51]

Alfred Barr, former director of the Museum of Modern Art and longtime close friend of Rockefeller's, stated that "Nelson had the most insatiable appetite for art I know. Works of art gave him a deep, almost therapeutic delight and refreshment such as other men may find in music or alcohol."[52]

René d'Harnoncourt, who collected art all over the world with Rockefeller, observed that "Nelson takes things in like a sponge . . . he reacted strongly to all objects of art and was remarkably free from prejudice. The kind of euphoria he received had nothing to do with that gambler's excitement characteristic of many collectors. It was not unlike benzedrine, it was a curious combination of excitement and relaxation. Call it solace, call it therapy. . . . Most men, after a hard day's work, want to relax. But Nelson was a man of such physical and intellectual energy that he preferred to go on working. . . . I mean by that, it is very hard work to look at paintings and sculpture as intensely as he does. One simply feels he enjoyed himself more profoundly, when he looked at art, than in any other activity."[53]

Rockefeller's collecting habits and the motivations behind them were unusual in the world of art. Barr sees his motives in collecting as being "exceptionally pure. Status, competition, investment, pride of possession, pride of taste, even a reputation for being a 'patron of the arts' did not interest him. Yet, beyond his private satisfaction there was a strong desire to share his treasures with others."[54] Rockefeller quickly dismissed the suggestion that he was building his collection for investment purposes and stated emphatically that "I could be just as happy collecting in a market in Mexico City in the early 1930s as I could in a gallery. It hasn't anything to do with monetary value."[55]

Rockefeller enjoyed the process of collecting immensely, especially amid the bustle and confusion found in a Mexican market. "He loved the physical and emotional contact a marketplace is all about," recalls Annie O'Neill. Again, reflecting on that last trip to Oaxaca, O'Neill says that "whenever Rockefeller bought a piece of art, he underwent a very personal experience. For him, the object had everything to do with the artisans, their pride and dignity, the transaction and the setting."[56]

Rockefeller always traveled with a camera so that he could capture a part of what he liked of the people and places he visited. During the 1978 trip, he took over 150 photographs, many of which deal with village life in Oaxaca. Many of them are of crowded market scenes and folk artists from Ocotlán and Coyotepec. They show women sitting on the ground behind neatly stacked piles of fresh fruit or hanging baskets and petals, or men tugging at animals reluctant to go on the selling block. Most photographs are taken from a spot central to the action and show that the photographer was surrounded on all sides by vendors, buyers, and merchandise. Very seldom did he photograph folk art objects by themselves, choosing to focus instead on the people who made, sold, and used them.

Rockefeller and his entourage returned to New York in early November. Work on the book began almost immediately. Objects were photographed and preliminary plans were drawn up for the organization of the book. Sadly, Nelson Rockefeller died only three months after returning from Oaxaca, and the folk art project was halted.

Fortunately, an important part of Nelson Rockefeller lives on through his Mexican folk art collection and his other collections of art. These collections reflect his constant faith in the inherent creativity of all people, regardless of cultural background or socioeconomic circumstance. His collecting, out of step with most of his peers, was directed not by fashion, price, or potential market value but by the intrinsic beauty and charm he recognized in the pieces themselves. He trusted his emotional response to art, and as the world now knows, he was usually right.

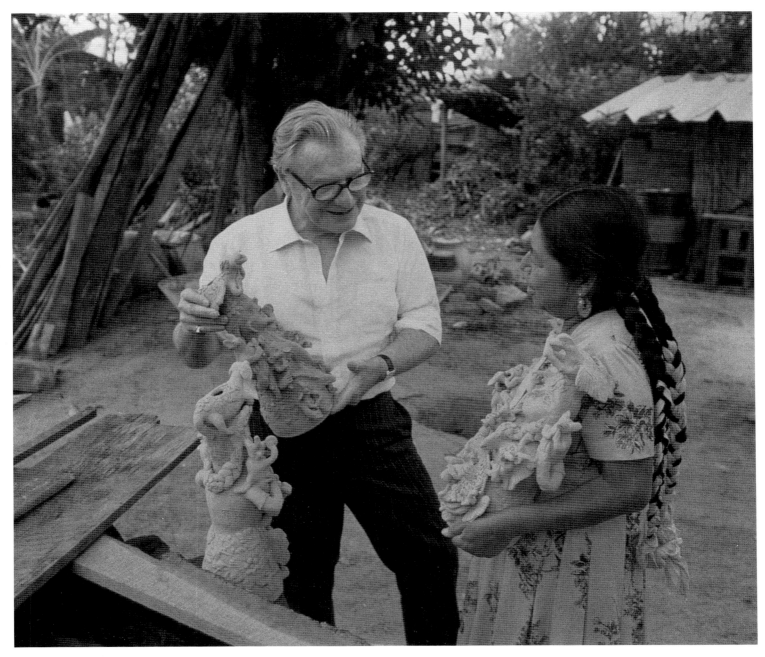

Rockefeller talking to Teodora
Blanco about her work at her home
in Santa María Atzompa, Oaxaca,
October 1978

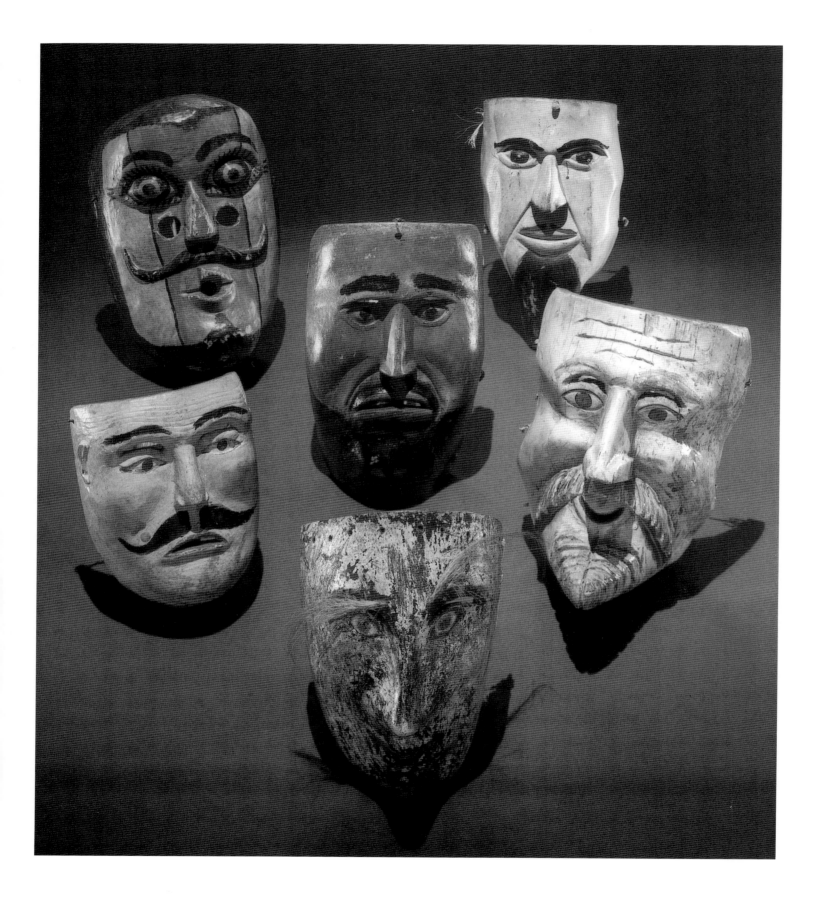

The Collection

Here is an art, almost unknown in the world today, a survival from
internal wars, conquests, many fusions; an actual thing full of breathing
vitality and meaning.

—Katherine Anne Porter[1]

Nelson Rockefeller's collection of Mexican folk art is both broad and varied. Parts of it are intensely personal and reveal Rockefeller's spontaneous collecting habits and lack of concern for representing all categories or for meeting a curator's stringent criteria. Other works—particularly the large number assembled by Roberto Montenegro for the 1940 Museum of Modern Art exhibition *20 Centuries of Mexican Art*—demonstrate a commitment to covering major historical, geographical, and topological areas of Mexican folk art.

The collection comprises objects ranging from colorful toys that dance and tumble, to sedate religious icons that tug at the soul. It contains objects of everyday use, with cool simple lines, and others whose warmth invites our touch. There are objects that represent love, hate, life, death, and many other states of the human condition. It is a collection that, when properly understood, reveals an important part of the essence of Mexican society and culture.

Plate 2
Masks
Various states of Mexico
1920s to 1930s
Painted wood, heights, 12½". MM
and SAMA

Modern masking in Mexico is firmly rooted in pre-Hispanic and colonial times. It can be found in most parts of Mexico and is an essential part of dance dramas dealing with moral and historical themes in celebration of important saint days and other religious events. Mask makers are primarily men; for its creator, mask making is often a fulfillment of a religious obligation to the community. Some masks are destroyed after the ceremony they are used for, while other masks are repainted each year. In some areas, such as Guerrero, it is believed that masks assume the spirit of the animals they represent and protect the wearer against evil during religious ceremonies.

These masks are all from the first decades of the twentieth century and are from various states of Mexico. They represent a broad range of themes and technical skills.

HISTORY AND IMPORTANCE OF THE COLLECTION

Beginning in 1933, with Rockefeller's first trip to Mexico, the collection grew over the years at an uneven pace, with inter-American politics, special museum exhibitions, and Rockefeller's periodic rekindling of interest in folk art playing important roles in its evolution and growth. He personally shepherded it for almost fifty years, and upon his death in 1979, it became part of his estate. Rockefeller's daughter Ann purchased it from the estate in 1982; owing to her efforts the collection found permanent homes in two museums important for their rich cultural connections to Mexico—the San Antonio Museum of Art and the Mexican Museum in San Francisco.

The collection now numbers slightly more than three thousand objects, from all over Mexico and made from a wide variety of materials using many different techniques. Interestingly, the size of the collection has decreased over the years. In a letter dated July 6, 1942, Rockefeller writes, "In making a check I find that there are more than four thousand objects making up the list of folk or popular art from Mexico."[2] Apparently, many of the objects listed were purely decorative and purchased for use in recreating a Mexican market in the garden of the Museum of Modern Art in 1940. Some pieces disappeared; others, being ephemeral art, simply deteriorated. Still others were given away by Rockefeller to friends. Susan Herter, who worked with Rockefeller during his days as coordinator for Inter-American Affairs, said that "if you admired [an object], he would often give it to you."[3]

As is characteristic of most collections of Mexican folk art, ceramic objects make up more than fifty percent of the Rockefeller collection. The collection of textiles, consisting of more than two hundred pieces, is small but provides a fine overview of textiles made since the turn of the century, especially non-Indian textiles. Objects of corn husks, wood, straw, paper, shell, glass, tin, silver, wax, and other materials constitute the remainder of the collection.

The majority of the pieces in the collection are by anonymous artists. Other works are by well-known personalities of the folk art world. The early part of the collection represents famous folk artists of the 1930s and 1940s, such as ceramists Doña Rosa of Oaxaca and Aurelio Flores of Izúcar de Matamoros, Puebla, and *popote* mosaic artist Felipe Olay of Mexico City. The part of the collection assembled after 1960 contains a large number of pieces by well-known modern folk artists: miniature–toy-maker Angel Carranza; ceramists Doña Teodora Blanco, Herón Martínez, the late Candelario Medrano, and the Aguilar family; internationally famous papier-mâché artist Pedro Linares; and others. In some instances, these pieces are signed by the artists, a custom that developed in response to commercial demand in the late 1960s.

In most cases, we know the provenance of objects. We also know something about the history of most objects after they left their places of origin. Some have impressive histories. The graceful lacquered gourd crane (pl. 125) from Olinalá, Guerrero, for example, first appeared in the 1930 *Mexican Arts* exhibition mounted by René d'Harnoncourt. In 1932 a picture of the crane was published in Frances Toor's magazine *Mexican Folkways* as part of an advertisement; presumably it was for sale at that time. Rockefeller possibly purchased the crane the following year, when he went to Mexico for the first time. It next appeared in public at the Museum of Modern Art in 1940, as part of the popular-art section of *20 Centuries of Mexican Art* but was not included in the catalogue. In 1969 it was shown again, this time as part of the exhibition of Rockefeller folk art at the Museum of Primitive Art. Several newspapers used a photograph of the by-then famous crane to illustrate their reviews of the exhibition. It was again displayed in 1984 as part of an exhibition at the Center for Inter-American Relations in New York and was prominently illustrated in the catalogue. When the Rockefeller collection was donated to the San Antonio Museum Association in 1985, the crane became a part of its permanent exhibition and is proudly displayed next to more recent lacquered pieces from Olinalá. Clearly, Rockefeller was very fond of the lacquered crane and thought that it was an important piece of folk art.

Another object with an impressive history of exhibition is the tin and

Plate 3
Vendor's Display of Milagros
Oaxaca, Oaxaca
1978
Cast metal, 15¾ × 12¼″. SAMA

This vendor's display of *milagros*
shows how these small offerings
typically are sold. A person has his
choice of a multitude of *milagros* and
is sure to find one corresponding to
a miraculous recovery, cure, or
change in events he has recently
experienced. The *milagro* is then
hung by the grateful person inside
the church near the saint who has
effected the miraculous event.
Milagros are small but significant
tokens of gratitude. Contemporary
milagros are made of cast metal and
affixed to shiny ribbons.

Surely the man outside a Oaxaca
church who sold his complete supply
of *milagros* to Rockefeller in October
1978 must have bought himself a
milagro in gratitude!

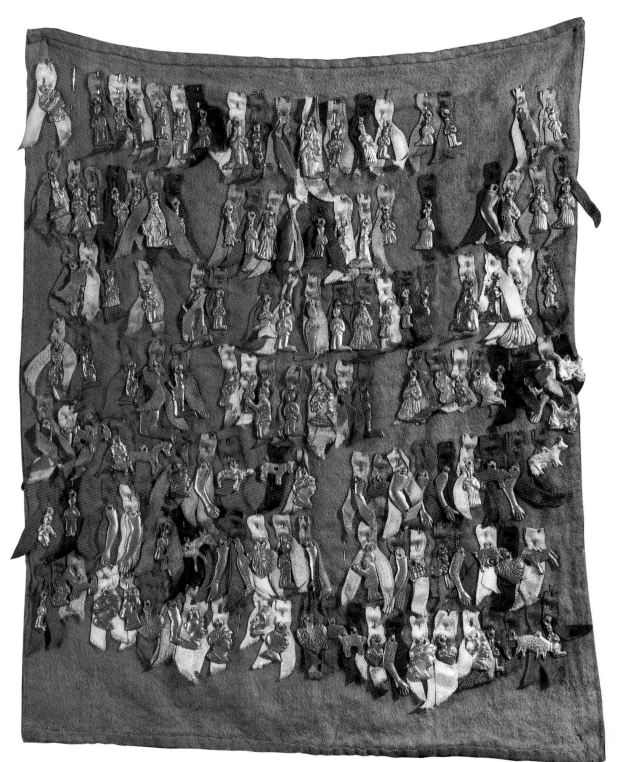

glass frame containing nineteenth- and early-twentieth-century silver *milagros* (pl. 54). This assemblage was part of the Museo de Artes Populares exhibition in Mexico City mounted by Roberto Montenegro and Moisés Saenz in 1934, and a photograph of it was later published in a short catalogue. Many pieces in the exhibition were from Montenegro's private collection, which was taken to New York six years later for the Museum of Modern Art exhibition. A photograph of it was published in the catalogue of that show, and the assemblage presumably became a part of the Rockefeller collection after the exhibition was concluded. Its subsequent history parallels that of the crane: It is now a part of the permanent exhibition of Rockefeller materials in San Antonio.

The collection has not been previously described and analyzed in detail, but numerous publications on various aspects of it have appeared.[4] Various reviews of exhibitions of the collection through the years are also available and provide useful comment on its nature and significance.

Several aspects of the Rockefeller collection set it apart from similar collections and make it unique. Clearly, its sheer size and scope make it one of the most comprehensive groupings of Mexican folk art in the world. Its greatest importance, however, lies elsewhere. First, in a field in which any object of more than twenty-five years is likely to be labeled "old," the antiquity of many of the pieces is important. The early part of the collection, particularly that assembled by Rockefeller with the assistance of Roberto Montenegro, contains extremely rare and important pieces from the eighteenth and nineteenth centuries—objects unmatched in collections elsewhere. Splendid folk objects such as the eighteenth-century centurion helmet mask from the State of Mexico (pl. 56), the exquisitely painted lacquered dish from Michoacán (pl. 116), the expressive set of *conchero* pull toys (pl. 92), and many other historically significant objects are without parallel in other collections.

Second, Rockefeller's treasures are a result of fifty years of collecting activity. In several important instances the collection contains folk art from the same village purchased during the 1930s, the 1950s, and the 1970s, allowing us a rare opportunity to identify patterns of continuity and change within a given area. Water-cooler supports from San Blas Atempa, Oaxaca, for example, span a century of production of this type of folk art in the Isthmus of Tehuantepec. The same chronological depth can be seen in dozens of other examples from the collection.

Finally, the collection—assembled by an unusually open-minded man with the assistance of artists, scholars, folk art connoisseurs, and dealers—represents Mexican folk art over the past fifty years and, in some cases, longer.

THE NATURE OF THE COLLECTION

There are many ways of organizing the objects in a collection as rich and varied as this one is. Perhaps the most useful way of grouping them, however, is according to their function, since folk art is best understood through consideration of the context in which the objects are made and used. Four basic categories suggest themselves: utilitarian—objects made primarily for day-to-day use with specific duties in mind; ceremonial—pieces used only within a particular ritual context; recreational—objects associated with play, fantasy, and entertainment; and decorative—objects created primarily for aesthetic reasons. These groupings are, admittedly, rough-hewn: while some objects fit into only one of the above categories, others might fit easily into two or three. For example, a painted clay skeleton with articulated limbs attached to a cord is ceremonial, because it was made to be used in Day of the Dead festivities. However, because the skeleton also functions as a toy, it might also be regarded as a recreational object. In what follows, an object's primary function will determine the category in which it is included.

UTILITARIAN OBJECTS

Today, as in the past, most Mexican folk art is primarily utilitarian. Carefully woven textiles used as clothing, cooking utensils, household fur-

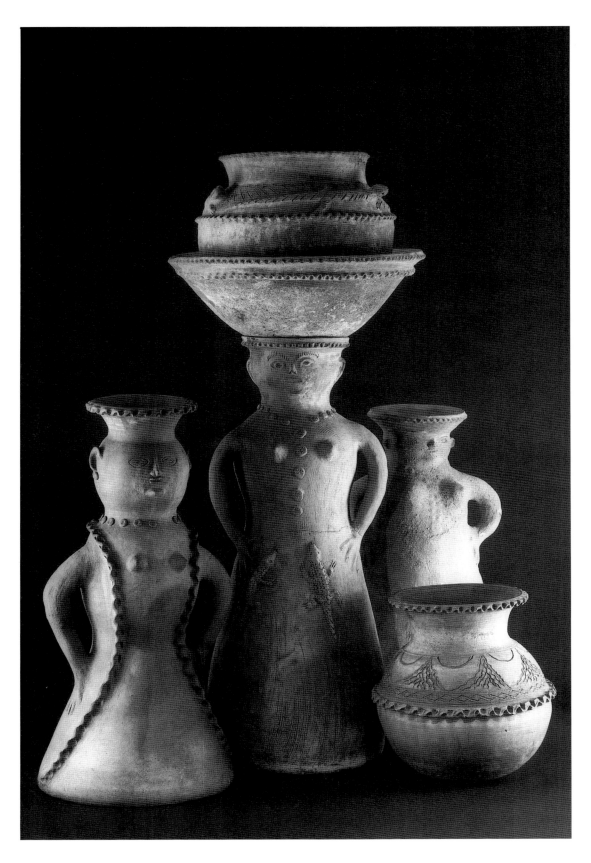

Plate 4
Water Coolers
San Blas Atempa, Tehuantepec,
Oaxaca
1940s to 1960s
Single-fired earthenware,
approximately 29 × 14″. MM and
SAMA

Keeping water cool and fresh is
critical in the hot Isthmus climate.
San Blas Atempa water coolers have
three parts. For this method of
cooling, the base, a traditional
female form, supports a shallow
flared bowl that holds the water jar.
Cooling is promoted through
evaporation. These bases bear an
abstract resemblance to the
Tehuanas—the fabled women of
Tehuantepec—whose distinctive and
imposing physical presence is
suggested by these solid and
dignified ceramic sculptures. The
three figures include a variety of
surface treatments. A fluted band
transforms a bare-breasted woman
into a cloaked figure, and lizards
crawl up the stomach toward a
necklace that also serves as
decorative buttons. The figure on
the right is an unadorned version
with little body contouring. Surface
paint has long since peeled off these
figures, bowls, and jars, which were
acquired by Rockefeller from the
garden of a Oaxaca family that had
transformed them into containers for
exotic semitropical plants.

Teodora Blanco, the great figural
ceramist from Santa María
Atzompa, was profoundly influenced
not only by these forms but also by
the highly stylized faces that bear
resemblance to some pre-Hispanic
ceramics.

nishings, and handmade containers of every shape and size are still found in abundance all over Mexico—particularly rural areas—even though plastics and machine-made clothing and objects are making steady inroads. All of these objects reflect and embody family or local traditions; each is uniquely designed to meet specific demands made by temperature, pattern of use, sex of wearer (in the case of clothing), and a variety of other factors. In short, the forms of these objects follow their functions.

The ceramics of Tulimán, Guerrero, a Nahua Indian community in the hills of southeastern Mexico, are primarily utilitarian. For hundreds of years, potters from this small community have produced highly prized three-handled water jugs used in dozens of villages in the region. What makes these jugs attractive to the peasants who buy them is the ease with which they can be used to transport water from distant village wells to individual households and their suitability as storage containers. The lightness and shape of the vessel, the curve of the handles, and the size of the orifice all are calculated to ease the gathering and carrying of the water. Furthermore, the single-fired pottery of Tulimán is highly porous, so that the water remains cool through evaporation. Because they must "sweat" constantly and freely, these jugs have round bottoms to discourage their being placed on the ground or on top of a table—settings that would impede cooling—and the three handles allow them to be suspended from a pole or roof support. After meeting such primary functional requirements, the potters of Tulimán are free to embellish as they see fit. Two water jugs from Guerrero, one of them from Tulimán (pl. 8), illustrate varying degrees to which these vessels are decorated after the basic requirements have been met.

While utilitarian considerations are at the core of most Mexican folk art, few artists are content to let their skills and imaginations rest at that level. Roughly carved, squat stools are ingeniously transformed into armadillos, horses, and other animals. Strong, functional walking sticks become a tangle of serpents and vines. This tendency of Mexican folk artists, and indeed folk artists all over the world, not only to make, but also to create and to animate, gives folk art its special quality and justifies its classification as art.

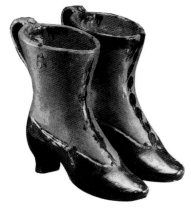

Plate 5
Boot Pitchers
Barrio de la Luz, Puebla
1930s
Painted and glazed earthenware,
11 × 9½ × 5″. MM and SAMA

Highly glazed, thick-walled boot pitchers for pouring pulque were mold-made by Barrio de la Luz potters. These asymmetrical pitchers are amusing representations of the high-heeled button-up shoes worn by the women of nineteenth-century Mexico.

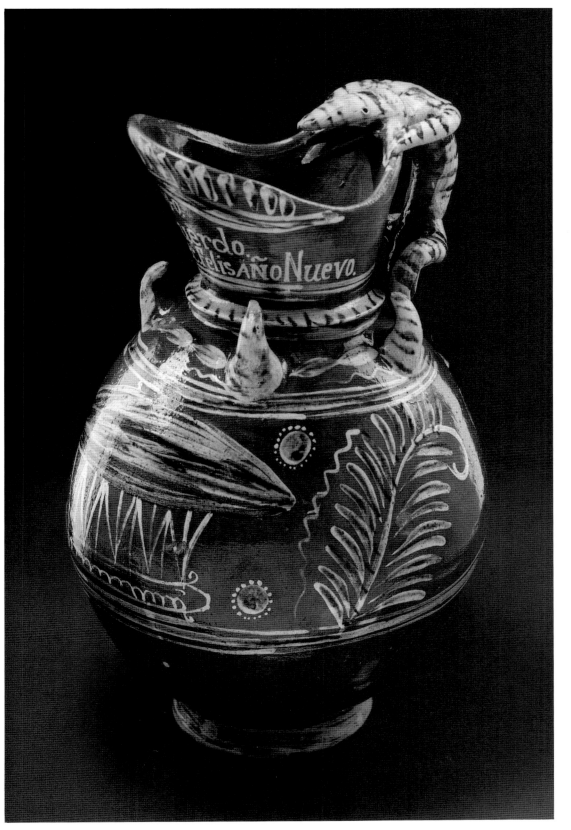

Plate 6
Pulque Pitcher
Metepec, State of Mexico
1940
Mold-made and hand-formed glazed earthenware, height, 16″. SAMA

A leaping lizard attempting to partake of pulque became the innovative handle of this pulque pitcher. Six cups that would have hung from the protrusions beneath the neck are sadly missing. The words "Recuerdo Feli[z] Año Nuevo" commemorate the New Year and help establish a memory for the purchaser. The exuberantly painted pitcher is a mix of energetic brushstrokes and floral motifs. The lizard takes us back to pre-Hispanic times, when innovative potters ingeniously used animals for spouts, handles, and relief decoration. The characteristic fine red Metepec clay shows through the glaze of this pulque jar.

Plate 7
Jar
Tulimán, Guerrero
1930s
Single-fired earthenware with
painted slip design, 13 × 13″.
SAMA

This large and graceful jar is
designed for storage. The symmetric
floral motif is painted with a natural
slip made from local ore. The pieces
are fired in large open fires with the
pottery piled up in the center of the
flames.

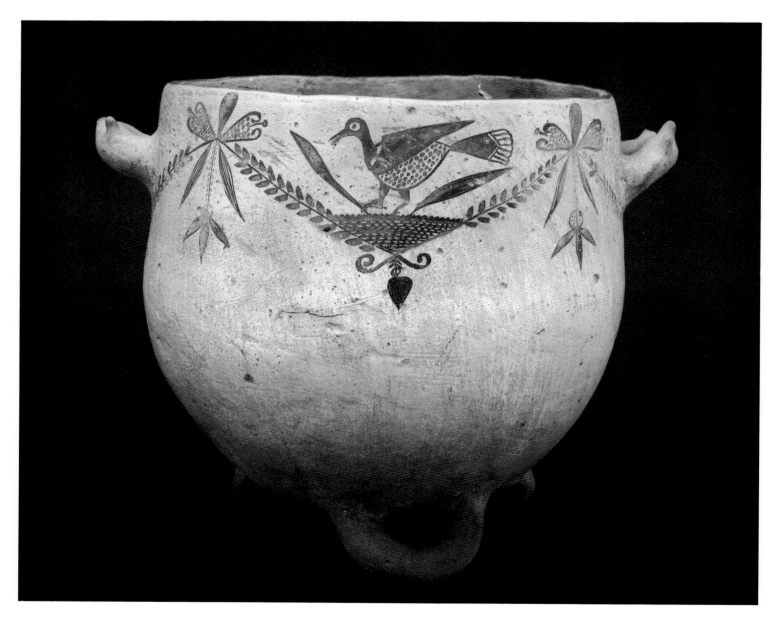

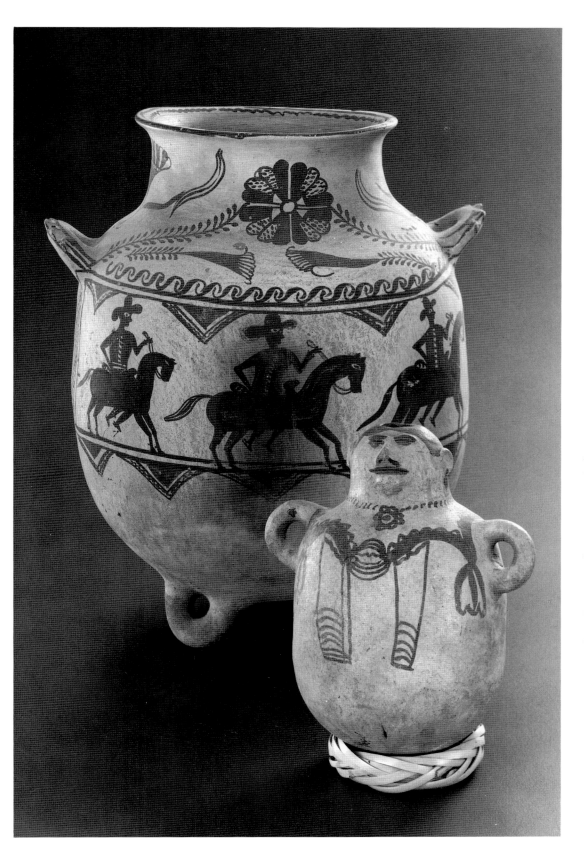

Plate 8
Water Jars
Mezcala region, Guerrero;
Tulimán, Guerrero
Left: Hand-molded, single-fired
ceramic with painted slip design,
18¼ × 15″; right: hand-molded,
single-fired ceramic with painted
slip design; bamboo base;
9¾ × 7½″. SAMA

A Nahua Indian area in the State of
Guerrero known as the Mezcala
region includes many pottery
villages still using pre-Hispanic
ceramic techniques. The artists of
these villages have always produced
a wide variety of utilitarian pottery
and in recent years have produced
new and decorative pieces.

On the left, the large *cántaro*,
designed for home water storage, is
made of a very porous clay that
enhances cooling through surface
evaporation. The three legs that
elevate the *cántaro* above the ground
assist with cooling. An almost
identical piece was included in the
Museum of Modern Art's 1940
exhibition, *20 Centuries of Mexican
Art*. The traditional design shows
charros on western-type saddles. The
decorative painting style is always
free and confident, whether it
consists of loose, repetitive
geometric motifs or profiled
horsemen or animals. On the large
cántaro the elegant horsemen face
the viewer while the horses' legs
suggest a canter.

The smaller piece is an
anthropomorphic canteen. Rope
strung through the handles makes it
easy to hang at home or carry back
from the river or stream.

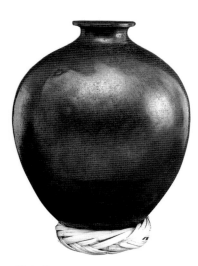

Plate 9
Doña Rosa Real de Nieto
Water Jar
San Bartolo Coyotepec, Oaxaca
1930s
Burnished earthenware; bamboo
base; 15½ × 13½". SAMA

This elegant black clay *cántaro*
(water jar) epitomizes Doña Rosa's
achievement as a folk artist. It is
difficult to imagine how this small
and fragile woman could hand-throw
large and graceful jars on a
primitive wheel. In her last years
Doña Rosa became a living legend.
Visitors and collectors from all over
the world came to San Bartolo
Coyotepec, a pottery center outside
Oaxaca, to see her black clay
pottery.

Black pottery is not black to
begin with. At a critical point in
firing, fuel is added to the fire, and
the potter rapidly seals all openings
to the kiln, producing thick smoke
that impregnates the pieces with
carbon. Before firing, the surfaces of
the jars are burnished with a quartz
burnishing stone. When the pieces
are removed, they are polished with
animal fat, wax, or oil that seals
them and produces a high luster.
Doña Rosa's early pieces impressed,
among others, Edward Weston, who
photographed the classical shapes of
her *cántaros*.

Ceramic Vessels

Among the objects whose function is mainly utilitarian, the most
impressive are perhaps the ceramics. These range from undecorated cooking
vessels from dozens of small Indian villages throughout Mexico to objects
that are embellished to a point that almost obscures their function.

The collection contains several splendid examples of highly burnished
black-ware made by the Zapotec potter Doña Rosa, of San Bartolo
Coyotepec. A large water jug (pl. 9) illustrates the sophistication of Doña
Rosa's work and the inherent strength of her plain but elegant ollas. It also
demonstrates her mastery of the coloration process achieved through
reduction-firing, a technique in which carbon residue is bonded to clay in an
airtight kiln. The handsome decoration of some Coyotepec earthenware is
achieved through selective surface burnishing into geometric or floral designs prior to firing.

Other fine examples of purely utilitarian earthenware come from the
State of Guerrero. Atzacoaloya, a small Nahua village outside the town of
Chilapa, produces elegant *cántaros* that are highly regarded throughout the
region for their shape, durability, and effectiveness (pl. 10). Still other
excellent examples of water vessels come from Zacualpa, Tulimán, and
Zumpango del Río, Guerrero. Another representative piece of utilitarian
Guerrero pottery is a water jar (pl. 8) probably from San Agustín de las
Flores, a Nahua village in the Mezcala region. This graceful jar was designed
for water storage in the home. The highly porous clay and the three supports
elevating the vessel above the floor permit maximum cooling. But, going
well beyond these basic requirements, the creator of this jar painted a lively
horizontal band of six horsemen, each of which has its own individual
personality and design quality. Rockefeller purchased this piece in the 1960s,
shortly after it was made, but it is strikingly similar to pieces from the same
village made in the 1930s.[5]

Majolica pottery, a high-fired, glazed pottery introduced to Mexico by
the Spanish in the sixteenth century, is a utilitarian ware strongly represented
in the collection. Rare nineteenth-century plates and platters from Guana-

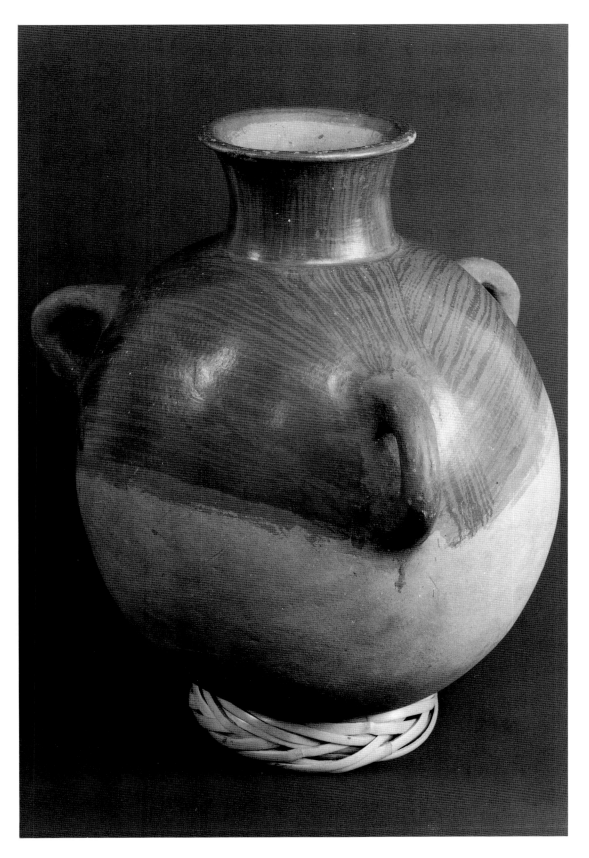

Plate 10
Water Jar
Atzacoaloya, Guerrero
1930s
Single-fired, burnished earthenware;
bamboo base; 14 × 12″. SAMA

This *cántaro*, from a Nahua village
near Chilapa, Guerrero, is a classic
example of utilitarian pottery. The
globular shape with three handles is
carried on burros, balanced on
heads, and hung at home. It is made
of a porous buff-colored clay that
allows the evaporation necessary for
cooling. The bamboo ring elevates
the piece above the ground.
Atzacoaloya produces other
utilitarian ware with similar surface
decoration of roughly burnished
sienna slip on their upper surfaces.
The touch of the potter is felt not
only in the traditionally hand-built
form but also in the vigorous
burnishing strokes.

Plate 11
Platters
Coroneo, Guanajuato
Late 19th century
Glazed and incised earthenware,
8½ × 6½". SAMA

Folk artists often find an outlet for humor on serving platters. In these examples, amusing and primitive animals are incised in the clay and painted with a runny glaze. The effect is spontaneous and uninhibited. This very engaging utilitarian pottery seems to be a rural interpretation of the already-decadent majolica produced in nearby Dolores Hidalgo.

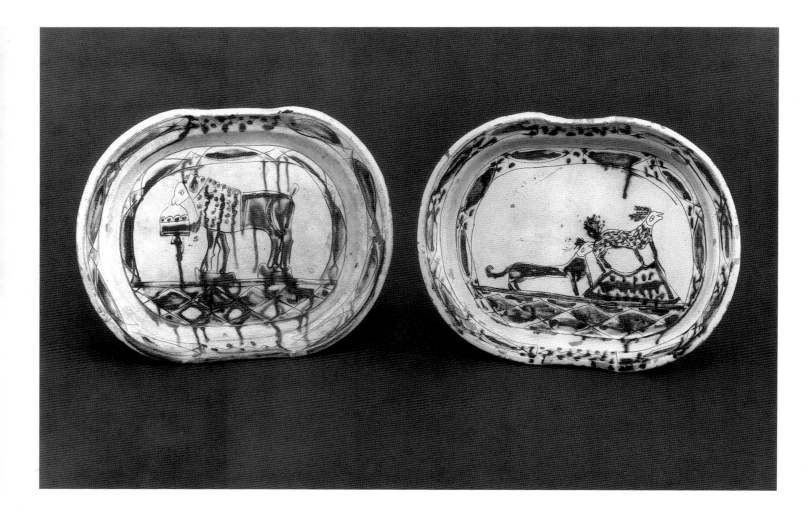

juato (pl. 11) and Talavera-style objects from the same period in the city of Puebla are excellent examples of a type of Mexican pottery with strong Mediterranean roots.

Most of the early majolica in the Rockefeller collection is elaborately decorated with figural motifs and arabesque floral designs typical of this ceramic ware. Later examples in the collection, made in this century, also come from the states of Puebla and Guanajuato. The collection contains more than a dozen examples of majolica ware made by the well-known Guanajuato ceramist Gorky Gonzales, who was instrumental in the rebirth of early majolica designs in Guanajuato; his fine pieces are now marketed all over the world.

There are also many ceramic pitchers, primarily utilitarian but decorated in ways that are both beautiful and amusing. The exquisitely worked amber-colored pitcher (pl. 12) illustrates the delicate touch of some unknown nineteenth-century potter.[6] Portrait pitchers from the states of Michoacán, Mexico, and Puebla were all used for the festive consumption of pulque.

Perhaps the most important utilitarian ceramic objects are the water cooler assemblages from San Blas Atempa, a Zapotec Indian community in the Isthmus of Tehuantepec. The collection has six fine examples. As mentioned earlier, one is from the nineteenth century, another from the 1940s, and the rest are relatively modern, dating from the 1960s and 1970s. Each cooler set consists of three pieces—a figural base, a shallow bowl, and an olla—which, together, maintain the freshness of a day's water supply. The cooler base in this piece (pl. 20) is extremely rare and may be the earliest surviving example of this folk art form anywhere.

Wooden Containers

About half of the fourteen wooden chests in the collection date from the nineteenth century, the rest from this century. Unquestionably, one of the most unusual is an elaborately carved chest (pl. 15) inlaid with woods of lighter hues. It is in superb condition. Unfortunately, little is known of its history, and its provenance is unknown. It is, however, typical of nineteenth-

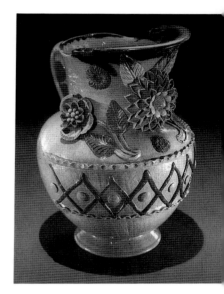

Plate 12
Pitcher
Oaxaca, Oaxaca
19th century
Glazed, hand-formed earthenware,
12¼ × 8″. SAMA

This charming pitcher is one of the rarest ceramic pieces in Rockefeller's collection. It was shown in the 1940 *20 Centuries of Mexican Art* exhibition at the Museum of Modern Art, with a caption that described it as a "type of ornamental jar unfortunately no longer made." The Spanish translation called it a rare sample of a lost art. The pitcher combines many stylistic techniques: press-molding, hand-forming, fluting, and relief work. It almost feels as if a potter and a baker collaborated to produce this very special piece.

Plate 13
Pot
Dolores Hidalgo, Guanajuato
Late 19th century
Glazed and painted majolica,
13 × 12″. SAMA

The tradition of Guanajuato
majolica dates back to the eighteenth
century. This type of majolica,
similar to the Talavera ware of
Puebla, was brought to the newly
wealthy, silver-rich Guanajuato by
the Spaniards long after the Puebla
potteries were established. In the
nineteenth century, Padre Hidalgo,
who later became known as the
father of Mexican independence,
encouraged the Indians of Dolores
to produce the type of decorative
wares being made in nearby
Guanajuato. He is credited with the
birth of Dolores Hidalgo majolica.
This hand-thrown piece is glazed
with traditional green, black,
orange, sienna, and yellow over a
creamy white opaque background.
Floral and bird motifs are
energetically painted in a more free-
flowing style than that of Puebla.

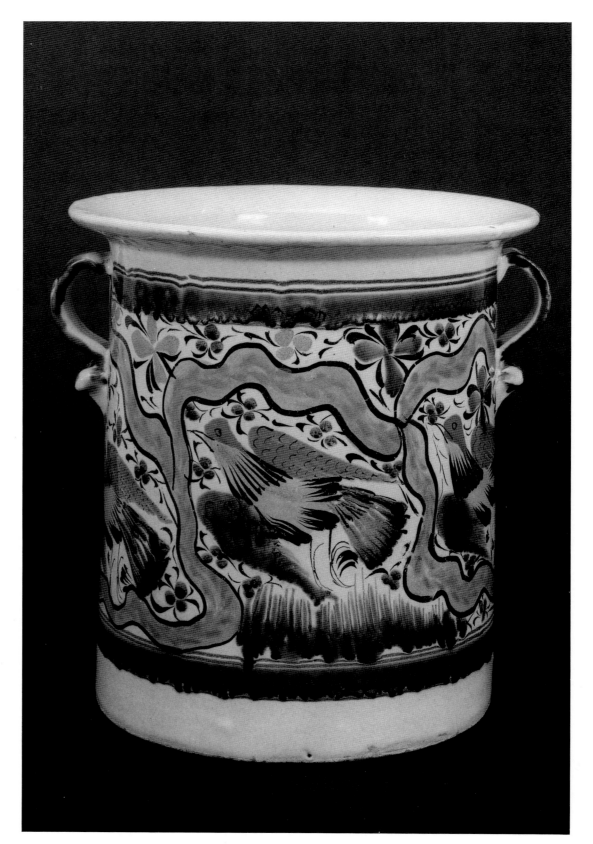

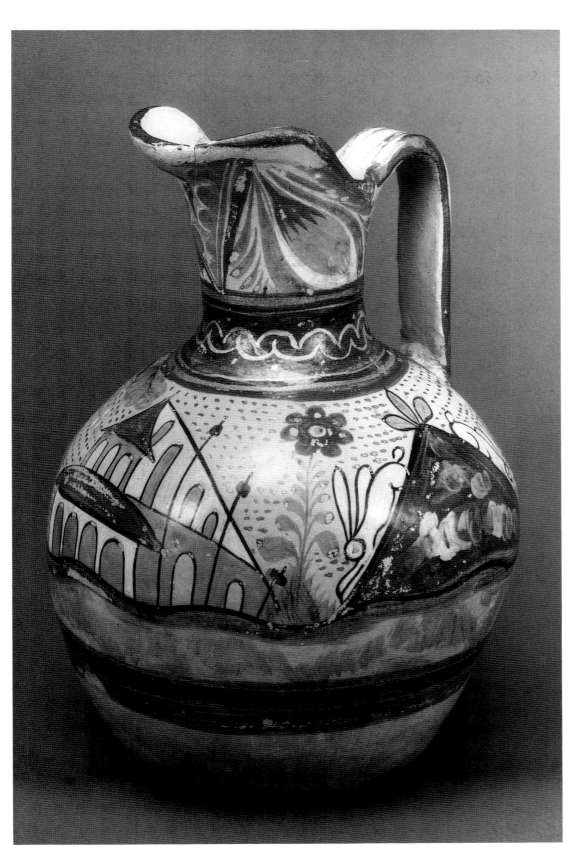

Plate 14
Pitcher
Tonalá, Jalisco
Late 19th century
Single-fired earthenware and
metallic paint, height, 10″. SAMA

This late-nineteenth-century Tonalá
pitcher is probably one of the few
surviving pieces with painted gold
decoration. Pitchers from Tonalá
were used to keep water fresh and
cool, and the excellent clay often
imparted a fragrant taste and smell.
This mold-made piece is hand-
painted with what appears to be a
spontaneity of brushwork. Bounding
rabbits were popular animal motifs,
along with songbirds, birds in flight,
and elaborate floral designs, and it
was not unusual at that time to paint
images of village chapels. These
early pieces, once painted, were
given a coat of clear varnish.

The palette used at the turn of the
century was somewhat different than
Tonaltecan color of today. All the
colors were natural pigments mined
locally. Today's combinations are
earthy colors with a dominant light
blue, pale green, or cream
background. Rose, red, and yellow
were once more fashionable. Much
like the ancient murals and wall
paintings, it is often hard to know
just how brilliant the original colors
were. They age gracefully and settle
into pastels of time and wear.

and early-twentieth-century inlaid furniture from the Mexican provinces, especially Oaxaca, Guerrero, and Puebla, and reflects the strong Oriental influences found in much of the furniture of that period.[7]

Another important and quite interesting piece is a leather-covered wood chest (pl. 16). This shallow trunk is rare both for its shape and for the materials used in its manufacture. The hand-painted designs are a mixture of neoclassical architectural motifs associated with the early nineteenth century and floral designs. The iron hardware that secures the top, while suggestive of an earlier, perhaps colonial, period, is probably nineteenth-century, as is the iron key. Like the inlaid chest, it is an outstanding example of furniture of the hinterland during the nineteenth century and early part of the twentieth. Its provenance, similarly, is unknown.

The largest selection of chests in the collection comes from Olinalá, Guerrero. Made from a highly fragrant *lináloe* wood, richly lacquered and painted, they manifest many of the finest folk qualities in Mexican painting and lacquer work (pls. 17, 18). Used primarily to store household linens and other valuables, these chests were greatly valued in rural Mexico as wedding gifts or as part of a dowry. Many were custom-made and dated, and they frequently included dedicatory verses.[8]

Olinalá chests are now shipped to all parts of Mexico and exported in great quantities to many places outside the republic. The collection contains several outstanding examples of these brightly colored chests. Most are richly painted on three sides and the top, inside and out. Street scenes from neighboring areas such as Izúcar de Matamoros and the city of Puebla are often included on the front panel (pls. 18, 24). The artists' concern for detail can be seen. Soldiers, flags, animals, and other scenes of nineteenth-century life are depicted in a fanciful, yet straightforward, fashion. Nationalistic emblems, most frequently the Mexican eagle atop a cactus and flags, are often part of the design motifs of trunks from Olinalá.

Other lacquered chests in the collection come from Michoacán and are richly decorated in a manner distinct from those of Olinalá.

Also in the collection is a large and impressive assortment of lacquered

Plate 15
Chest
Possibly from Olinalá, Guerrero
Early 1920s
Inlaid wood and metal,
32 × 14 × 17½". SAMA

This inlaid wooden chest is
reminiscent of nineteenth-century
work. In fact it was probably
commissioned in 1933 as a present
for Nelson's father, John D.
Rockefeller, Jr., as evidenced by the
initials "JR" on the front of the
chest. Since Nelson Rockefeller

never visited the remote Guerrero
village of Olinalá, it is likely that
Frances Flynn Paine, a great
champion of Olinalá lacquerware,
commissioned this piece. These
dowry chests can be found in many
Olinalá households but are rarely
made for external markets. The
inlaid floral designs are very similar
to delicate painted motifs found on
lacquered chests. Elements of
traditional work are also seen in the
geometric border designs that set
off the inlaid work on the body of
the chest.

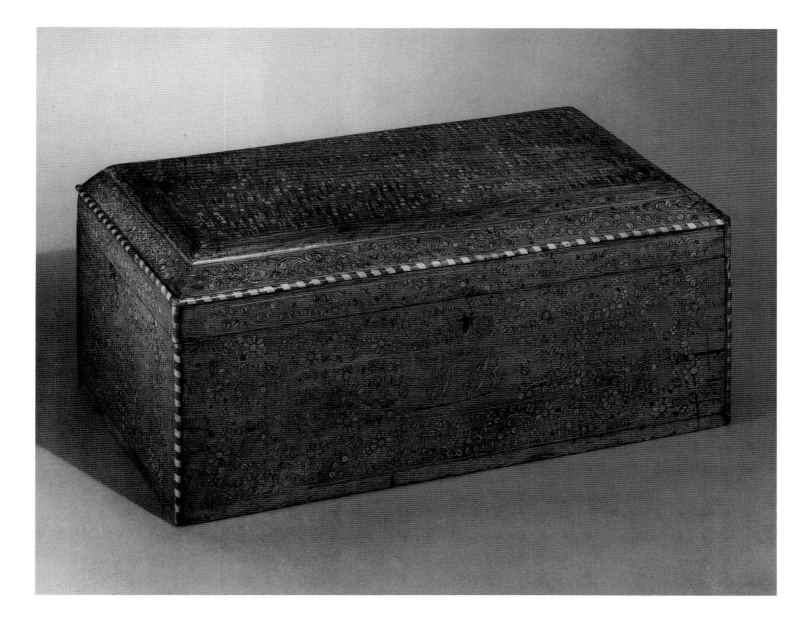

Plate 16
Trunk
19th century
Painted leather on wood,
29 × 16 × 10″. SAMA

Although the exact origin of this unusual leather-covered trunk is difficult to determine, it might have been found in a rural hacienda near Puebla because of its curious mixture of motifs: the popular floral designs seen on Talavera-style pottery from Puebla and neoclassical pillars from *portales*—those wonderful covered walkways that surround a town's central plaza. The use of ornate wrought-iron hardware shows a definite Spanish influence. The Spaniards brought wrought iron to Mexico; after the Conquest blacksmith guilds were divided into locksmiths and bladesmiths. Puebla and Amozoc were centers for most of the elaborate ironwork in Mexico. Leather-covered trunks were popular in colonial Mexico but are rarely seen today.

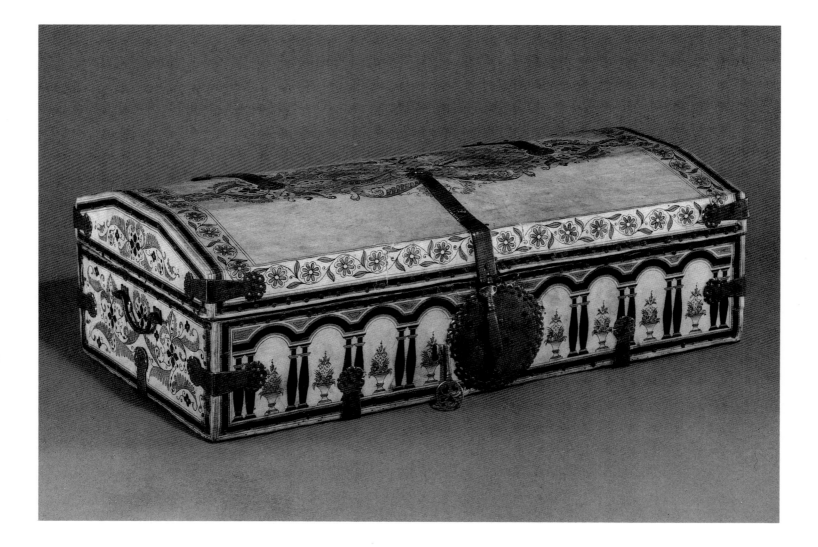

Plate 17
Chest
Olinalá, Guerrero
Late 19th century
Lacquered and painted wood,
12 × 29 × 15½″. SAMA

Lacquerware is one of Mexico's oldest crafts, and evidence of widespread pre-Hispanic Indian production is conclusive. When the Spaniards arrived in Mexico, they were stunned by the brilliant and diverse selection of lacquerware they saw in the Aztec marketplaces. Olinalá, a small village in the rugged Sierra Madre del Sur of Guerrero, was and still is devoted to this labor-intensive craft. The techniques of lacquerware have not changed significantly for hundreds of years.

The base material for Olinalá lacquer is chia oil extracted from the crushed and boiled chia seeds. After the first coat of oil and powdered dolomite is applied and burnished with the heel of the hand, layers of the oil and locally mined pigments are applied and polished, building up a very resistant base. This lacquered base can then be decorated with paints that nineteenth-century artisans made with natural pigments. The traditional base colors are a deep orange-red or black. Two techniques are now practiced in Olinalá, *rayado* (incised) and *dorado* (painted).

Rockefeller's collection of lacquered chests is a testimony to the splendid colonial and late-nineteenth-century work produced in Olinalá. René d'Harnoncourt and Fred Davis helped revive this craft in the late 1920s, and the late Carlos Espejel was instrumental in reviving it once again in the late 1960s, when the number of artisans had dwindled to seven. Lacquerware is now produced in most Olinalá households.

Today lacquerware is a communal craft involving many artisans who are specialists in the many techniques necessary to complete a piece. Five or more artisans work on one painted dowry chest. A carpenter makes the wooden chest from the highly fragrant *lináloe* wood harvested in the tropical areas of Guerrero. Various family members collect the minerals and make the oil and pigments. A woman generally performs the critical burnishing of the base coat.

Polishing is performed by a specialist, and a painter completes the work.

This extraordinary dowry chest is one of the earliest pieces of lacquerware in the Rockefeller collection. An abundance of large, loosely painted flowers and foliage surrounds mounted horsemen and figures on a rich burnt-orange lacquered background. The panels are framed with simple bands of colors unlike the patterned border designs seen on other Olinalá chests. Time has faded the once-brilliant pigments to subtle autumnal hues. The painter of this trunk skillfully integrated the figures, animals, and floral motifs into a structured yet freely executed design.

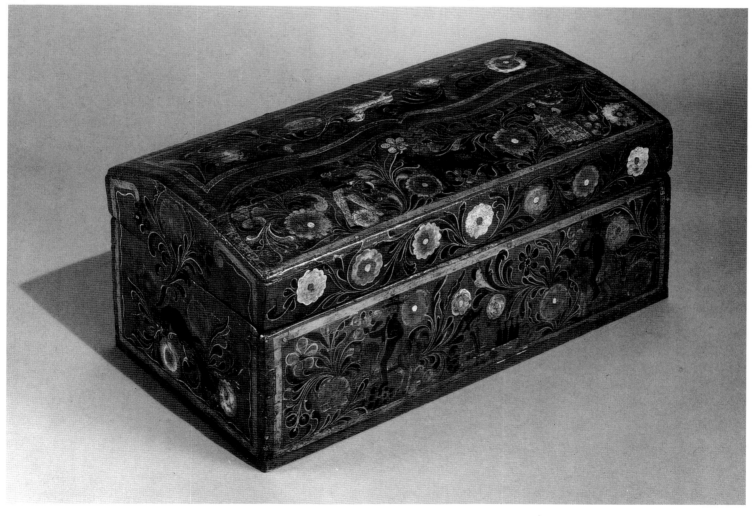

Plate 18
Chest
Olinalá, Guerrero
Late 19th century
Lacquered and painted wood,
13⅞ × 28 × 13¾". MM

This dowry chest is typical of the
nineteenth-century style of pictorial
decoration popular in Olinalá.
Although the village was in a
remote part of the Sierra Madre del
Sur, the artisans took pleasure in
copying urban scenes they found in
books. The curious painting on the
front panel combines cathedrals and
colonial buildings against a
backdrop of mountains. The
charming confusion of perspectives
is very common on these lacquered
chests. The top of the trunk is
decorated with the ever-popular
patriotic motif of the eagle, cactus,
and serpent surrounded by Mexican
flags. Pelicans, cranes, flowers, and
a variety of border designs complete
this very traditional chest. The
background color is a rich burnt
orange.

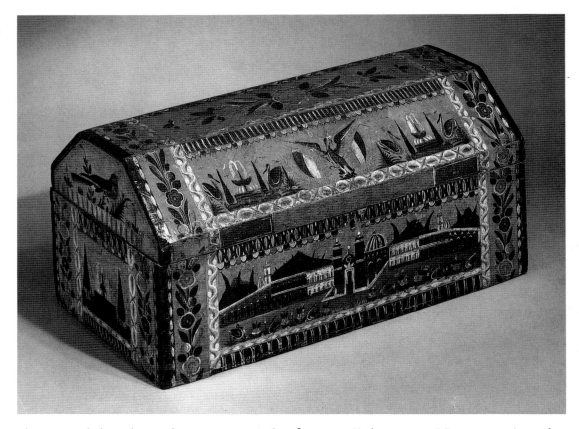

plates and bowls and trays, mainly from Michoacán. Here, again, the variously shaped objects, decorated with floral motifs typical of the nineteenth century, show an Oriental influence. Trays from Uruapan (pl. 28), decorated using an inlaid lacquer technique, are interesting for comparison with the other pieces.

Textiles

The collection has more than 150 textiles, the majority of which are from the twentieth century. With few exceptions, they are in excellent condition. Most are mestizo textiles, produced on Spanish-style looms in weaving centers such as Chiconcuac, State of Mexico; Santa Ana Chiautempan, Tlaxcala; and Teotitlán del Valle, Oaxaca. Less numerous but of no less importance are the Indian textiles, most of which were produced on back-strap looms. *Huipiles, quechquémitls, fajas, bolsas,* and other items from Indian Mexico provide an interesting contrast to the large collection of non-Indian materials.

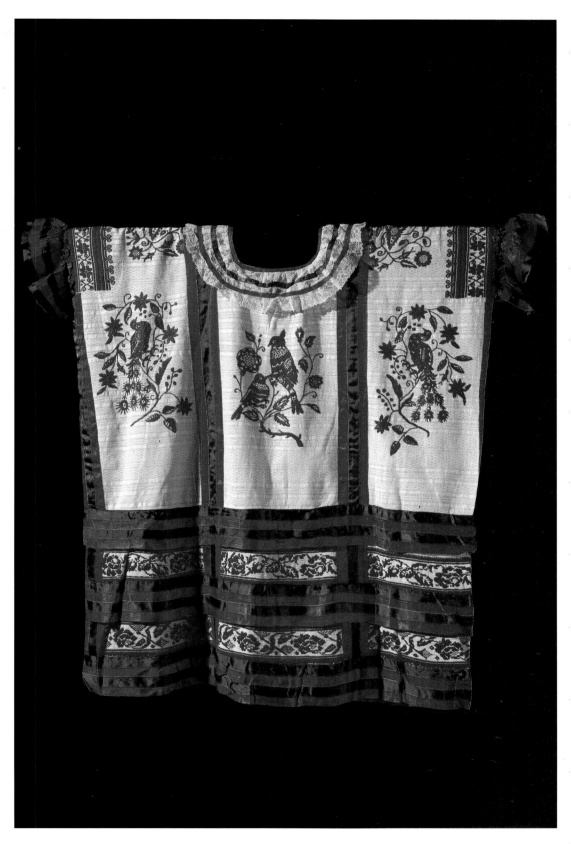

Plate 19
Fiesta Huipil
Huatla de Jiménez, Oaxaca
1920s
Hand-loomed cotton, silk, ribbons, and lace, 36 × 25″. SAMA

This classic fiesta *huipil* from the mountainous Mazatec region of Oaxaca is worn for ceremonial occasions. There is a striking contrast between the carefully woven open-meshed strips and the wildly exuberant silk ribbons that join them. The central panel is embroidered with a stylized parrot and a hummingbird partaking of floral nectar. Floral bands circle the bottom of the *huipil* and help to reinforce the weave at the shoulders. Imported silk threads are used for embroidering.

The *huipil,* a woman's tuniclike costume, was called *huipili* by the Aztecs. It is the most commonly worn garment in Indian Mexico. It is made by joining rectangular strips woven on a back-strap loom. The weave can vary from gauzelike fabric to tightly woven cotton. The surface can be adorned with intricate or simple embroidery in geometric or floral and animal motifs. The embroidery stitches include a great variety of techniques, from simple cross-stitch to elaborate brocading. These loose-fitting garments are made for everyday use and for ceremonial occasions. A finely woven *huipil* is expected to last a lifetime and often is a symbol of status for the weaver.

Plate 20
Water Cooler
San Blas Atempa, Tehuantepec,
Oaxaca
Late 19th century
Painted, single-fired earthenware,
36 × 16″. SAMA

This classic late-nineteenth-century
tinajera (water cooler) is one of the
most important pieces in the
collection. The three-part set is
missing the shallow bowl that
ordinarily sits on top of the figure
and holds the jar of drinking water.
Water is cooled through the process
of evaporation, made possible by the
highly porous clay the piece is made
of. The flared bowl, placed between
the figure and the *cántaro,* is filled
with sand to absorb excess moisture
and promote further cooling. These
pieces are a sculptural translation of
the traditional water-carrying
posture.

These anthropomorphic figures
are traditionally women, but this
unusual piece appears to be a male
with a black beard and stylized
mustache. A pendant adorns his
neck, and his torso is decorated with
a floral motif. The water jar is very
coarse clay with a fluted coil circling
the piece. A floral design incised on
the upper part of the jar is similar to
pre-Conquest decoration.

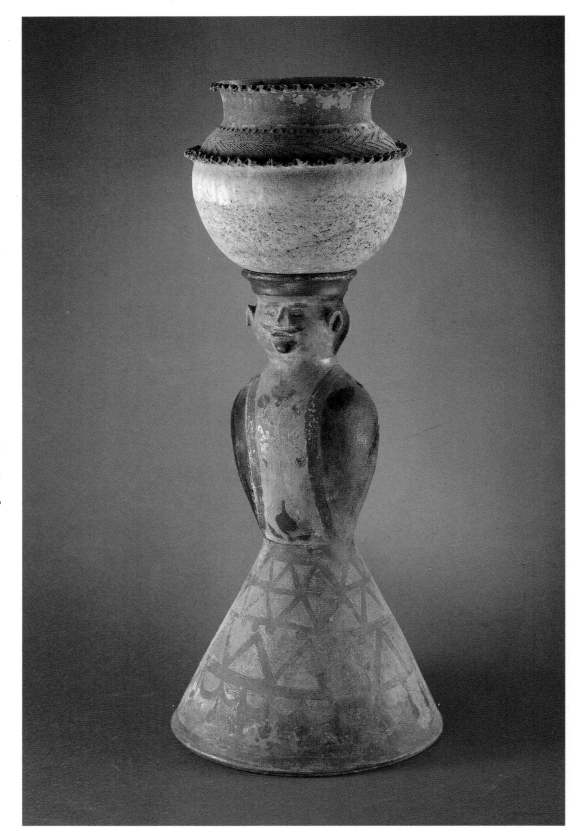

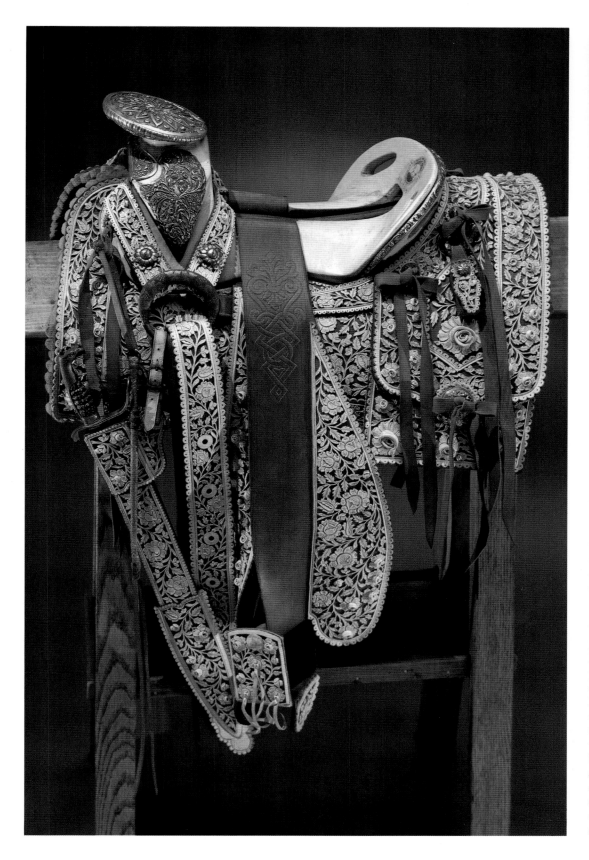

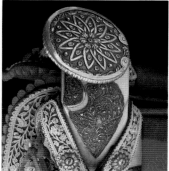

Plates 21 and 22
Saddle and Detail
Amozoc, Puebla
Early 20th century
Leather, silver, metal, and bone,
40 × 29 × 20″. SAMA

The art of saddlery was taken very seriously in Mexico, where not only transportation but entertainment for wealthy Mexicans revolved around horses. Horseback riding, introduced by the Spaniards, is considered a national sport in Mexico. Shortly after the Conquest, the Mexicans were forbidden to ride by the Spaniards, who set themselves apart by lavish displays on horseback, including processions, promenades, and competitions. But the inevitable occurred on provincial ranches, where successful Mexican landholders bought horses and took up riding. They dressed in elaborate costumes adorned with silver and embroidery and outfitted their horses similarly. They were called *charros*, meaning "loud and flashy."

This saddle would have been used by a *charro* in a parade on a national holiday or in a *charreada*, where all kinds of equestrian events take place. It is made of carved and appliquéd leather with elaborate leather roses. The metalwork of engraved and encrusted steel is a traditional craft in Amozoc, Puebla, where artisans make elaborate spurs, bits, and decorative accessories for *charros*. The whole effect is one of opulence, a carryover from the sixteenth century, when class divisions were intensified by this sport's lavish manifestations.

Plate 23
Chest (front panel)
Quiroga, Michoacán
19th century
Lacquered wood,
16¼ × 30½ × 14½". SAMA

This nineteenth-century chest
documents the elegant costumes of
high-ranking military officers in
Mexico's struggle for independence
from Spain. These splendid
uniforms, inspired by European
military fashion, were decidedly
French, with occasional Spanish
influence. Paintings of Mexico's

fight for independence show Agustín
de Iturbide, General Antonio López
de Santa Anna, and other important
officers impeccably dressed in white
breeches with tiny gold buttons, red
and white tight-waisted short jackets
elegantly trimmed with gold
epaulets and braiding, and gold-
tasseled cummerbunds. Hats were
copies of a French military style.
Rifles and bayonets were often
skillfully engraved. The border
designs and floral motifs around the
soldiers are classic Uruapan patterns
used on Michoacán lacquerware.

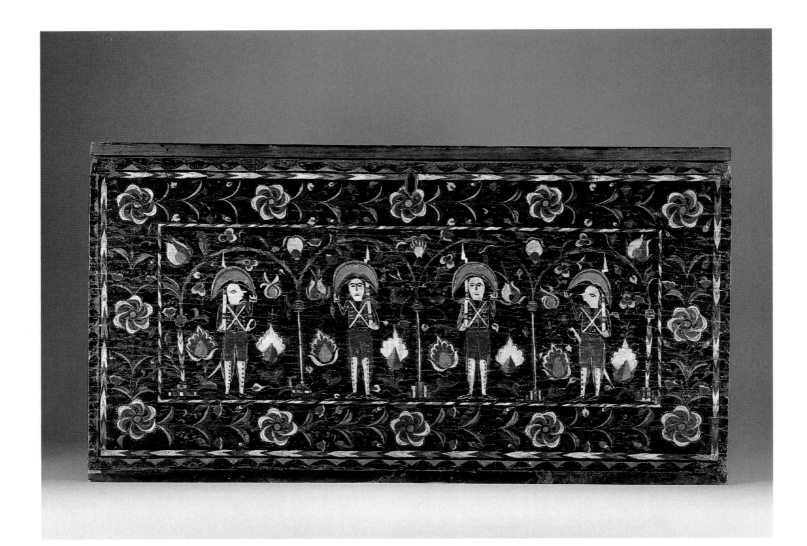

Plates 24 and 25
Chest and Detail
Olinalá, Guerrero
Late 19th century
Lacquered and painted wood,
16½ × 30 × 16″. SAMA

This classic Olinalá piece was intended to be a dowry chest. Many colonial chests had panels painted with charming and idealized scenes of rural and urban life, such as those depicted here. The more sophisticated urban scenes were copied from books and have a distinctly naive quality. The border designs are a mix of geometric and floral motifs. The front panels are colonial scenes of the city of Puebla or Cholula with their magnificent central squares, imposing stone buildings, and impressive churches. The side panels are pastoral scenes located in and around Olinalá with vistas of the surrounding mountains. The side panels of the lid are decorated with cranes—popular with Olinalátecos.

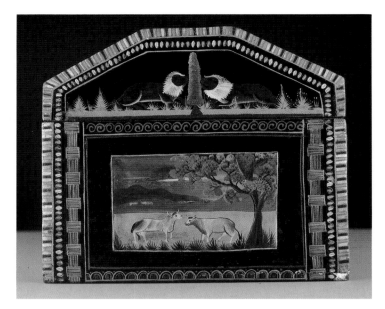

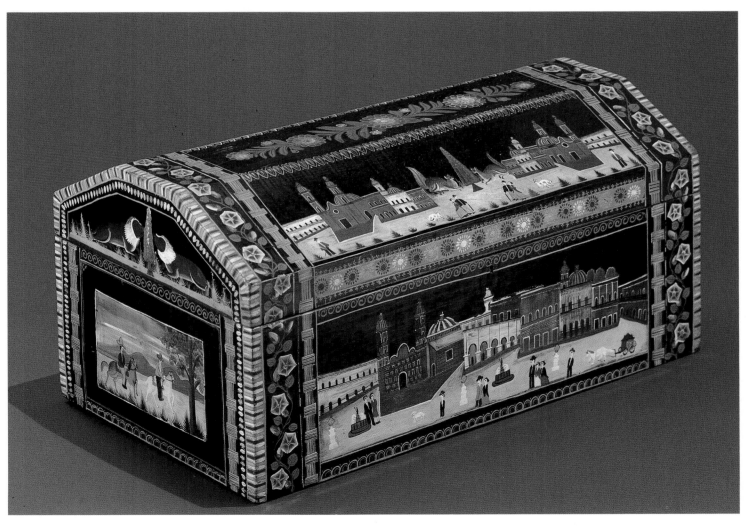

Plate 26
Chest
Olinalá, Guerrero
Late 19th century
Lacquered and painted wood,
14¾ × 33 × 16⅝″. SAMA

This chest has a traditional deep orange-red lacquered base painted with a profusion of floral, animal, and architectural motifs. A colonial panorama is set behind a grassy courtyard filled with a menagerie of rabbits, ducks, cranes, pelicans, and dogs. They are larger than the trees. The lid is painted with the ancient eagle-and-serpent motif surrounded by Mexican flags. Nineteenth-century dowry chests were painted a solid color on the inside. It is common to find the initials of the young woman for whom the chest was made on the inside of the lid, surrounded by decorative motifs.

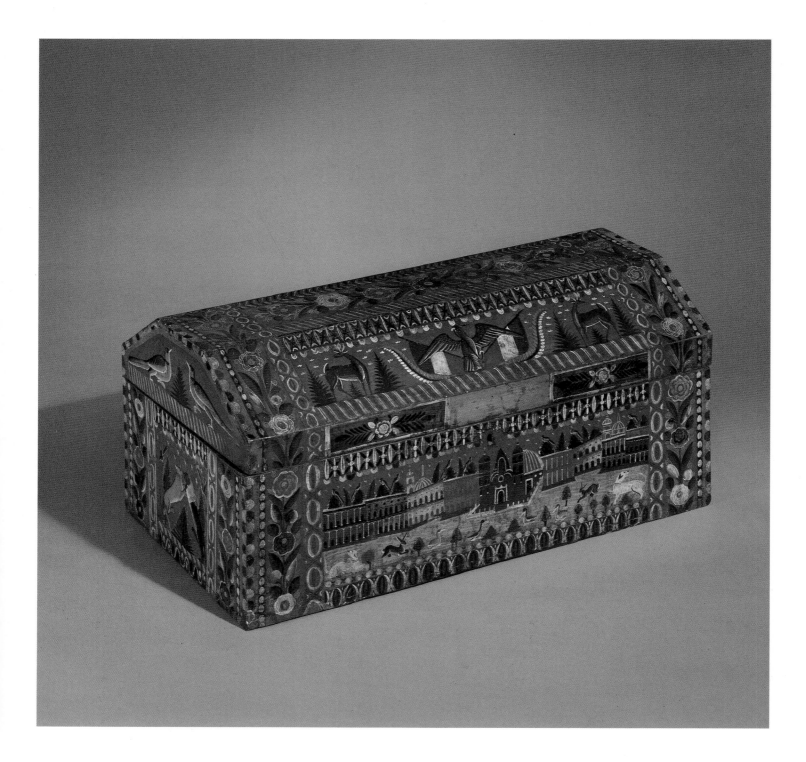

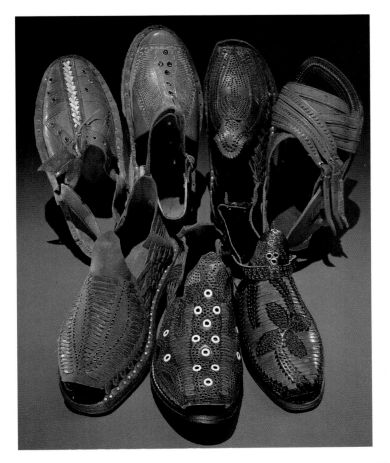

Plate 27
Huaraches
States of Jalisco, Michoacán, and
Oaxaca
1930 to 1960s
Leather, grommets, nails, and
rubber tire treads, 10½ × 3½" to
11¾ × 4⅜". MM and SAMA

Huaraches are the footwear of
Indian Mexico. They are
traditionally worn by men—Indian
women in the past usually went
barefoot. They have been worn in
Mexico since pre-Hispanic times
and are well-documented in all the
early codices. Stylistic variations
appear from state to state and
developed according to terrain and
climate. Huaraches are almost
always made of leather. The soles
were once made of laminated leather
but are now made of rubber
automobile tire treads. Huaraches
can be laced, lashed, buckled on, or
just slipped into.

Plate 28
Tray
Uruapan, Michoacán
Early 20th century
Encrusted lacquerware and wood,
diameter, 22½". SAMA

This early-twentieth-century *batea*
(tray) is typical of the traditional
embutido (encrusted) technique of
lacquerware practiced in Uruapan
since organized guilds were set up in
the sixteenth century under the
direction of Don Vasco de Quiroga,
who introduced this elegant craft to
the Tarascans in Uruapan, Periban,
and Quiroga.
    Many steps are involved in
making this tray. After the first coat
of lacquer is hardened, the design is
incised with a very sharp metal tool
and hollowed out. These hollowed
areas are filled with lacquer—
colored mineral powders mixed with
the fat extracted from boiling *aje*
insects—and rubbed vigorously with
the palm of the hand to achieve a
high luster. Many colors can be
used on one tray for the inlaid
design. In the old days the colors
were natural pigments mined in the
area. Recipes for these colors were
passed down for generations within
families. The early pieces had a
refined delicacy and austere
symmetry that have given way to
profuse decoration. This *batea* has
delicate floral motifs surrounding
two stylized figures and their
animals. The geometric border
design is a classic Uruapan design
used on gourds and trays.

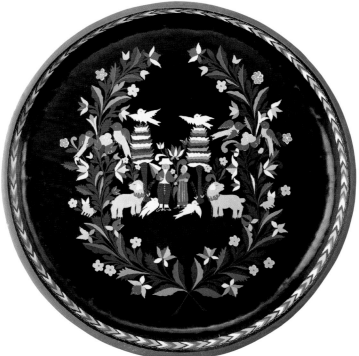

Plate 29
Sarape (detail)
Saltillo, Coahuila
Early 20th century
Wool, cotton, and aniline dyes,
45 × 88″ (full size). SAMA

This detail is of the central section
of a "portrait" sarape in vogue in
the late nineteenth and early
twentieth century in Zacatecas and
Saltillo. In the midst of the striking
and complex triangular patterning
are two mustached *charros*, one
toasting the other with his glass of
tequila and the other raising a knife.
Are they engaged in a drinking bout
or toasting an occasion? These
sarapes were often commemorative,
the central motifs portraying
political heroes, national symbols,
and popular themes. The shredded
areas of the sarape reveal the
underlying white cotton warp
threads.

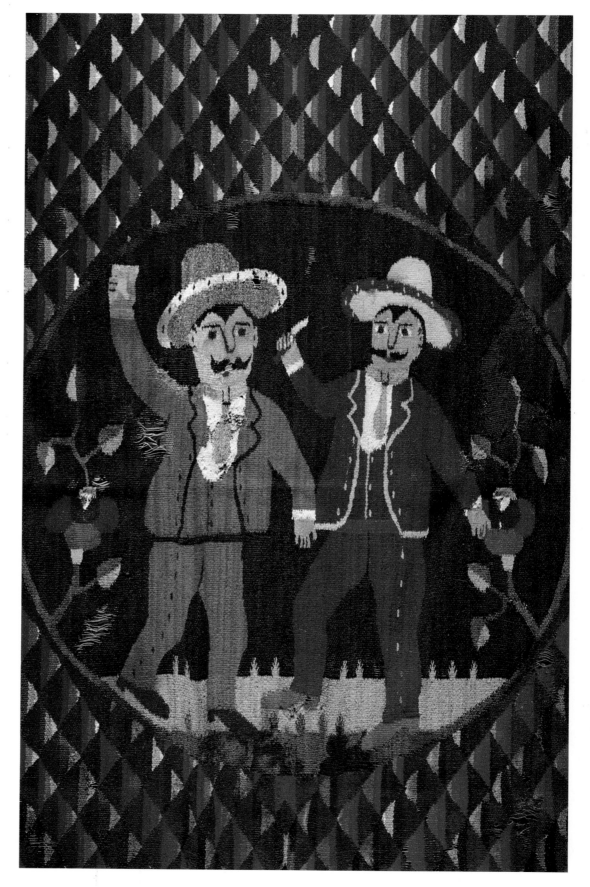

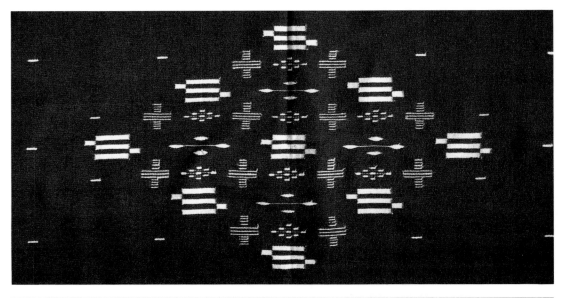

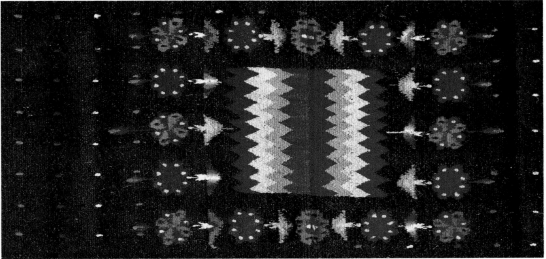

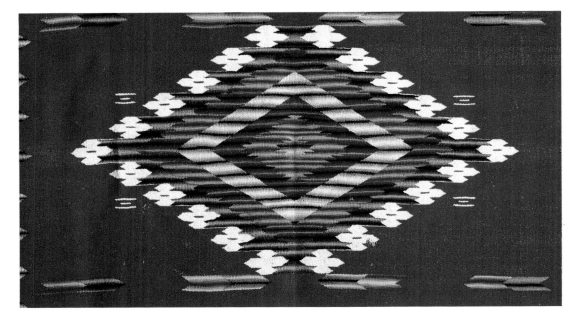

Plates 30, 31, 32
Sarapes (details)
Top to bottom: San Bernardino
Contla, Tlaxcala; Texcoco, State of
Mexico; Santa Ana Chiautempan,
Tlaxcala
1930s
Wool, 6'4" × 4'5" to 7 × 5' (full
size). MM and SAMA

In pre-Hispanic times, Indians wore
a capelike garment similar to a
sarape but woven of cotton or other
plant fibers. Upright treadle hand
looms were introduced to Mexico by
the Spaniards, who also taught the
Indians how to gather and spin
wool, profoundly influencing the
development of the sarape.

A sarape, generally the size of a
blanket, is usually made of wool and
can be woven in one or two pieces.
As an all-purpose part of a man's
costume, it can be folded and worn
decoratively across his shoulders or
worn as a cloak. It can also be used
as a blanket or as a ground cover for
displaying market wares. Many
sarapes have a slit in the center so
they can be slipped over the head,
becoming useful for riding, rainy
weather, or walking. Mexican
weaving centers are identified by
their sarape designs. Rockefeller,
particularly fond of sarapes from
San Bernardino Contla, Tlaxcala,
continued to collect sarapes into the
late 1970s.

The central design seen in the
detail at top is a variation on the
traditional diamond pattern—a
broken diamond combining
geometric motifs. The warp is
cotton and the weft naturally dyed
indigo. The center detail depicts a
central design of zigzags surrounded
by floral and abstract bird motifs.
The bright colors are repeated in
the border designs and as
background accents. The exciting
optical pattern in the detail at
bottom is a variation on the serrated
diamond motif, surrounded by
serrated hourglass shapes. Diamonds
within diamonds were used in
traditional Tlaxcala and Saltillo
sarape designs. Another traditional
motif, the chevron, is used as an
overall accent and on the borders.
Aniline dyes are responsible for the
vivid colors.

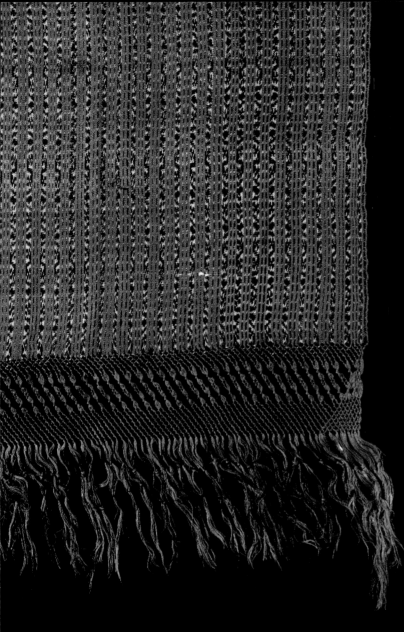
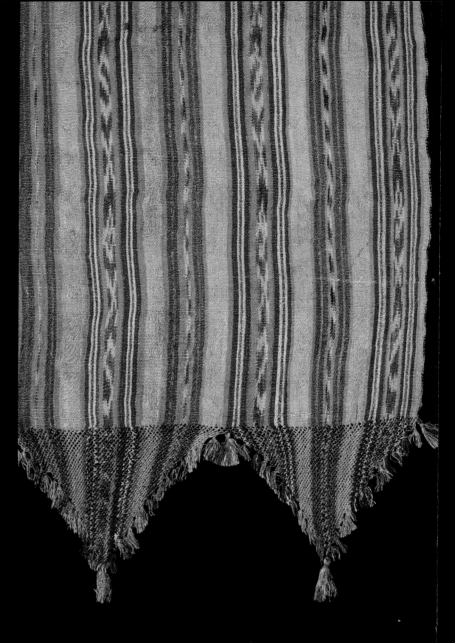

Plates 33 and 34
Rebozos
Santa María del Río, San Luis
Potosí
Late 19th century
Silk, cotton, natural dyes, and gold
thread, approximately 97 × 33″ (full
size). MM and SAMA

A rebozo is an indispensable part of
the mestiza and Indian woman's
wardrobe. It serves as a shawl, a
baby carrier, a head covering, a
support for a basket or *cántaro*, and
is used in certain indigenous dances.
It can be intricately woven in
complex *ikat* patterns or coarsely
woven of cotton or wool. In the

eighteenth century, it was stylish to
embroider the surface with rural
scenes. Rebozos were originally
woven for mestiza women who
would not dress like the Indians and
yet could not afford Spanish finery.
They have since been adopted by
Indians.
The rebozos in Rockefeller's
collection come from Santa María
del Río and Tenancingo, where the
finest rebozos in Mexico were woven
on back-strap and upright looms.
These rebozos can easily take over a
month to make, since the process
involves complex tie-dyeing and
loom setup. The weaving takes at
least two weeks, and the elaborate

fringe must be finger-knotted into
complex patterns learned when the
artisans are children.
In the detail on the left, one can
see this rebozo's lacy, weblike
pattern, called *granizo* (web or cloud
over the eyes). On the right is a
detail of a particularly beautiful
rebozo that combines naturally dyed
yellow silk with gold threads. The
method used to make the delicate
fringe dates back to the early
eighteenth century. The fringes of
Rockefeller's rebozos all have
different patterns. Each of these fine
silk rebozos weighs approximately
¾ pound and often has over 7,000
weft threads. The very finest rebozo

can be pulled through a wedding
ring. The silk threads traditionally
were dyed with plants, nuts, and
insect dyes. The purple dye in the
example on the left comes from
cochineal, a dye made from cactus
parasites.
Deciphering the various threads
of the rebozo's history is complex.
The multitude of influences was
global—Chinese silk and scarves,
Southeast Asian *ikat*, shawls that
arrived with the Manila galleon,
pre-Hispanic woven garments, and
Spanish and Moorish designs. The
blend of cultures in this traditional
Mexican shawl is as varied as its uses.

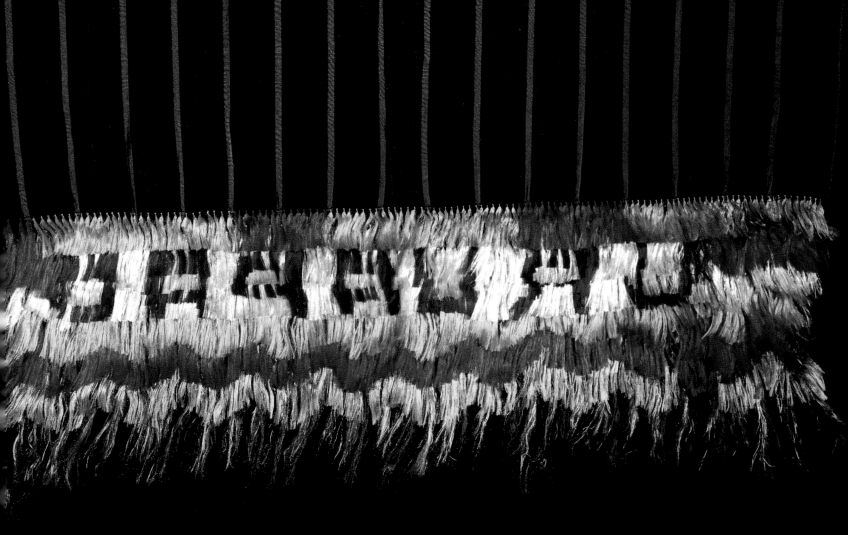

Plate 35
Rebozo Fringe
Michoacán
1930s
Cotton and synthetic silk, width, 9″.
SAMA

Elaborate fringes are the glorious finales of rebozos. Threaded in purple into this layered fringe of dyed synthetic silk is the name Uruapan, a principal city in the Tarascan sierra. The fringe is reminiscent of the fine-feathered lower edge of the unique tuniclike costumes worn by the ancient Tarascan warriors. At the time of the Spanish Conquest, the craftsmen of this region were well known for their luxurious featherwork, illustrated in the *Relación de Michoacán*, a sixteenth-century book by Spanish missionaries. The tightly woven black and indigo-blue fabric is still made in the sierra of Michoacán, where different villages each have individually and imperceptibly modified this traditional style.

Plate 36
Feliciana Martínez
Embroidered Sampler
Central Mexico
Late 19th century
Cotton and silk; tin frame;
26 × 18″. SAMA

Mexican samplers are a
compendium of stitchery and
popular embroidered designs. They
differ from the traditional American
samplers that incorporate a poem or
text. The Spaniards brought many
of their skills to Mexico after the
Conquest, and their traditions,
mixed with centuries of Moorish
occupation, created a wealth of craft
techniques easily transmitted to the
highly skilled and artistic indigenous
population. Young Mexican girls in
convents were trained by devout
Spanish nuns, who taught them all
they knew about stitches, fabric
making, and design. These highly
skilled girls went on to adorn
servilletas, altar cloths, and clothing
for clerics and the wealthy, whose
finery reflected their status.

This large sampler includes cross-
stitch, herringbone, satin stitch,
reverse satin stitch, fish bone, stem,
and feather stitch. This piece is
relatively elementary—there is no
drawn or gauze work. Samplers are
always signed and usually dated.
This sampler, made by a seven- or
eight-year-old, reads "Lo iso
Felisiana Martines." It should have
read "Lo hizo Feliciana Martínez"
("Made by Feliciana Martínez").

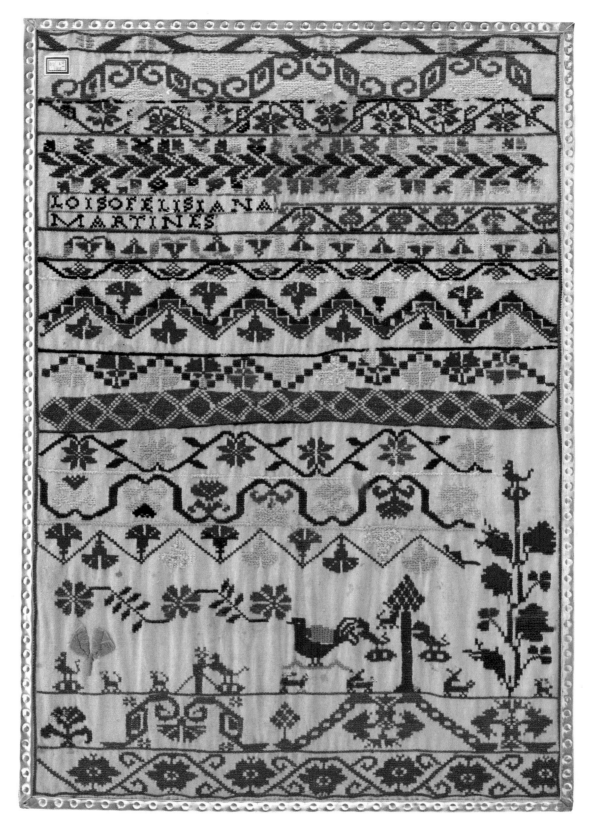

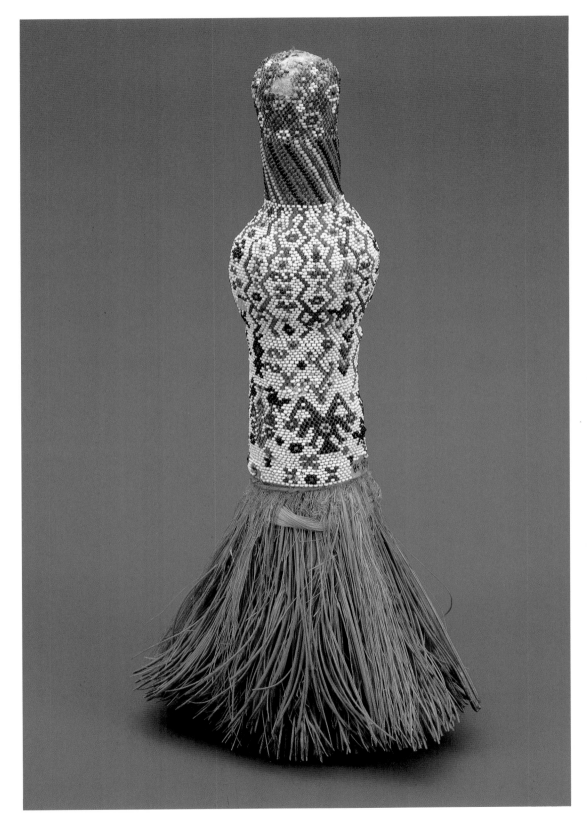

Plate 37
Rebozo Whisk Broom
19th century
Broomstraw and beads, 8¼ × 1¼".
SAMA

When rebozos had elaborate silk
fringes it was often necessary to
comb out and unsnarl the tangles
that developed in storage or in use
or after washing. Each woman had a
small broom used to straighten out
the thousands of threads left after
the fringe has been designed and
macraméd. There is an old proverb
to the effect that a woman's beauty is
judged "by her braids and by her
rebozo."

This nineteenth-century whisk
broom has been gathered at the top
with delicate beading in a
combination of floral and geometric
patterns and the ever-present double-
headed eagle. It was probably
bought along with the many
exquisite silk rebozos Rockefeller
collected.

Plate 38
Uriarte family
Talavera Jar
Puebla, Puebla
Late 19th century
Painted and glazed earthenware,
19 × 12″. SAMA

Talavera poblana is the Mexican variation of Spanish majolica ware produced in Talavera de la Reina and other Spanish cities. Spanish majolica was derived from Italian Renaissance majolica, with Moorish, Islamic, and Far Eastern influences. The craft was brought to Mexico immediately following the Conquest when the Spanish settled the city of Puebla. This very beautiful glazed pottery was originally produced in Puebla only by Spanish artisans under strict guild control. Glazing had been unknown in pre-Hispanic Mexico. The stylish pottery was produced in great quantities by well-organized potteries to meet the need for tableware, architectural tiles, and utilitarian pottery in the New World. Today only a few workshops exist that make this elegant cobalt blue and white pottery according to the original Spanish method. Talavera pottery was enormously popular in colonial Mexico. Over seventy-five potteries were still at work in 1890. A century later there are only five.

Blended clays are mixed and prepared according to strict formulas. The rich opaque undercoat glaze is a perfect base for the thick cobalt oxide (blue) outer glaze. The long firings give these pieces their brilliant surface. This large, lidded jar combines traditional decorative motifs and stylized floral arrangements on an Oriental form. It was made in the Uriarte ceramic factory, one of the oldest family potteries in Puebla.

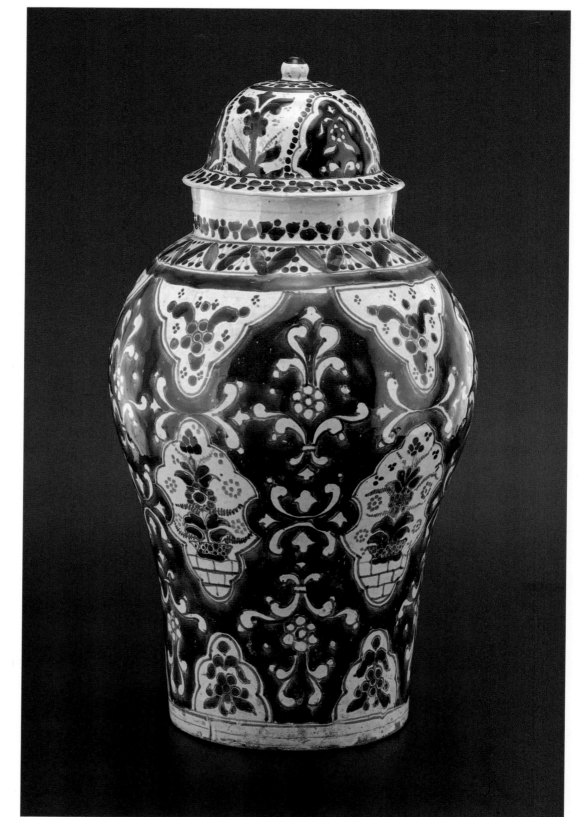

Plate 39
Portrait Pitchers
Metepec, State of Mexico; Santa Fe
de la Laguna and Quiroga,
Michoacán
Late 19th century to 1930s
Single-fired, glazed, and painted
earthenware, 6″ to 13¼″. MM and
SAMA

Portrait pitchers have a long history
in Mexico, where commemorative
and patriotic ceramics were popular
in the mid-nineteenth century. Just
as the gourd is a natural container,
heads and torsos suggest a variety of
pitcher forms fulfilling different
purposes. The two pitchers in the
foreground are made in similar

molds but painted and glazed for
different effects. The late-
nineteenth-century pulque pitcher in
the center of the photograph is
hauntingly and delicately painted.
Some of these pitchers combine
hand-thrown forms with press-
molded features.

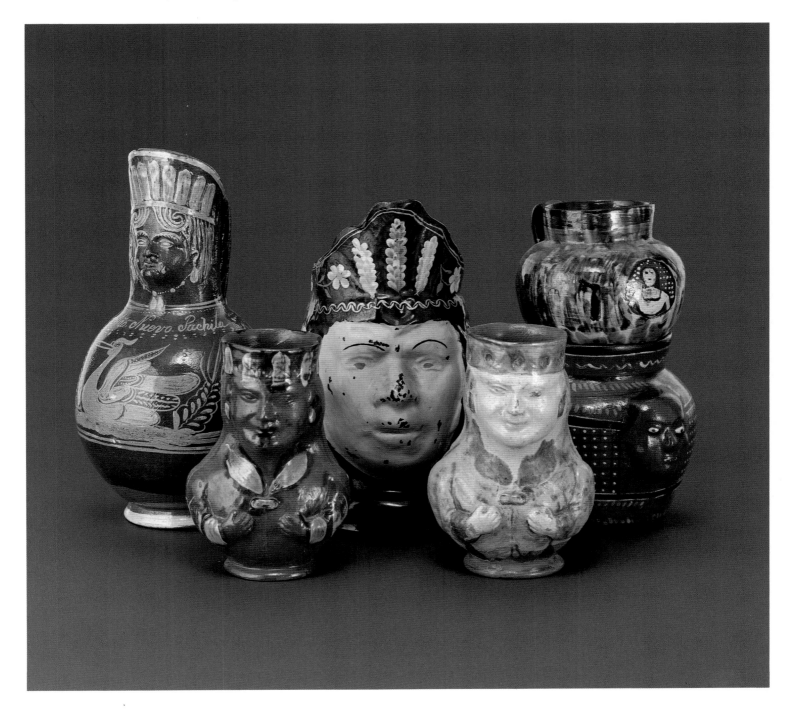

Plate 40
Mescal Container
San Bartolo Coyotepec, Oaxaca
1930s
Black pottery, 10 × 4½″. SAMA

This very wide-eyed monkey,
holding a small jar that says
"Salero" (saltcellar), is a container
for mescal, a potent alcoholic drink
made from the maguey plant. The
jar is for holding the salt that is
often eaten as an accompaniment to
drinking mescal. Perhaps this piece's
monkey form implies that after one
drink you start to act like an
energetic monkey, losing some
inhibitions and careening about.
Oaxaca is famous for its mescal, and
these monkeys are filled, often
painted, and then wrapped in a sisal
net as a holder—a perfect souvenir
to carry away from Oaxaca!

Many of these monkeys are mold-
made and hand-finished, giving each
one an individual expression.
Mexicans favor ancient symbols, and
the monkey has been one of their
favorite animal motifs since pre-
Conquest times.

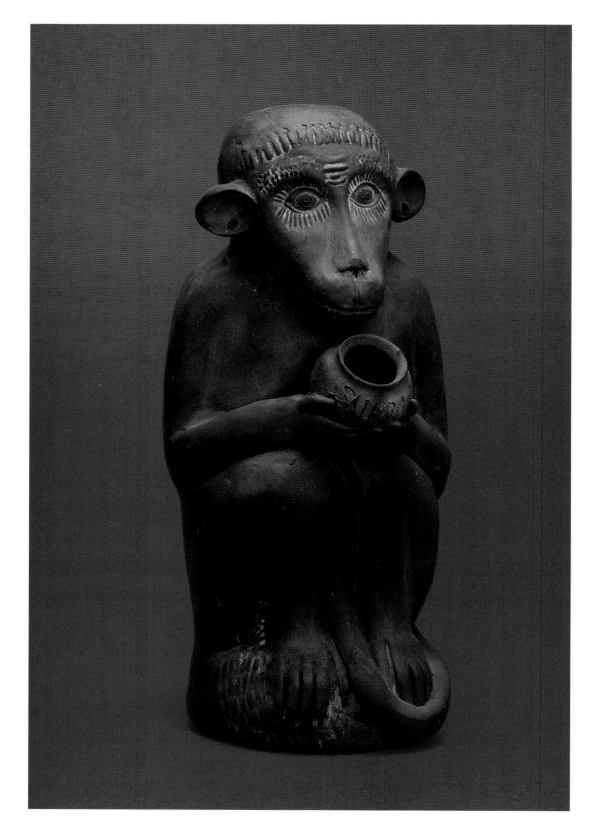

In general, the quality of Mexican textiles has declined sharply since the 1950s. By and large, later textiles reflect an increasing lack of attention to tightness of weave, consistency of dyeing, intricacy of embroidery, and other measures of excellence. Most of the textiles in the Rockefeller collection come from an earlier period, when a high standard was maintained.

The collection contains many fine examples of the tightly woven wool sarapes made during the first quarter of this century for *charros*.[9] Made on Spanish-style looms—as opposed to the back-strap loom, which predates the Spanish conquest—these sarapes are usually composed of solid or repeating motif fields, decorated with traditional geometric designs, such as stepped-fret motifs. Technically, they are of very high quality and compare favorably with superior twentieth-century sarapes in other collections.

A sarape from northern Mexico, possibly Saltillo or Zacatecas, was acquired by Rockefeller in the 1930s. Although it has suffered insect damage, it is an excellent example of the degree to which textiles are sometimes embellished. The multicolored field is woven in a complicated diamond/triangular pattern. The medallion in the center (pl. 29) shows two men dressed in clothing typical of rural Mexico in the early twentieth century. What is going on between them is not entirely clear, but they appear to be engaged in a drinking bout. While the content of this medallion is unusual, the use of decorated center medallions in Mexican sarapes goes back to the eighteenth century in Saltillo. It is still found in Zacatecas and other weaving centers of northern Mexico, where center sections often contain portraits of political leaders and famous figures from Mexican history.[10]

The collection contains an exceptionally fine selection of rebozos, mainly from Santa María del Río, San Luis Potosí, and Tenancingo, State of Mexico. The rebozo, once an essential element of rural and urban dress, especially for the lower classes, was among the most utilitarian of textiles. Today, it is still used by peasant women to keep warm, to haul wood, to carry and clean infants, to block the hot rays of the Mexican sun, to preserve the warmth of tortillas, to cushion against a hard stone bench, and to drape

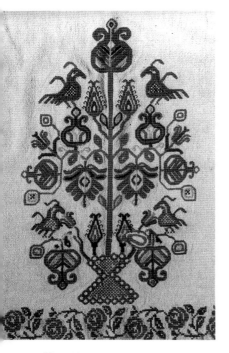

Plate 41
Bed Cover (detail)
Huixquilulcan, State of Mexico
Early 20th century
Hand-loomed wool,
8' × 6'4" (full size). SAMA

This hand-loomed embroidery is covered with a profusion of cross- and satin-stitch animals, flowers, birds, and deer, with a dominant tree-of-life motif. The tight cross-stitch creates a raised surface design. Many of the embroidery motifs are similar to the popular designs seen on eighteenth- and nineteenth-century samplers and have been part of Mexico's design vocabulary for hundreds of years. Floral and bird motifs, which are thought of as purely decorative, often had symbolic meaning in the past. The tree of life is a popular design throughout Puebla and is often incorporated into Otomí and Nahua embroideries.

themselves with while attending Catholic Mass. Rebozos are wrapped, tied, and hung in dozens of different ways, each a special response to the particular situation at hand. Rebozos for everyday use, some richly dyed and woven using the traditional *ikat* method, are represented in the greatest number. The truly important rebozos, however, are those that were meant to be worn on special occasions by the well-to-do. A rare, early-twentieth-century rebozo from Santa María del Río was acquired by Rockefeller in the 1930s. This silk rebozo (pl. 34) contains threads of gold interwoven with bands of *ikat*-dyed designs. The elaborately knotted fringe is reminiscent of the fringes of elegant rebozos from the eighteenth century.[11]

Of the Indian textiles in the collection, two *huipiles* from the Mazatec region of the State of Oaxaca are among the most important. One was worn by a child, the other (pl. 19) by an adult from the village of Huatla de Jiménez, an isolated community renowned for its ritual use of hallucinogenic mushrooms. Both are outstanding examples of Indian weaving and embroidery characteristic of festive dress during the first half of this century.

Another exquisite textile from Indian Mexico is a beaded blouse (pl. 43) from the Sierra de Puebla, acquired during the 1930s. Blouses, introduced from Europe, have replaced *huipiles* in many Indian villages in Mexico but often continue to exhibit old traditional design motifs. Today, in the State of Puebla, Nahua and Otomí Indians wear them on special occasions. This example is noteworthy because of its rarity, fine condition, and exceptional quality.

Quechquémitls from the Huastec region of Mexico and other areas, *fajas* from Oaxaca, Michoacán, and the State of Mexico, and intricately woven Huichol and Otomí *morrales* from the states of Nayarit and Hidalgo, respectively, comprise the rest of the Indian portion of the textile collection.

In summary, the textile portion of the Rockefeller collection of utilitarian objects is small but of consistently high quality. The sarapes, *huipiles*, rebozos, and other objects collected during the 1930s are rarely found in museum collections today.

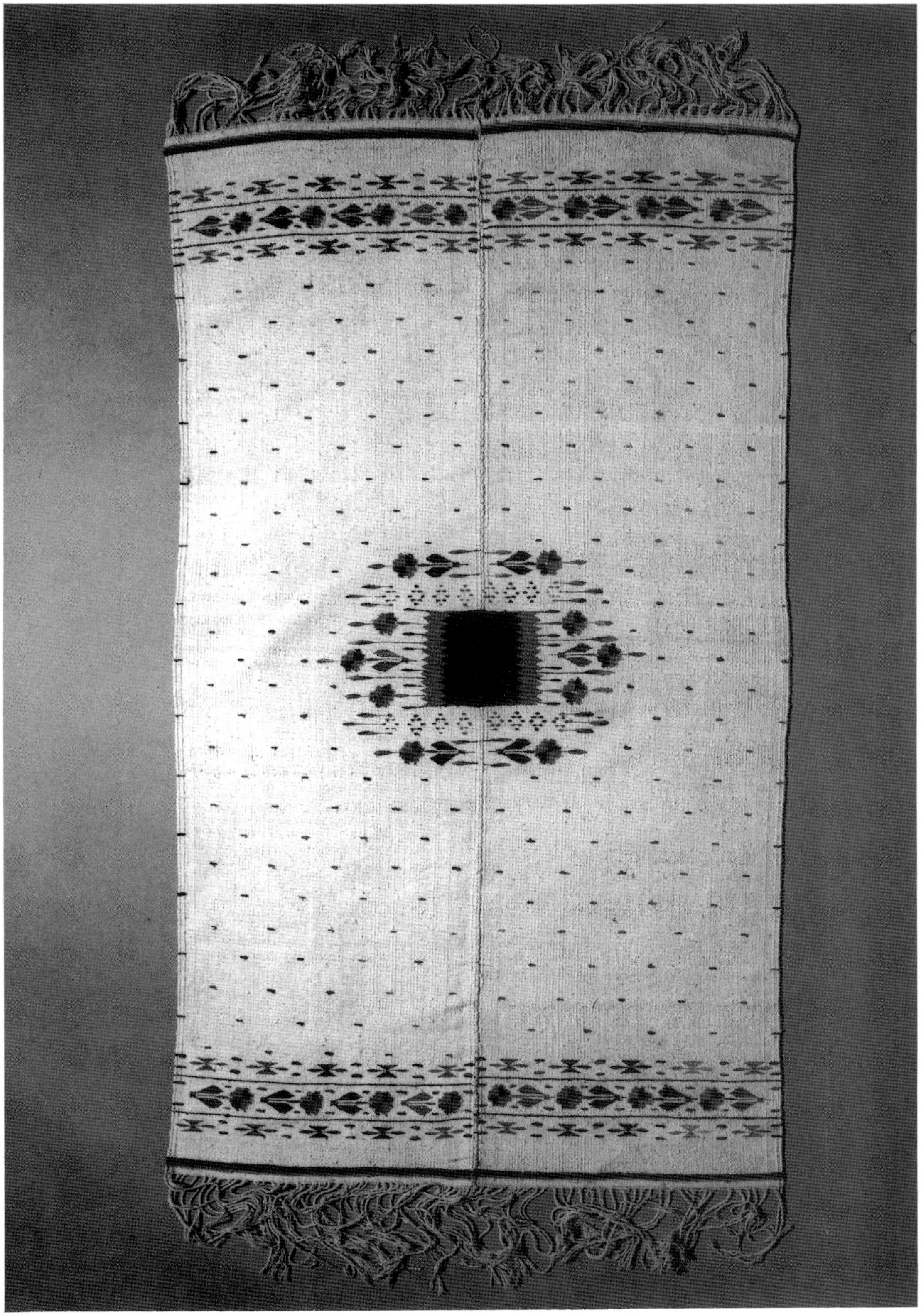

Plate 42
Sarape
San Bernardino Contla, Tlaxcala
1930s
Wool, cotton, and linen,
75½ × 38½″. MM

This elegant sarape has a natural
background with the design accented
in deep red and black. The warp is
linen and the weft is handspun wool.
This sarape was part of a group of
Tlaxcala sarapes that Rockefeller
treasured and hung in his summer
home.

Tlaxcalans were engaged in
weaving long before the Conquest.
They were enemies of the Aztecs and
allied themselves with Cortez in
toppling Montezuma's empire, for
which the Spaniards gave them
special privileges and favored status.
Soon after the Conquest the
Spaniards further developed
Tlaxcalan weaving to supply their
colonists with fabric. By the mid-
sixteenth century they were weaving
wool, and with the introduction of
the treadle loom, Tlaxcala became
the first major center of wool
production in New Spain. A group
of Tlaxcalans was then sent north to
the Saltillo area as colonists, giving
birth to the Saltillo sarape, whose
influence is felt all over Mexico. It
is not clear whether the sarape
depicted is influenced by Saltillo
designs or whether the pattern is a
traditional Tlaxcala design that
might have pre-Hispanic origins.
This traditional piece has a central
motif that incorporates zigzags,
diamonds, and stylized floral shapes.
The border design repeats the
central elements and contains a
popular hourglass pattern.

Plate 43
Beaded Blouse
The Sierra of Puebla
1930s
Cotton and black and gold glass
beads, 18½ × 24½″. SAMA

Beaded blouses from the highlands
of Puebla are used by Nahua and
Otomí women for ceremonial
occasions. This striking beaded
blouse with finely smocked sleeves is
designed in the same way as a
traditional embroidered blouse.
From a distance, the beading is
easily mistaken for a floral and
cross-stitched design. In times past,
Indian women would bring a few of
their beaded blouses to Oaxaca to
sell at the Lunes del Cerro fiesta. As
the cost of beads increased, fewer
and fewer blouses were seen. Now
they are a disappearing folk art.

Chaquira (small beads) have a
long and popular history in Mexico.
In the nineteenth century, they were
incorporated into samplers and made
into pictures and decorative cloths.
Today they are used for Indian hair
cords and jewelry. The Huichol
Indians use them to decorate bags,
ritual bowls, wrist bands, and
sashes.

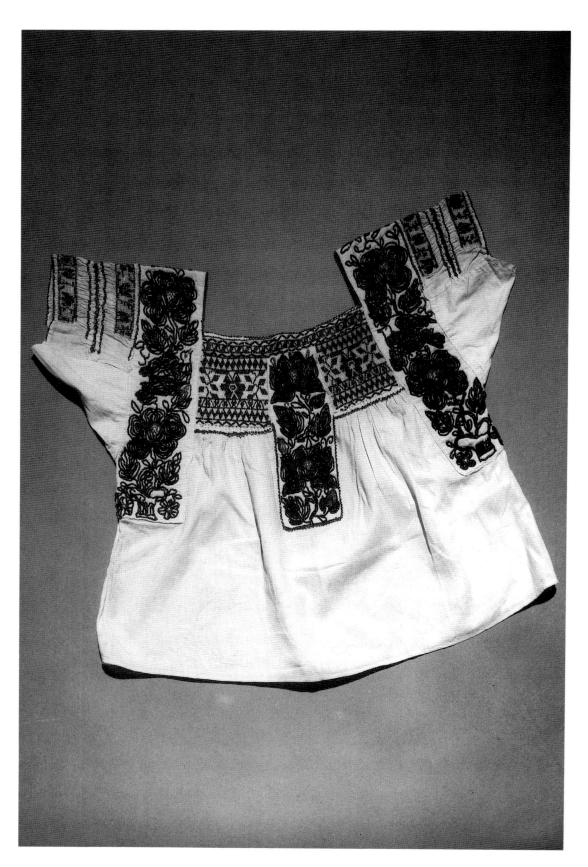

CEREMONIAL OBJECTS

The most dramatic objects in the Rockefeller collection are those associated with ceremony, primarily religious. Such works of art, intended for use in ritual and celebration, embody and proclaim the energetic spirit that infuses much of the folk art of Mexico. Through these pieces, Mexicans are able to commune with the saints, maintain continuity between the living and the dead, and strengthen the ties of family, community, and nation.

Every day of the year, somewhere in Mexico, ceremonial folk art is being used in ways prescribed by local tradition to celebrate religious or secular events. During certain times of the Catholic calendar — Holy Week, the Day of the Dead, and Christmas — the celebrations are particularly intense, involving the entire community, as well as the artists and artisans who produce the folk art objects associated with these occasions. In the semiarid parts of central Mexico, religious celebration intensifies during the end of the dry season and is designed to curry the favor of those who control the weather and the future of the crops. Masked dramas are performed, special altars are constructed in homes and churches, processions wind through the narrow streets of villages and small towns, and sky rockets are sent aloft proclaiming the devotion of those below and as a signal to the gods that they should pay attention to the beautiful preparations of the faithful.

Religious ceremonial folk art is often made as part of a *promesa* to a saint or to the Virgin, who in turn will bestow his or her blessings and good fortunes — health, prosperity, and love — on those seeking them. Young women cut their elegant braids and attach them to the figure of San Antonio de Padua, in appreciation for his assistance in finding a husband or redirecting one who has gone astray. Participants in dance dramas perform for hours in order to satisfy a pledge to their patron saint, whose intervention is essential to the maintenance of balance in the world. Altars are built; statues of saints are carved, or retouched, and carefully placed in small chapels; exotic floral arches are set in place; and special foods are prepared in anticipation of the main day of celebration. Folk art is everywhere.

The ceremonial folk art in the Rockefeller collection consists mostly of paintings, masks, incense burners, musical instruments, objects associated with the Day of the Dead, and miscellaneous religious paraphernalia.

Paintings

The religious paintings in the Rockefeller collection are among the most important objects in the ceremonial section. There are more than thirty, each a very special example of Mexican folk perspective and expression. *Retablos*—paintings usually on tin, copper, or canvas and located on or behind the altar—are represented in various forms. Ex-votive-type *retablos* are deeply personal accounts of miraculous interventions. Made in great numbers during the nineteenth century by itinerant folk artists, these paintings are part of a tradition that goes back to early colonial times and can be found in many parts of the Catholic world. Once painted and sold, they were placed by the devotee on the altar honoring the saint whose intervention is documented by and memorialized in the painting. In many churches throughout central Mexico, walls are covered with ex-votive *retablos*, providing a fascinating testimony to the power of religious personages.

Other nineteenth-century paintings on tin include representations of saints, typically attired in the dress of their time and order, together with special attributes associated with their lives—professions, stations of birth, martyrdoms, and so on. The subject of *El Niño de Atocha* (pl. 65), a popular manifestation of the young Christ, is always associated with specific attributes that set him apart from other images: a brimmed hat with a plume, a pilgrim's staff and a gourd, a basket containing flowers, spears of wheat and roses. The Niño de Atocha is the patron to whom people pray for the freeing of prisoners and for delivering people from all types of serious danger.

La Mano Poderosa (pl. 64) is impressive in terms of both its form and its content. It is a fine example of nineteenth-century folk painting, with characteristic soft-edged figures and flattening of perspective. The hand is that of Saint Francis of Assisi, who, according to legend, experienced the stigmata of Christ during a period of intense prayer. The arm is robed in a garment of the Franciscan order. The blood that cascades from the saint's

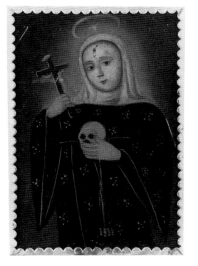

Plate 44
Santa Rita de Casia
Central Mexico
Mid-19th century
Oil on tin; tin frame; 9¾ × 6⅝".
SAMA

This *retablo* portrays Santa Rita de Casia, who is invoked in Mexico as the patroness of desperate or impossible situations and considered a model for married women. In the fifteenth century, late in her life, the widow Rita entered an Augustinian convent in Casia, Italy. In this very tender and youthful depiction, her childlike face, rosy lips, and demure look are disturbed by the stigmata on her forehead. It is thought to have been caused by a thorn from a crucifix during intense contemplation in her life of meditation and penance. In her left hand she holds a crucifix, and with her right hand she presses a skull, a symbol of mortality or penance, close to her body.

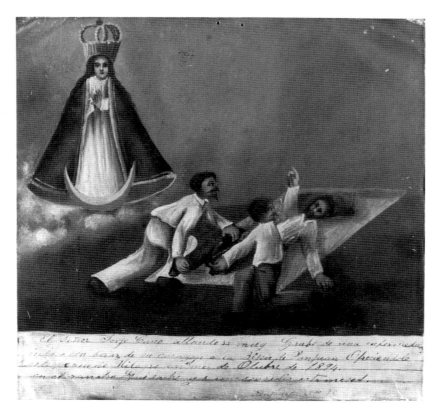

Plate 45
Ex-voto
Central Mexico
1894
Oil on tin, 10¼ × 10½″. SAMA

The text on this ex-voto reads, "Mister Jorge Cano, finding himself dangerously sick of some illness, prayed with all the fervor of his heart to the Virgin of San Juan for a cure. This small miracle is offered in the month of October 1894, on the Guisache Ranch, for granting me this favor." This small work on tin is an illustrative account of a miraculous intervention resulting in a cure.

In the nineteenth century at the height of the popularity of ex-votos, great quantities of these paintings were executed by unknown, informally trained, and often itinerant folk artists. They interpreted textual material into a very dramatic rendering of an event. Tin was the chosen material, replacing the canvas and copper used earlier for ex-votos commissioned by the wealthy. Devotees placed their small commissioned works on the altar honoring the saint whose intervention is documented and commemorated in the painting. This custom arrived with the Spanish and was immediately adopted by the Mexicans. In many churches throughout central Mexico, walls are crammed with hundreds of ex-votos offering a comprehensive glimpse not only of personal devotion and the power of religious personages but also of the social history and faith and dreams of the populace.

hand represents the blood of the Eucharist. The lambs who drink it are the faithful. At the end of each finger, from left to right, are images of Saint Anne, the Virgin Mary, the Christ Child, Saint Joseph, and Saint Joachim. This theme, associated with veneration of the Holy Family, was popular in nineteenth-century Mexico and remains so today.

One of the most technically impressive tin paintings in the collection shows Saint Francis embracing Christ on the cross (pl. 67). This powerful *retablo* is painted in rich colors with a sharply defined technique. The architecture of the buildings at the base is reminiscent of Italian structures and was most likely copied from European models.

Among the religious paintings not executed on tin, the most important is a series depicting twelve of the fourteen Stations of the Cross, dating from 1850 (pls. 68, 69). Station VI illustrates Veronica holding the cloth used to wipe Christ's brow. The attire of the woman on the right, whose back is to the viewer, is reminiscent of Mexican Indian dress of the nineteenth century. The predominant colors surrounding her are those of the Mexican flag—

green, red, and white. The other eleven paintings demonstrate similar regional qualities.

Finally, the most extraordinary religious painting in the Rockefeller collection is a scroll painting titled *Death of San José* (pl. 66). Painted during the early part of the nineteenth century, it shows, in a wonderfully "folk" manner, a grieving Mary and angels in the presence of the dying saint.

Masks

The Rockefeller collection contains a small but important group of masks from all over Mexico and made of many different materials. Most were used in a religious context. In a time when most mask collections to a large extent consist of decorative and commercial masks made for tourists, the Rockefeller collection is a refreshing exception. Of the sixty masks in the collection, only two were made for the tourist market.

The most important mask in the collection, and thought by some to be the most important object in the entire collection, is a centurion helmet mask (pl. 56). Masks of this type generally date from the late eighteenth century. Undoubtedly, the carving, gesso, and painting are of the type and style associated with colonial Mexico, but the mask may well be from the early nineteenth century. Although rare, similar examples are to be found in collections elsewhere—The Taylor Museum of the Colorado Springs Fine Arts Center, and the Museo Nacional de Arte in Mexico City. The provenance of these centurion helmet masks is uncertain; however, they are generally thought to have been made and used in an area around Toluca, State of Mexico. Worn to represent a Roman guard leading Christ to Calvary, this mask, with its movable jaw, oversize teeth, and ferocious facial features, is indeed impressive. It was made using the *estofado* technique, in which "the wood is covered with plaster, forming a relief design or sculpture, then painted and adorned with gold leaf."[12]

Another outstanding mask in the collection is a Negrito mask (pl. 59) from the State of Michoacán, probably in or near the village of Nahuatzín. Symbolizing that which is good and admirable in life, this mask was used in a

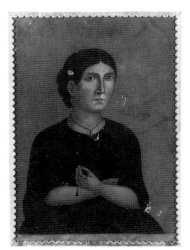

Plate 46
Portrait
Central Mexico
Mid-19th century
Oil on tin; tin frame; 13¾ × 9¾".
SAMA

This austere painting of a woman, possibly in mourning, is a classic mid-nineteenth-century portrait painted on the standard 10-by-14-inch tin sheet popular with *retablo* painters. It is encased in a more contemporary cut tin frame. The woman is wearing black, a color that was noted by nineteenth-century visitors to Mexico as being the predominant color of wealthy Spanish or mestiza women or children after the struggle for independence. Her necklace, a braided black cord, is loosely draped with a small knot below the neck. She is holding one end of the necklace between her fingers. The classic hairstyle of the nineteenth century was severe, with a central part dividing coal-black hair drawn tightly back into a large bun. Women often wore hair ornaments of filigreed or repoussé silver.

line dance, and masks of this kind were worn by several members of the troop. The attached multicolored satin ribbons and glass beads provide a sense of movement to the dance, which itself is usually performed very slowly. One remarkable feature of the mask is the way its fixed facial expression shifts when the mask is slightly tilted to one side or the other.

Another impressive mask in the collection is a late-nineteenth-century jaguar mask from the State of Guerrero (pl. 60). Jaguar masks, still popular in many parts of southern and central Mexico, are among the few masks still used that are rooted in pre-Columbian ritual. In the State of Guerrero, where they are used with the greatest frequency, they are worn in dance dramas related to the agricultural cycle as well as during ritual battles between neighboring communities and barrios. Some jaguar masks are thought to assume the spirit of the animal they represent and to protect the wearer from witchcraft during dance performances. This mask, rare because of its age and fine condition, may well be the earliest example of a jaguar mask surviving today.

Not only does the collection contain masks that are historically significant, it also contains objects that tell us about the often-complicated process of mask-making. Twenty well-worn earthenware papier-mâché mask molds from the State of Guanajuato constitute a significant part of the collection. Although these molds are an important part of the masking phenomenon, they are rarely found in collections today. The masks produced on them are worn all over Mexico during carnival celebrations, particularly in areas where local mask production has died out. The collection also includes several dozen papier-mâché masks from Celaya, Guanajuato, similar to those made from these molds (pls. 2, 57, 58).

Finally, the collection contains objects associated with masquerade dance dramas. A delightfully carved wooden horse associated with the Dance of Saint James (Santiago) is among the most unusual objects (pl. 78). Strapped to the waist, this sculpture is quite different from the more frequently used hoop-style, which slips over the dancer's body and has a horse's rump.

Plate 47
Torito
Oaxaca, Oaxaca
Late 1960s
Papier-mâché, paint, split cane, and
bamboo, 27 × 28″. MM

A Mexican fiesta is never complete
without spectacular fireworks. The
fireworks attached to the bamboo
structure on this *torito* (little bull)
are set ablaze by a *cohetero*
(pyrotechnician), who holds the
sparkling piece above his head and
charges bull-like through a
screaming crowd. While the
fireworks explode in bursts of
rainbow-colored sparks, he cavorts
with the high-spirited onlookers. He
might be followed by other *toritos*
who help keep the crowd amused
and moving in an evening
entertainment that never fails to
excite both children and adults.

    Toritos can be small, or they can
be as tall as a man. The taller and
more complex the bamboo towers to
which fireworks are attached, the
more dazzling the display. Mexican
castillos (fireworks castle towers) can
be many stories high and are often
the spectacular half-hour culmination
of a fiesta. It might take more than a
week to construct and fit a large
tower with fireworks. This very
technical and precise craft is often
passed down in families through the
generations.

    Pyrotechnics have a long history
in Mexico, and old engravings show
that *castillos* were being constructed
in the eighteenth century. The
Spaniards brought gunpowder to
Mexico, and it was quickly adopted
by the Mexicans, who were
enchanted by the magical
possibilities of light and sound.

    This small *torito* was purchased on
a Oaxaca street where it was
hanging to indicate the home of a
fireworks artisan. It can be used
over and over again, with only
minor repair necessary between
fiestas.

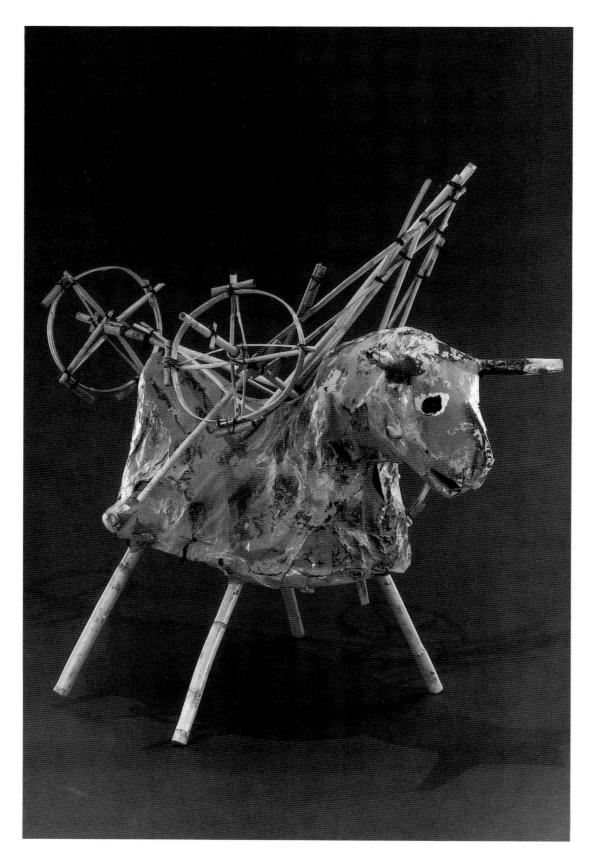

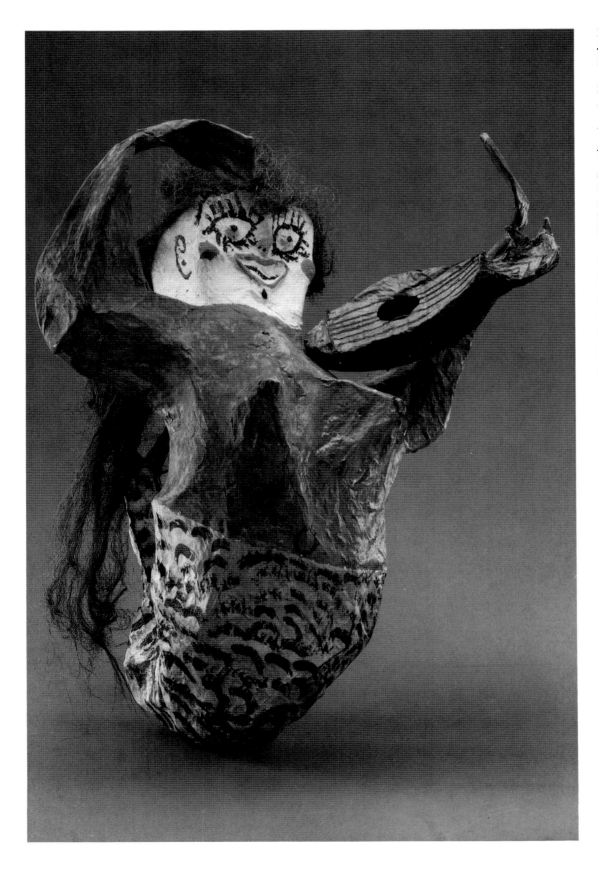

Plate 48
Judas Figure
Mexico, D.F.
1970s
Painted papier-mâché and horsehair,
3 × 2′. SAMA

This oversize, exuberant siren is a Judas figure, one of the cast of unsavory, nefarious characters that are fashioned out of papier-mâché for Holy Week. The tradition of making and then destroying Judas figures is a fascinating Mexican interpretation of a Spanish custom.

In the old days, on the day before Easter a huge paper Judas figure (often twelve feet high) would be hung up in a village or barrio and then destroyed by fireworks or by burning. Noisy and excited crowds gathered to see the Judas extinguished—a symbolic destruction of evil. This ephemeral art form is meant to be sacrificed. The tradition of making Judas figures is still alive, on a reduced scale. Peddlers still sell brightly painted paper figures of devils, bandits, sirens, evil politicians, villains, and skeletons, but today communities rarely get together to burn the oversize Judas figures.

This hot-pink, silver-scaled siren represents a temptress of the most dangerous sort, who will snag the unsuspecting with a tune from her *conchero* guitar and a sly look from her wide-eyed painted face.

Plate 49
Tree of Death
Metepec, State of Mexico
1978
Single-fired earthenware,
42 × 29 × 8″. SAMA

The Day of the Dead inspires
artisans all over Mexico. October is
a free-for-all of ceramic production
in Metepec, culminating on All
Saints' Day, November 1, and All
Souls' Day, November 2. This
pottery village on the outskirts of
Toluca produces brightly
polychromed pottery and elaborate
trees of life. Each year the trees
become larger and more intricate.
Metepec potters have adapted their
kilns to accommodate these trees that
defy tight stacking.

This imaginative unpainted
earthenware tree of death is crowned
with five skeletons, and atop the
upper branches five more leering
calaveras have candle-holders
emerging from their skulls. Nestled
in the tangle of leaves and flowers
are more skeletons—a man and
woman going to market, two men
enjoying food and drink, and a jolly
pair perched high up on the tree.

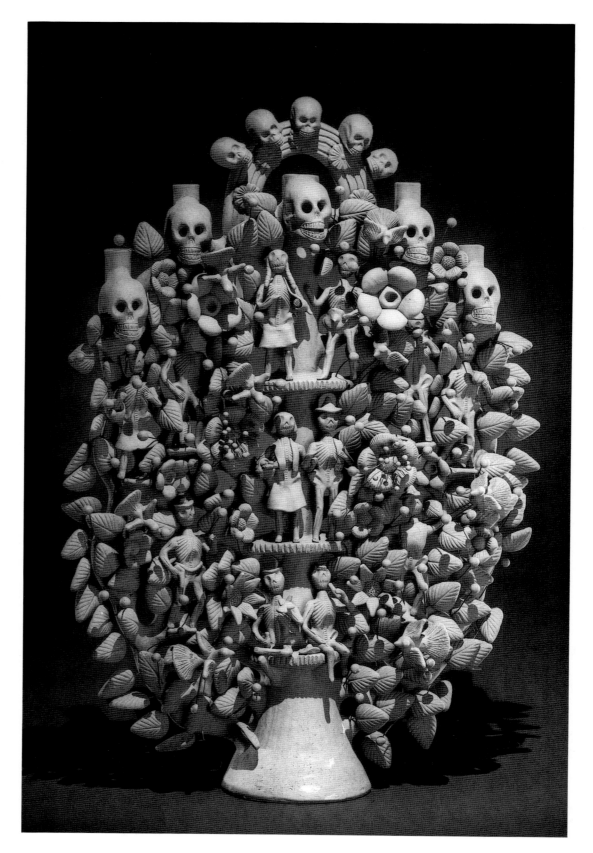

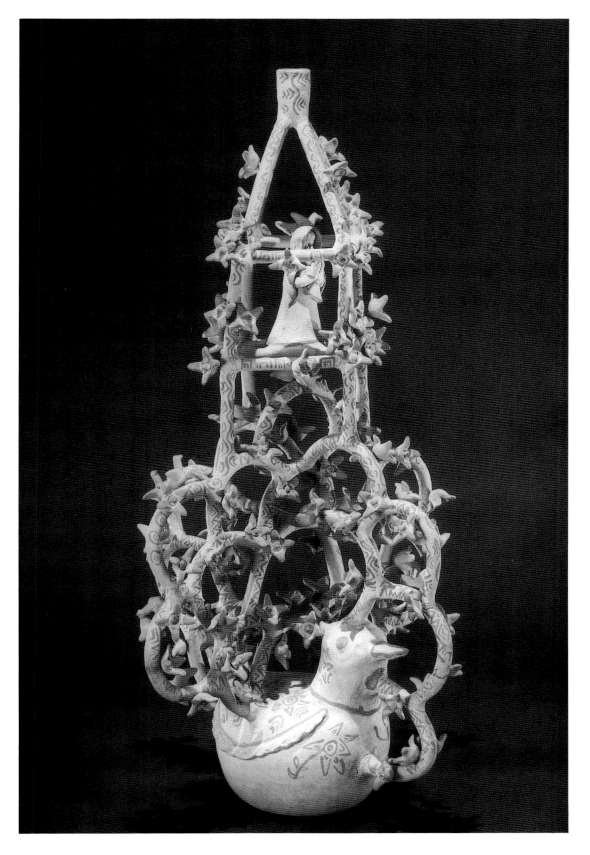

Plate 50
Herón Martínez
Tree of Life
Acatlán de Osorio, Puebla
Late 1960s
Single-fired, slip-decorated
earthenware, $40 \times 23 \times 19''$. MM

Herón Martínez is one of Mexico's
great contemporary folk artists. In
this piece he pushed the limits of the
tree-of-life form by making it a tree
in the round. His home, Acatlán,
Puebla, has always been an
important pottery center producing
everyday utilitarian pottery and a
famous barrel-shaped pot invented
by Martínez when he first began
working. After abandoning pottery
for many years, a Oaxaca craft
dealer encouraged Martínez to
develop new forms. His pieces have
influenced the direction of
traditional Acatlán potters, who now
produce ornamental pottery for an
external market. Martínez' work has
evolved from single-fired, slip-
decorated earthenware pieces to
intricate multicolored trees with
white backgrounds to his more
recent highly burnished slip-
decorated trees, insects, wall
planters, and stacked animals.

This tree employs various ceramic
techniques: coiling, press-molding,
hand modeling, convex molding,
and lump molding. The slip, called
tinta, is obtained from mineral-rich
rocks from a mine nearby. Short
lengths of galvanized wire hold the
tree sections together and connect
the leaves and birds to the branches.
A complicated tree of life takes at
least a week to construct.

Plate 51
Incense Burner
Barrio de la Luz, Puebla
1930s
Glazed earthenware, 19¼ × 12¼".
SAMA

Few religious ceremonies are
complete without an incense burner.
Folk artists produce an endless
variety of containers to burn copal.
Copal permeates churches all over
Mexico, saturating the olfactory
senses of the faithful and
intensifying the visual stimulus of
the paintings and statuary. Incense
burners are carried in processions,
adorn home and church altars, and
are placed near gravestones during
the Day of the Dead.

This mold-made piece with
appliquéd hand-formed decoration is
topped with a crucifix. It was made
in Barrio de la Luz, an old section
of the city of Puebla, where the
Spaniards established potteries under
Spanish colonial grant. These guild-
system shops were governed by
intricate and rigorously enforced
codes. The metallic black glaze is a
hallmark of Barrio de la Luz
pottery. The form is reminiscent of
hanging brass church pieces from
Spain and the Middle East.

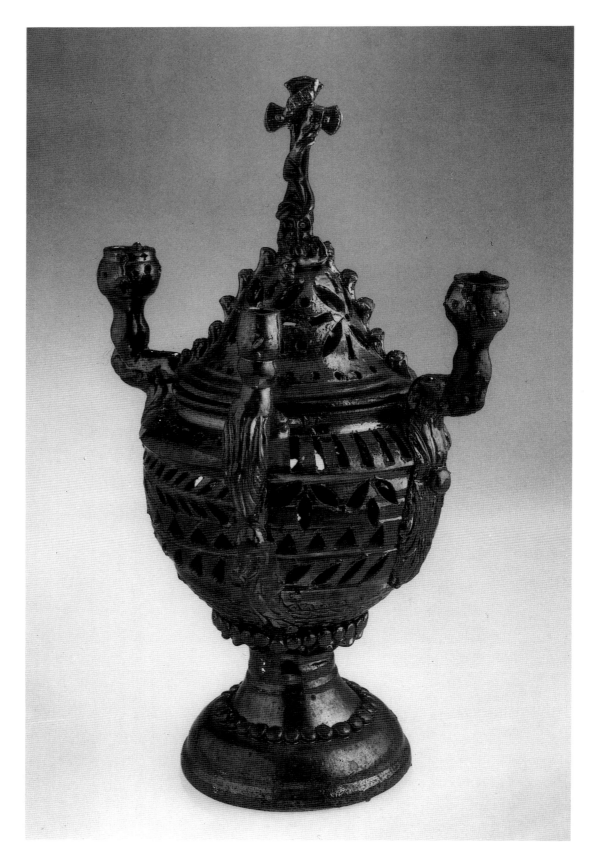

Incense Burners

No religious ceremony in Mexico is complete without the presence of incense, or copal. Dating back to pre-Hispanic times, copal plays a key role in purification and is considered essential for the creation of the proper ambience in which rituals are conducted. The odor of copal permeates churches all over Mexico, saturating the olfactory senses of the faithful while intensifying the visual effect of paintings and statuary. Incense burners of varying sizes, colors, and shapes are carried in solemn procession through the streets of small villages, used on the altars of local churches and chapels, and placed on the graves of the deceased during the Day of the Dead. The Rockefeller collection contains several excellent examples of traditional incense burners, some dating from the early 1930s, including a highly glazed, metallic-like incense burner from Barrio de la Luz, Puebla (pl. 51). More gaily painted burners from Oaxaca, Tonalá, and Guanajuato are also represented.

Musical Instruments

Music is another key element in Mexican celebrations. Village bands, comprising peasants with little or no formal training in music, are part of every festival. Participation is frequently due to a *promesa* between the musician and local saints. Flutes, guitars, violins, and drums are standard instruments for almost all religious events, but brass and other instruments are also used on occasion. These rustic bands set the cadence for dance dramas and religious processions, and the musicians work hard to make certain that their music can be heard above the din of other sounds in the celebration.

The collection's most important ceremonial musical instrument is a *conchero* guitar (pl. 62) made of armadillo shell, wood, mother-of-pearl, and various other materials. *Concheros* are brotherhoods formed to dance in honor of saints or other religious images for the well-being of a neighborhood, community, or region. Although these brotherhoods grew up as part of an Indian revitalization movement that began at the end of the nineteenth century, their roots go back much earlier. Each *concha* has its own name and

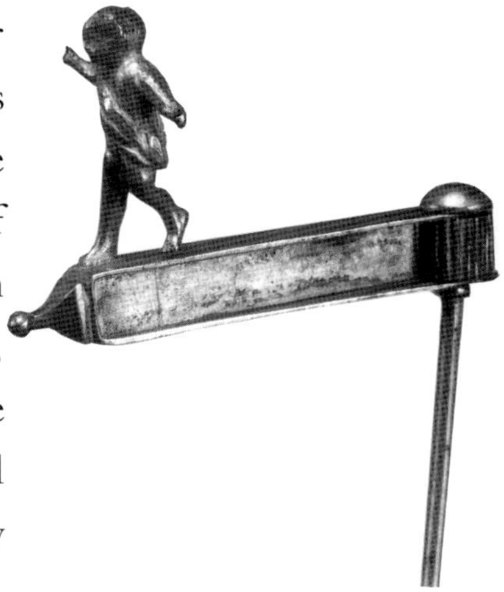

Plate 52
Noisemaker
Mexico, D.F., or Puebla, Puebla
19th century
Sterling silver, 4⅝ × ⅞ × 2¼″.
SAMA

Delicate silver *matracas* were used during Holy Week in colonial Mexico. On Good Friday, the Catholic Church prohibits the ringing of table bells, and during the week-long celebration church bells are silenced until Easter Sunday. Masses are announced by an orchestration of noisemakers. The wealthy Mexicans bought small silver noisemakers for Easter gifts.

Rockefeller bought this piece from a folk art shop in Mexico City owned by Fred Davis. Davis had an enormous collection of these finely crafted silver noisemakers. On this *matraca* a small child is carefully running down the piece, making you feel he will maintain his precarious perch even when he is swung around.

must have been ritually consecrated during a *velación* before its effectiveness can be assured.[13]

Another instrument used in religious celebrations is the *matraca*. Of the several fine examples in the collection, the rarest and most interesting is a miniature silver *matraca* with a dancing figure on top (pl. 52). During the nineteenth century wealthy Mexicans used noisemakers of this kind to celebrate Holy Week. Today, *matracas* made of wood, tin, and other inexpensive materials are used by all classes throughout Mexico.

Day of the Dead Objects

Nelson Rockefeller's last trip to Mexico took place during the time when preparations were being made for the Day of the Dead festival, and he purchased many objects associated with the celebration. Although some were of such an ephemeral nature that they have since disintegrated, other objects fortunately remain—sugar animals, candles, bread dolls, and tissue-paper figures bought from street vendors in Oaxaca and the State of Mexico. Papier-mâché masks from Celaya and large expressive figures made by the Linares family in Mexico City are also part of the Day of the Dead materials in the collection. A skeletal figure (pl. 77) made by Miguel Linares in the mid-1970s satirizes a traditional Mexican street peddler who sold small birds from the lake areas that originally surrounded Mexico City.[14]

Another outstanding Day of the Dead object is a large, unpainted earthenware tree of life (including death) from the famous pottery-producing town of Metepec, State of Mexico (pl. 49).

Other Objects of Celebration

Also quite rare and significant are the three wooden molds used for making tortillas (pl. 53). The special tortillas made on this type of mold—made only in Vizarrón, Querétaro—are served at family reunions and religious events.[15] These examples were purchased in the late 1960s for inclusion in the Museum of Primitive Art exhibition.

Other ceremonial objects in the collection include ordinary and fancy candles, altar textiles, and Huichol *tablas*.

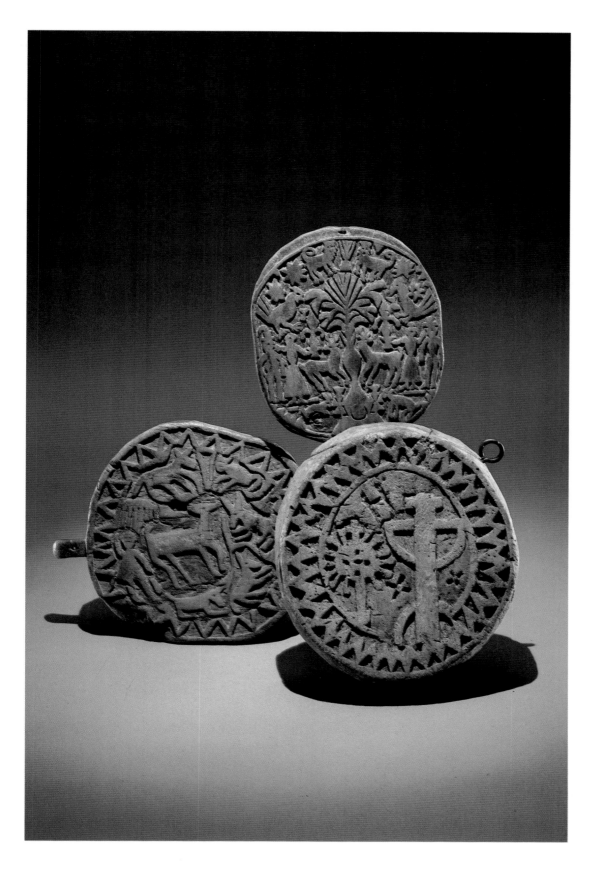

Plate 53
Tortilla Molds
Vizarrón, Querétaro
1930s
Carved wood, approximately
10 × 2″. MM and SAMA

Tortillas, the staff of Mexican life,
are consumed in all states of the
country. The clapping of hands
making tortillas is one of the
rhythms of everyday life in Mexico,
or at least it was. In many towns and
villages the thin round pancake
made of *masa harina* (corn flour) is
now processed from start to finish by
a machine at the *tortillería*. But in
the recent and distant past, tortilla
making was an important part of a
woman's daily life. These tortilla
molds, unique to Vizarrón, are
made of hand-carved mesquite with
animal, religious, patriotic, and
floral motifs. Carefully and
colorfully decorated tortillas made in
these molds were used for religious
ceremonies and family celebrations.

Plate 54
Milagros
Late 19th, early 20th century
Milagros: silver, ½" to
1" × ¹⁄₃₂" × ¹⁄₁₆"; case: tin, glass, and
velvet, 26 × 16 × 3". SAMA

This tin mirrored frame topped by
an angel houses a collection of
nineteenth- and early-twentieth-
century silver *milagros*. In gratitude
for a cure, a recovery, or a
miraculous change in a difficult
situation, a devout Mexican will buy
a *milagro* from one of the many
vendors seen outside of churches and
hang it inside the church as an
offering to the appropriate saint.

Arms, legs, hands, eyes,
huaraches, women's heads, burros,
pigs, and praying figures are
popular subjects for a silversmith.
The small silver pig might have
been offered by an individual to
thank a saint for a pig's recovery
from infection. Or perhaps the pig
had many piglets, and the owner felt
divine intervention accounted for its
fertility. Kneeling figures indicate
that a prayer was successfully
answered.

From the sixteenth to the early
twentieth century, *milagros* were
handmade by silversmiths and
commissioned by the thankful.
Eventually they were cast in silver
but hand-finished. There was an
enormous variety of shapes since you
could commission almost anything—
a vase, an instrument, or even an
insect if you had recovered from a
serious sting. Today they are usually
cast in metal, sewn onto colorful
ribbons, and pinned on brightly
hued cloth along with hundreds of
others.

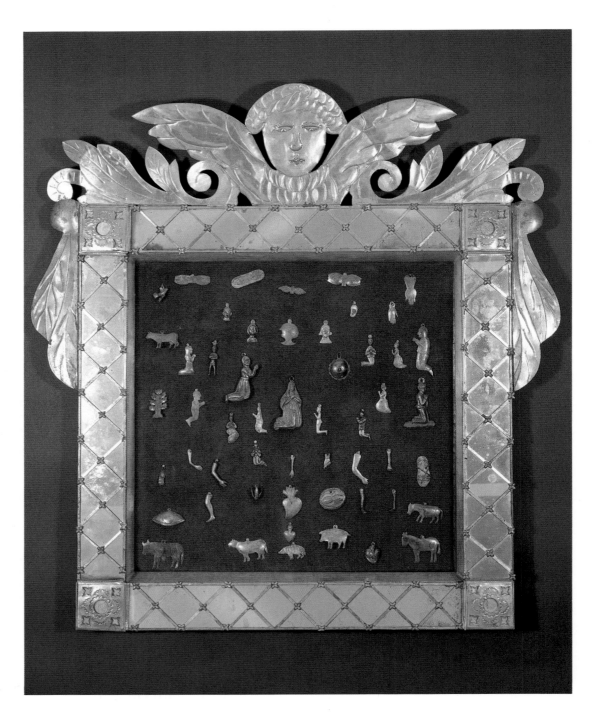

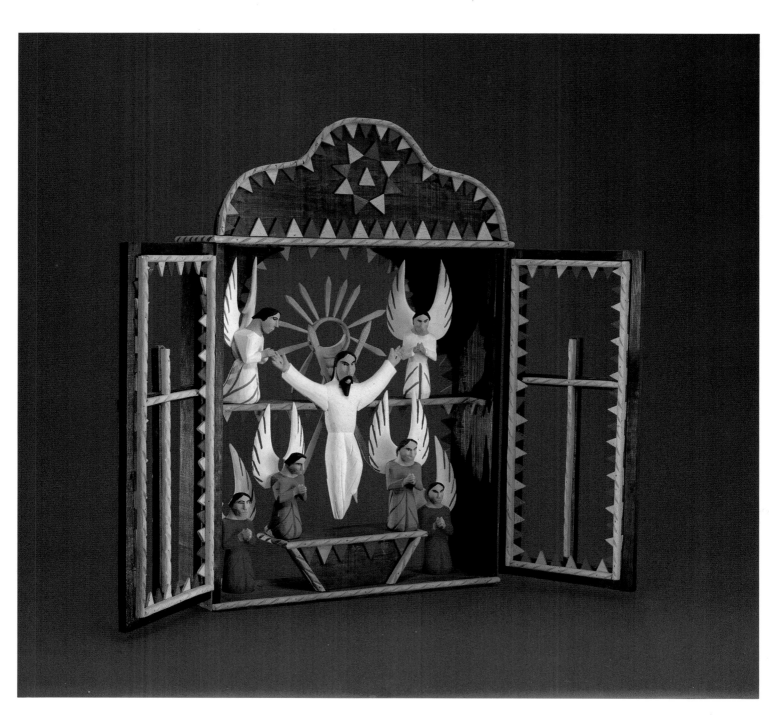

Plate 55
David Villafáñez
The Glorious Ascension of Christ
Oaxaca, Oaxaca
Late 1960s
Carved and painted wood,
33½ × 25 × 7". SAMA

This triptych represents the Ascension of Christ, his ascension to heaven at the end of his earthly ministry when he finally entered into divine glory. He is surrounded by angels. Ascension Day is the most important part of Semana Santa (Holy Week), and this piece was carved by Villafáñez to commemorate the great Christian event. He carves many religious tableaux and altars in a highly stylized and deliberate manner. His colors are very simple and complement the purity with which he treats his subjects. He has influenced many contemporary carvers in the Valley of Oaxaca.

Plate 56
Centurion Helmet Mask
State of Mexico
Late 18th century
Wood, gesso, paint, and gold leaf,
15½ × 10 × 13″. SAMA

This eighteenth-century centurion
helmet mask is one of the oldest and
rarest pieces in Rockefeller's
collection. It represents a member of
the Roman guard that led Christ to
Calvary. It is one of the few
remaining masks of this type in
existence. These masks are
attributed to the Valley of Toluca in
the State of Mexico.

This powerful piece is carved of
wood and covered with thick gesso.
The gesso can also be carved before
the piece is painted and gold-leafed.
The jaw is articulated with leather
straps allowing the dancer to move
the mouth and appear more
menacing.

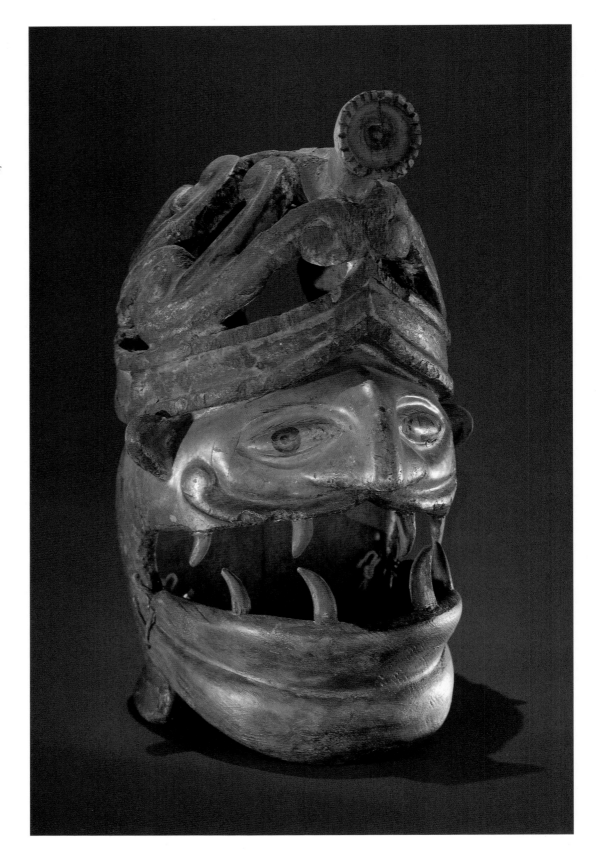

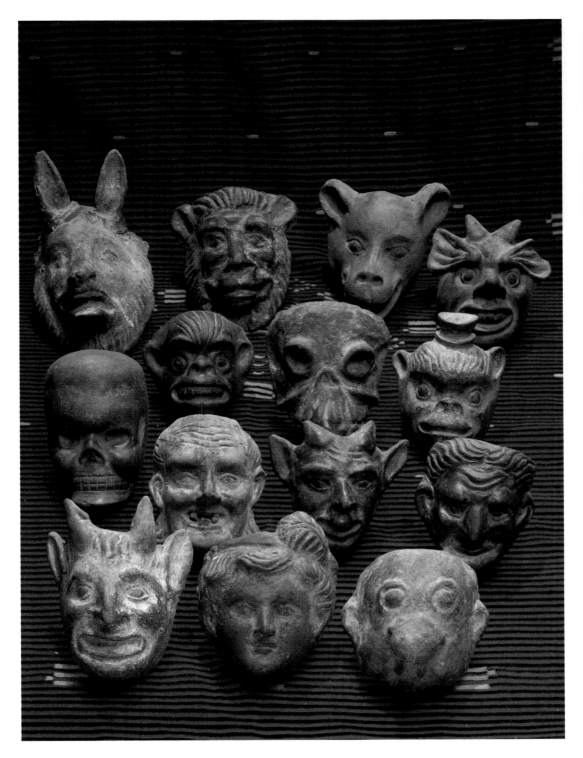

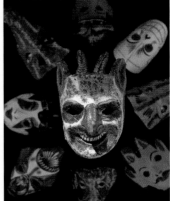

Plates 57 and 58
Mask Molds and Masks
Celaya, Guanajuato
1930s to 1960s
Molds: earthenware; masks: painted
papier-mâché; 10½ × 6″. MM and
SAMA

Ceramic molds are used to make the
famed papier-mâché masks sold in
Mexican markets for fiestas and
holidays. They reflect the Mexicans'
obsession with celebration and
transformation and connect both
children and adults with ritual.
Skeletons are made for the Day of
the Dead, Moors and Spaniards for
Carnival, *viejitos* (old men) for the
Dance of the Old Men, and devils
and an entire imaginative zoo of
animals for other celebrations.

These classic molds, saturated
with animal fat, have an
extraordinary patina built up over
years of use. The masks are made by
pressing two or three layers of
papier-mâché onto the mold; when
dry, the mask is lifted off the mold.
Masks are first painted with calcium
carbonate, and then the real
decoration begins as mask makers'
fantasies are unleashed. The
accenting red and black paint often
appears glossy since the pigments are
mixed with *cola*, a gelatinous fish
mucilage. It is interesting to note
that in the classic period of
Teotihuacán, molds were being used
to cast clay heads and figures. Well
over fifteen hundred years ago, the
Mexicans found an expedient way to
fulfill a popular demand.

Plate 59
Negrito Mask
Area of Nahuatzín, Michoacán
1930s
Carved and lacquered wood, silk
ribbons, cloth, beads, and foil, 4'
(with ribbons). SAMA

This splendid mask, with four feet
of cascading silk ribbons, a
profusion of cloth flowers, and
beaded and foil adornments, is worn
for the Danza de los Negritos
(Dance of the Black Men) in
Michoacán. The lacquered mask has
European features and is associated
with wealth and power.

Black people have a long and
extensive history in Mexico,
particularly in Michoacán. They
were brought there as slaves by the
Spanish colonists and imparted great
status to their owners. Their
elaborate costumes are recorded in
mid-sixteenth-century writings.
When blacks first arrived in
Mexico, they were perceived by the
Indians as being very powerful and
were accorded great status.
Tarascans applied soot to their faces
before defending themselves in
battle to acquire some of this power.

The first Negrito dance grew out
of religious brotherhoods of blacks
dedicated to the Virgin. The Danza
de los Negritos takes many forms,
with Negritos often masquerading as
clowns, controlling crowds, or
paying homage to saints. The
dancers perform many times during
the year, singing or reciting verses
at churches and homes, in honor of
saints, the Holy Child, the Virgin,
and village elders.

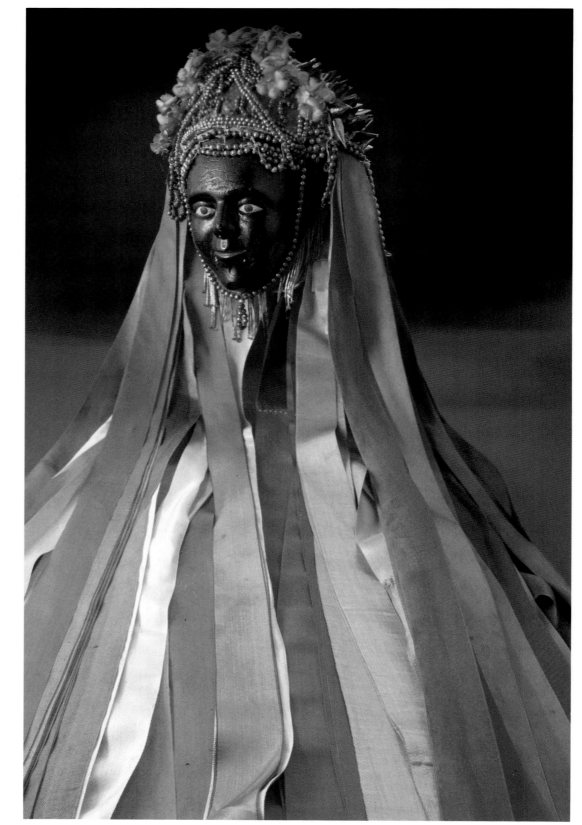

Plate 60
Jaguar Mask
State of Guerrero
Late 19th century
Painted wood, animal teeth, boar
bristle, and glass, 14 × 12 × 7½".
SAMA

Jaguar masks are used in many parts of Mexico. The jaguar was one of the most powerful pre-Hispanic symbols and could be found on Mayan stelae, Aztec altars, Toltec, Mixtec, and Olmec carvings, and was depicted repeatedly throughout the early codices. The jaguar, arrogant and powerful, was considered lord of the animals. He represented the night and symbolized war. Jaguars were connected to caves, to fertility, and to the hostile forces of the natural world. The jaguar was considered a supernatural force to be reckoned with. Many versions of the *tigre* (jaguar) dance exist: El Tigre, Tlacololero, and Tecuani. In these dances, the jaguar is eventually chased, captured, and killed, symbolizing the power to change a threatening world into a protective one. Often these dance dramas are related to the agricultural cycle or are performed as ritual battles between neighboring communities or barrios. This spectacular mask is one of the oldest of its kind to have survived.

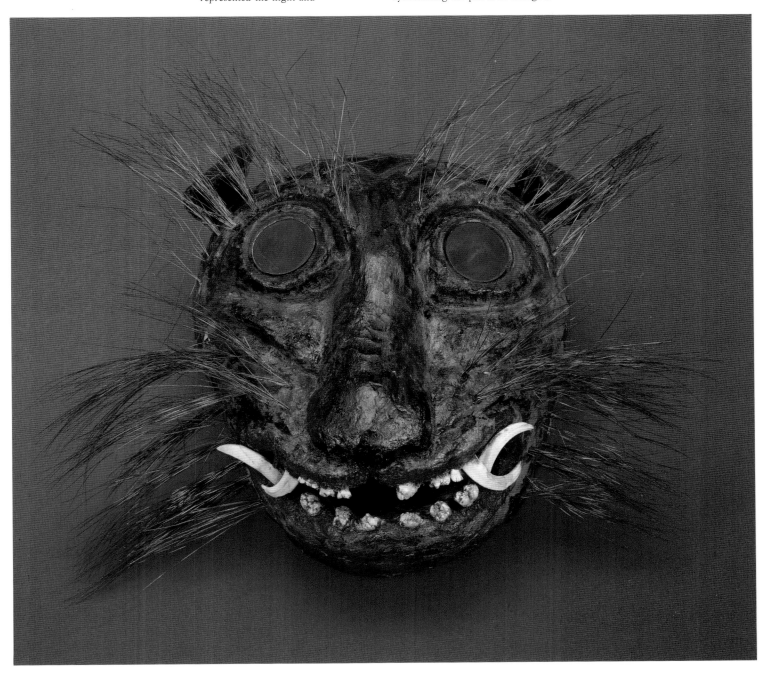

Plate 61
Aurelio Flores
Tree of Life
Izúcar de Matamoros, Puebla
1930s
Single-fired, painted, and varnished
earthenware, 18½ × 16½″. MM

The tree of life symbolizing
fertility, the life cycle, and rebirth is
a concept artisans find inspiring
because of its design potential.
Mexican trees of life are adorned
with flowers, birds, animals, and
leaves. The base figure can vary
from Madonnas and saints to Adam
and Eve or skeletons, depending on
the purpose of the piece. This
traditional ceremonial tree is made
by Aurelio Flores, whose family
members are the sole producers of
this tree and traditional incense
burners. It is not clear where this
form originated, although Flores
said they were originally used on
wedding altars in Izúcar. He still
makes special ritual trees for yearly
ceremonies. Perhaps the work was
inspired by the ornate baroque
carving found in the churches of
Tonanzintla, Acatepec, or Atlixco,
Puebla. Parts of the tree are mold-
made with additional press-molded
and hand-formed pieces. After
firing, the piece is whitewashed with
a mixture of zinc oxide and calcium
carbonate. It is painted with a
mixture of aniline dyes and tempera
and then coated with a homemade
varnish of a tree resin mixed with
prickly pear juice. This gives the
paint a brilliant glaze that eventually
turns the base coat a warm creamy
yellow.

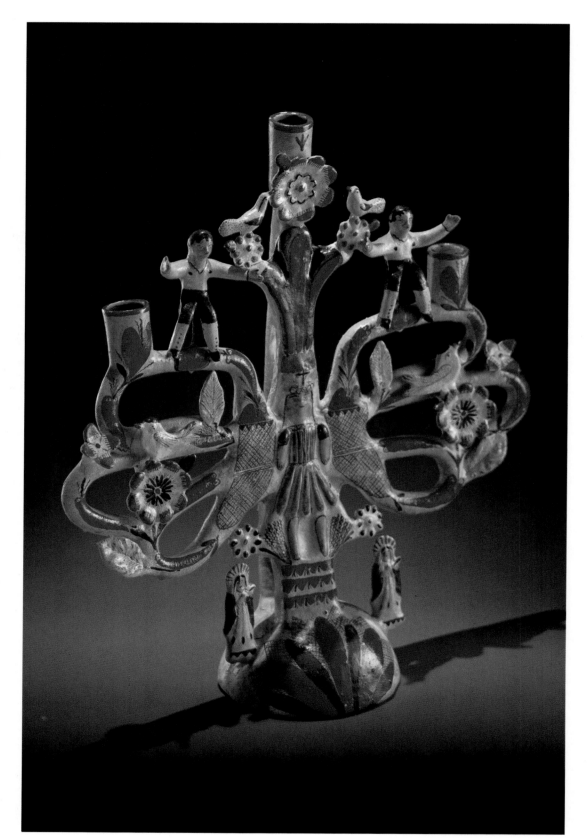

Plate 62
Concha
State of Guanajuato
1930s
Inlaid wood, armadillo shell,
mother-of-pearl, wire, and
embroidered fabric, 35½ × 10″.
SAMA

The *conchero* dancers are known by
many names: Soldiers of the
Conquest, People of the Shells, and
Chichimecas (after the ancient
Mexicans). They are tightly knit
and rigidly organized brotherhoods
that dance in honor of saints at
religious ceremonies and fiestas.
Concheros adhere to strict and formal
fraternal obligations and rituals in
their devotion to the cardinal points
of the cross. Their dance costumes
are elaborate and include ornate
feathered headdresses with mirrors,
beads, tassels, and fringed or
feathered layered wraparound skirts.
The combinations are a dazzling and
showy array of vibrantly dyed
feathers, ribbons, cloth, and
sequins. These dances are
romanticized versions of the Aztecs'
dances and are closely connected to
feelings of nationalism.

During their vigorous dance, they
play the *concha*. This twelve-stringed
instrument looks like a mandolin but
is tuned like a guitar. Each *concha* is
consecrated in a special ceremony
and has its own name; this one is
inscribed with "C.M." A complete
armadillo shell makes up the back
part of the instrument and is
responsible for its unusual sound.
Small *concheros* painted on the front
surround the symbol of the four
winds of the cross. The sound hole
is surrounded by delicate inlaid
work, and the stem is inlaid with
mother-of-pearl. The elaborate
instrument strap is intricately
embroidered and bordered with
mirrors.

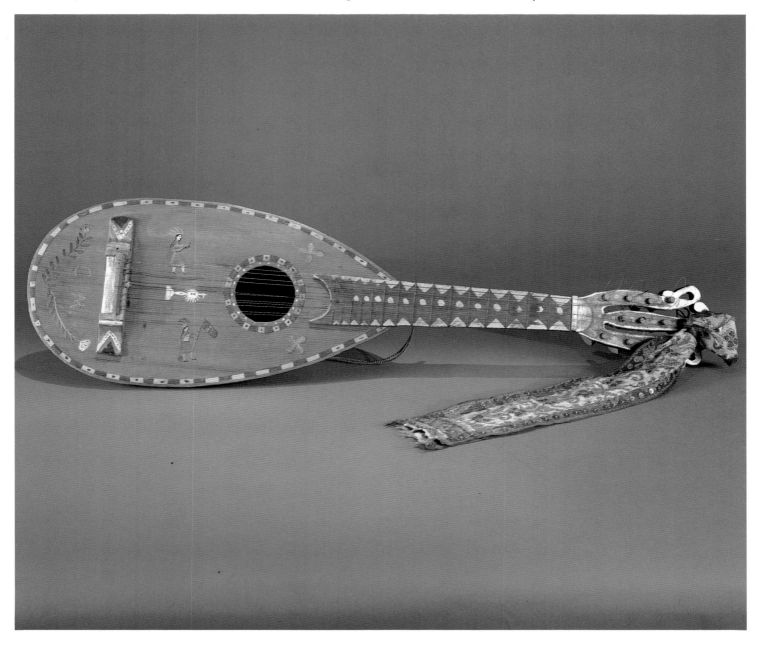

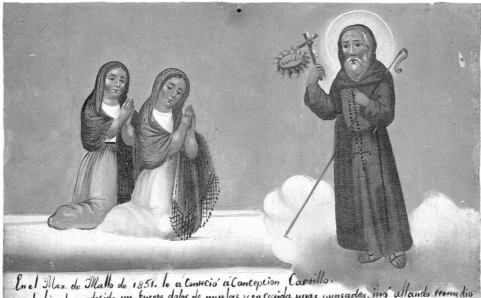

En el Mes de Mayo de 1851. le a Contecio a Conception Castillo. que hubiendo padecido un fuerte dolor de muelas, y en ceguida unas punsadas. ino allando remedio en lo humano, aClamo a S. S. Francisco de p.a y Juntamente su niña Crucita por lo que Fue reestablecida de su salud.

Plate 64
La Mano Poderosa
Central Mexico
Mid-19th century
Oil on tin; tin frame; $13 \times 9\frac{5}{8}''$.
SAMA

La Mano Poderosa, an image associated with the veneration of the Holy Family, was one of the most popular and common colonial *retablo* themes. The artist used a painterly technique to emphasize the work's dramatic subject: the hand of Saint Francis, dripping with blood, emerging from a billowing cloud. The blood symbolizes the Eucharist, and the lambs who drink it are the faithful. From left to right, images of Santa Ana, La Virgen María, El Niño Jesús, San José, and San Joaquín correspond to the five fingers of San Francisco.

Plate 63
Ex-voto
North central Mexico
1851
Oil on tin, $7 \times 10''$. SAMA

Ex-votos are small commissioned works painted to commemorate recovery from an illness or escape from serious danger because of the intervention of a holy being. These small paintings are then placed in churches by the recovered or saved in gratitude for the miraculous and divine powers that came to their aid. The paintings by informally trained artists are often incredible renderings that vary from the childlike to sophisticated, from cartoon to realistic, but are always inventive, devout, and full of visual emotion. This tradition arrived with the Spanish, was adopted first by the wealthy, and following independence from Spain, achieved widespread popularity among all Mexicans. The ex-voto is often divided into two parts, a charming and pictorial representation of the occurrence and the divine intervenor and an accompanying narrative and devotional text. In this small piece, a woman, Concepción Carillo, is thanking the Franciscan San Francisco de Paula for helping her recover from a painful toothache she was stricken with. She is portrayed in the ex-voto with her daughter. The Franciscan saint is pictured with his staff and cross. Ex-votos are often valuable tools for studying regional customs and costumes. The women in this ex-voto, who look more like sisters than mother and daughter, are wearing traditional *ikat* rebozos from Santa María del Río, San Luis Potosí, enabling us to attribute this painting to north central Mexico.

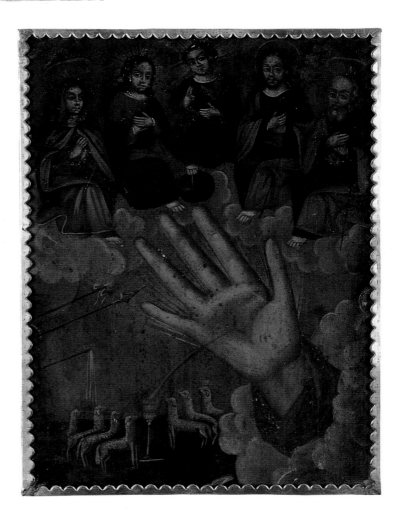

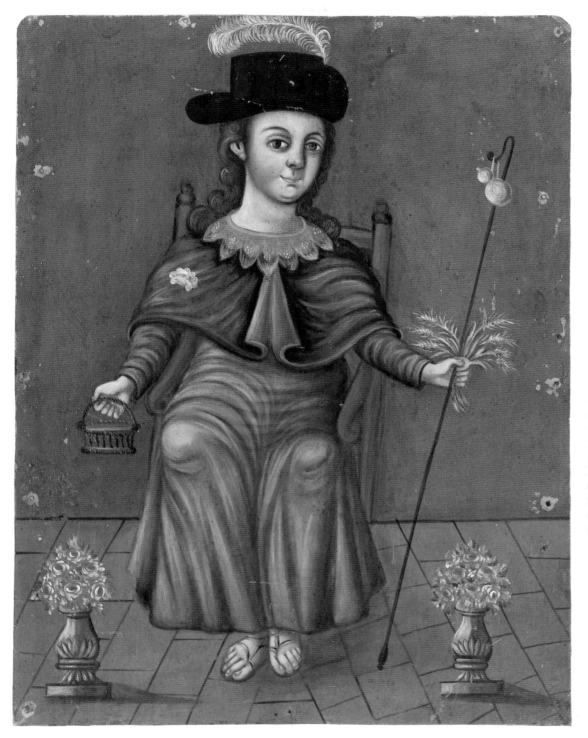

Plate 65
El Niño de Atocha
Central Mexico
Mid-19th century
Oil on tin, 12¾ × 9¾″. SAMA

El Niño de Atocha, one of the most common folk *retablo* themes, is a popular manifestation of the young Christ. This image had its origin in Atocha, Spain, during the Moorish invasion. The tyrannical Moors, so the story is told, forbade anyone except for young children to visit the incarcerated Christians on errands of mercy. The prisoners were starving, and the Atochans prayed fervently for their deliverance. When a young child dressed as a pilgrim with a staff, a water gourd, and a basket of food arrived, their prayers were answered. Miraculously, there was still food in his basket and water in his gourd even after all the prisoners were fed.

El Niño de Atocha is the patron to whom people pray for the freeing of prisoners, for protection from violence, and for deliverance and rescue from serious dangers encountered during travel. The Niño's attributes remain constant in *retablos:* a brimmed hat with a plume, a pilgrim's staff, a gourd, shafts of wheat, and a basket containing flowers or bread.

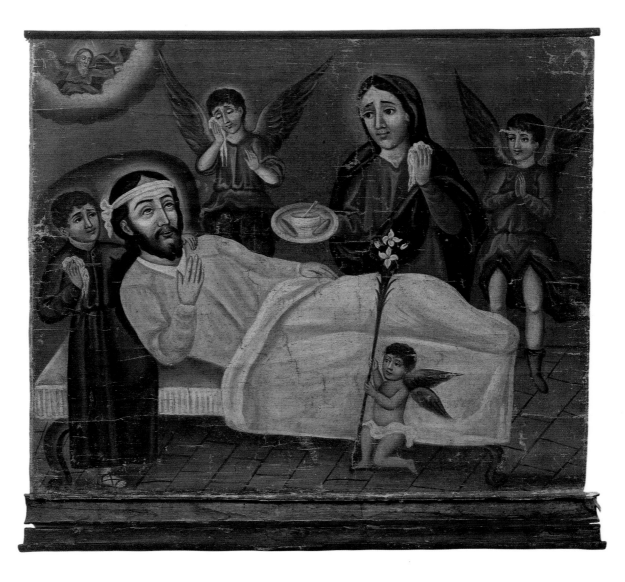

Plate 66
The Death of San José
Central Mexico
Early 19th century
Oil on canvas; wooden sheath;
32 × 35½". SAMA

This timeworn canvas, designed to
be rolled up into a cylindrical
wooden sheath, illustrates the death
of San José. Scroll paintings were a
convenient way for itinerant priests
and friars to carry religious material
to the many village churches in their
parishes. They originated in Europe
to facilitate storage. This painting
can be attributed to the early
nineteenth century by its depiction
of neoclassical bed legs and the tiled
floors. The predominant red, white,
and green coloration reflects the
artist's patriotism.

San José's main attribute is a
flowering staff, which is said to have
blossomed while he was courting
Mary. He was selected as the
successful suitor because of this
miraculous occurrence. The staff
also symbolizes the coming of
Christ. The staff in this painting is
held by an angel. The dying saint is
attended by his weeping wife, Mary,
while two archangels, recognizable
by their wings and footwear, sadly
look on. San José is the patron of
the family and fatherhood. He
symbolizes protection for those in
search of a home and for a good
death. He is always portrayed as a
gentle and compassionate saint. This
moving and tender scene is
reinforced by the youth and
innocence of the angels and by the
boyish priest who appears to be an
acolyte. Waiting in heaven to receive
San José is God the Father,
identified by the triangular shape
behind his head—a symbol of the
Holy Trinity.

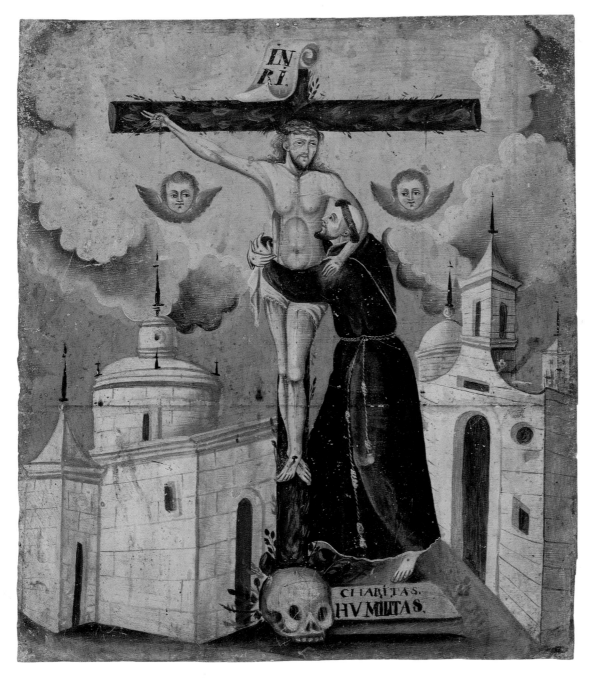

Plate 67
San Francisco Embracing Christ
Central Mexico
Mid-18th century
Oil on tin, 14 × 16¾″. SAMA

This *retablo* of San Francisco
represents the visionary saint's
devotion to Christ and symbolizes
the ideal penitent. Saint Francis,
born in the late twelfth century, was
known for his espousal of poverty,
chastity, and obedience. In this
retablo he is wearing the habit of the
Franciscans, an order he founded.
In 1523 Franciscans arrived in
Mexico to convert Indians to
Christianity. San Francisco, who
had a vision of Christ crucified,
received the stigmata during a time
of intense prayer and contemplation.
He is portrayed tenderly supporting
the bleeding Christ while two angels
look down upon them. The
buildings are a blend of Italian and
Mexican Franciscan church
architecture. He is standing behind
a foliated skull—a symbol of
mortality and penance—and a
plaque that reads "Charitas HV
Militas." The awkward perspective
is characteristic of the work of
retablo painters, who often relied on
a verbal account of the subject
without a visual prototype to work
from.

Plate 68
Stations of the Cross (Station II)
Central Mexico
1850
Oil on canvas, 19 × 24½″. SAMA

The fourteen *Stations of the Cross*, of which twelve are in the Rockefeller collection, recount the route of Christ on his way to Calvary. Station II depicts Simon carrying Christ's heavy cross. Simon rushed out of the crowd to help a weary Christ when the cross became too heavy for him to bear. Christ's arm appears merged with Simon's in a touching artistic gesture of thankfulness. Simon is dressed in red, white, and green, colors that emphasize the Mexicanization of the religious theme. A centurion is reining in a very stylized horse that has partially entered the painting from the right. The background, with its curious perspective, the street's surface, and the figural highlighting reflect the engaging style of the painter whose lack of formal training never detracts from the descriptive and emotional power of this series.

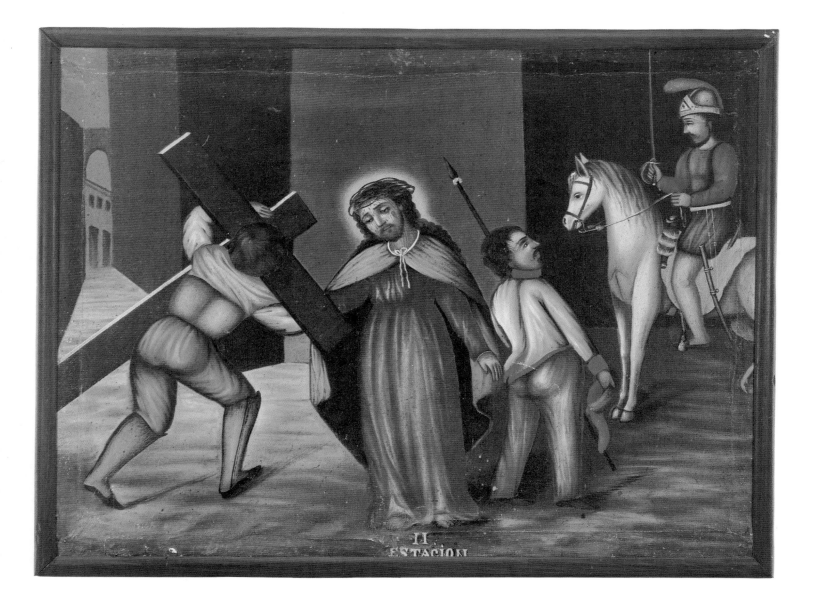

Plate 69
Stations of the Cross (Station VI)
Central Mexico
1850
Oil on canvas, 19 × 24½″. SAMA

Station VI portrays the moment when Christ bearing the cross is approached by the pious woman Veronica, who will mop his brow; according to legend, the image of the face of Christ later appeared on the cloth she used. In this painting, the veil of Veronica has three identical images of Christ, representing the Holy Trinity. Rome considered the three faces of Christ motif heretical, but in Mexico it was a popular way of explaining the mysteries of the Trinity. Veronica and Christ are surrounded by young soldiers.

The paintings in the *Stations* series are excellent examples of the blending of popular Mexican painting and Christian symbolism with regional details. In this painting, the Indian woman on the right is wearing a traditional large, capelike rebozo around her shoulders. Her elaborate hairdo has decorative hair cords and gleams with the sheen of vegetable or nut oils, whose use was popular with Indian women. A red, white, and green patriotic color motif is used throughout this series.

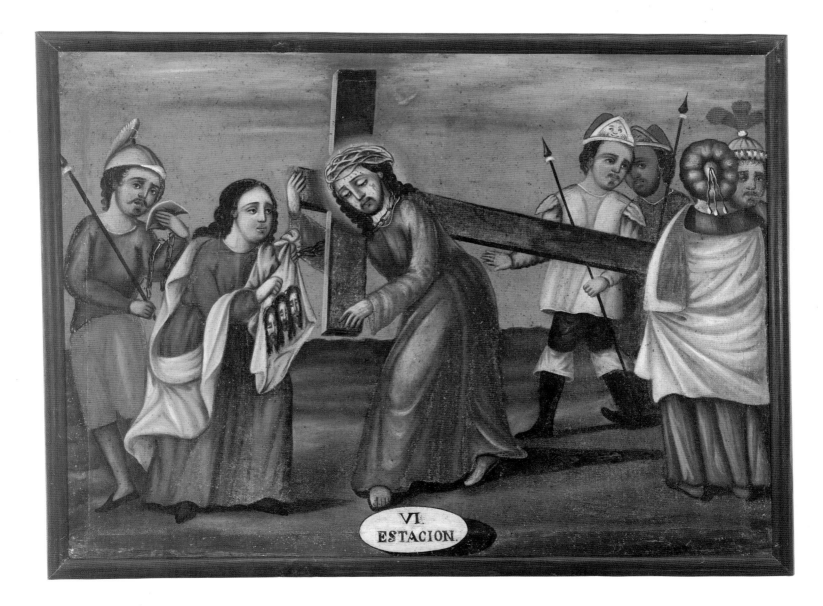

Plate 70
Day of the Dead Toys
Toluca, State of Mexico
1978
Alfeñique and pumpkin seed paste,
1½″ to 6½″. MM and SAMA

These delightful and fragile pastel
figures are traditional objects made
only in Toluca during the last days
of October. The recipe for *alfeñique*
(sugar paste) dates back to colonial
times and combines potatoes, sugar,
egg whites, lime, and food coloring.
The dough is pressed into two
molds; the two halves are then
joined and decorated.
    The rather crude embellishments
of these figures account for their
naive charm. They are made by a
few women who use molds passed
down for generations. The animals
are also made of *alfeñique*, the
parrots of pumpkin seed paste.

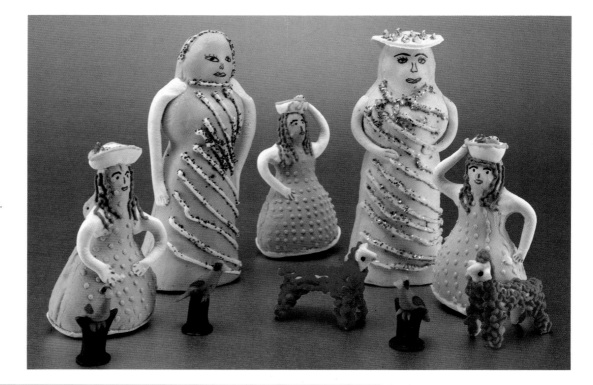

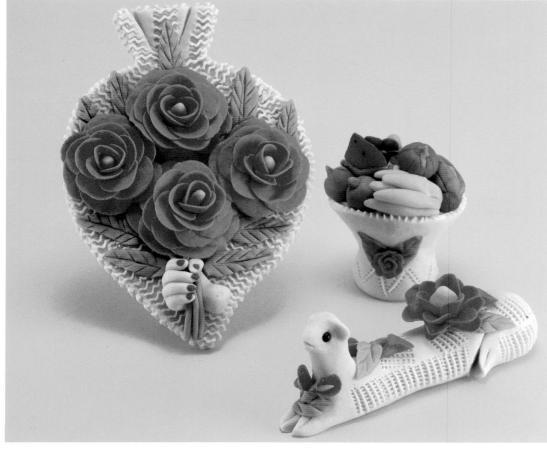

Plate 71
Day of the Dead Offerings
Puebla, Puebla
October 1978
Pumpkin seed paste and food
coloring, 1½″ to 6″. MM and
SAMA

These charming pieces made by a
Puebla confectioner are elegant,
edible offerings. The Day of the
Dead calls forth a burst of creative
confectionery despite its ephemeral
nature. Temporary street stalls sell
sweets, flowers, and breads, while
local candy shops and bakeries offer
brightly painted and tinted
temptations. The visual effect is
dazzling.
    Pumpkin seed paste can be hand-
formed, extruded, or press-molded,
before being elaborately decorated.
A woman's delicate hand offering
four vivid, perfect roses to her
beloved deceased makes a poignant
statement. The fruit bowl contains
picante peppers and some of the
ninety-eight tropical fruits available
in Mexico.

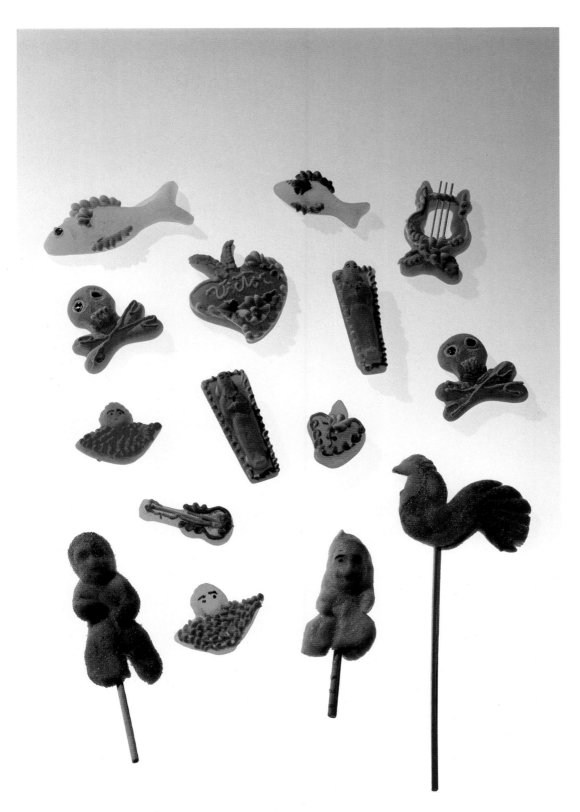

Plate 72
Day of the Dead Offerings
Oaxaca, Oaxaca
1978
Molded sugar, 1″ to 2″. MM and
SAMA

Sweet offerings are just a small part of the culinary delights placed on an altar to tempt the returning souls. After feasting on the smells of mole, tastes of tamales, and swigs of beer, it might be time to indulge a sweet tooth and have a fish or a small guitar or a coffin filled with sugar water. Along with the customary sugar skulls that each child buys, these little candies are a cherished part of the celebration and can be eaten with pleasure when the dead souls depart. Often these delicately colored confections are decorated with glitter and foil, turning them into objects to treasure but not to taste.

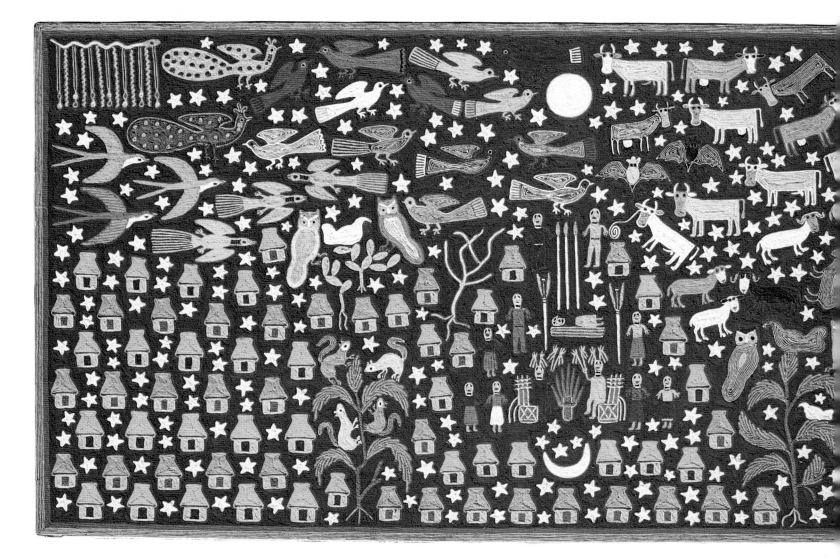

Plate 73
Elena Carillo and Pablo Cosillo
Hernández
Huichol Tabla
Mexico, D.F.
1978
Yarn, beeswax, and plywood,
48 × 96″. SAMA

This complex *tabla* is a
contemporary *Nearika*, a Huichol
term for ritual art depicting an
enormous variety of symbols and
representations used to communicate
with their gods. This piece was
made in Mexico, D.F., by Elena
Carillo and her husband, the shaman
Pablo Hernández, while they were
working as informants for well-
known Mexican anthropologists. It
depicts a funeral scene of a woman
being sent to the gods as two
shamans, sitting on their chairs,
pray over a quiver containing
Tateway, the old grandfather fire
god. The stars represent the souls of
various gods and shamans. The
moonlike disk is the symbol that
identifies the *tabla* as a *Nearika;* it is
where a mirror representing the
central deity Tateway would be
placed. The little buildings are
xiriki (gods' houses); each represents
a specific deity. The yarn colors used
are sacred colors to the Huichols.

Decorative yarn paintings are an
urban Huichol folk art not practiced
in their home villages in the remote
and rugged sierra of Nayarit.

Making these *tablas* is an alternative
to the demanding seasonal day labor
on the coast that the Indians do to
supplement their income. The *tablas,*
outgrowths of sacred boards, are
storytelling devices that are very
popular with the Huichol "urban
professional artisans" who have
temporarily moved to large cities.
They often work communally to
produce these fascinating
storyboards that depict a wealth of
personal and religious mythology.

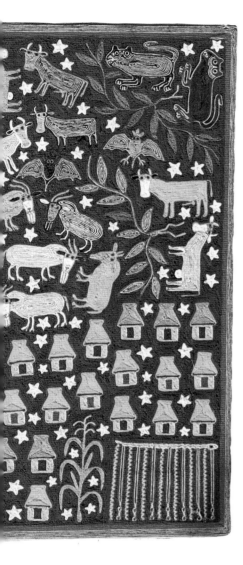

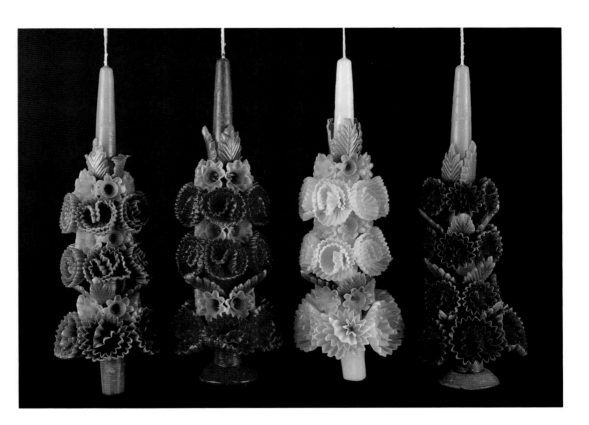

Plate 74
Ceremonial Candles
Michoacán or Mexico, D.F.
1978
Molded and hand-formed wax,
height, 14½″. MM and SAMA

It is hard to envision Mexico
without the candles that burn
continually in churches and small
chapels, adorn home altars, and are
carried in religious processions, lit
for the dead, and used for
illumination. Who can forget the
magic of a candle-lit cemetery
during the Day of the Dead, a
nighttime funeral procession making
its way through a small village, or
an Easter Sunday as hundreds of
Indians march with candles and
offerings?

Elaborate wax candles are one of
the fragile ephemeral arts of
Mexico—a selfless art where all is
subjugated to the ceremonial
purpose. In Michoacán the delicate
art of molded wax flowers is
renowned throughout Mexico.
Multitiered floral arrangements of
white wax with gold or silver
stamens or pistils might surround a
three-foot candle already entwined in
colored foils. These candles are a
tribute to the artisans who are called
for ceremonial occasions to patiently
create something that will survive
only a few bright hours.

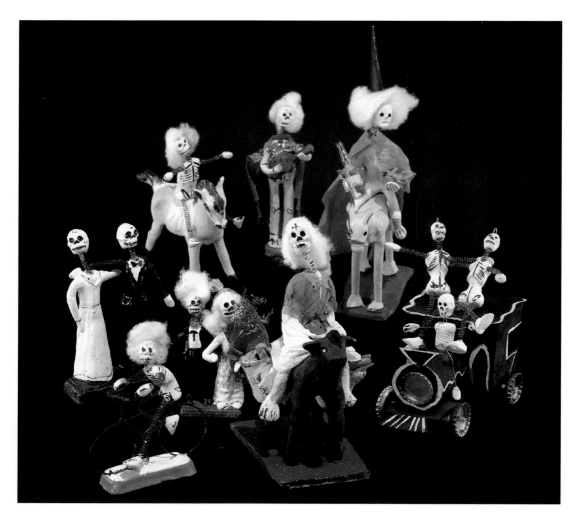

Plate 75
Day of the Dead Figures
Valley of Oaxaca
1978
Paper, earthenware, wire, cotton, bottle tops, and wood, 4″ to 10¾″. MM and SAMA

Each year during El Día de los Muertos dead souls return to earth to celebrate with friends and family. The festivities begin October 31, when the *angelitos* (children who have died) start arriving, in time for All Saints' Day on November 1. November 2, All Souls' Day, is devoted to departed adults. In preparation, elaborate altars with foods and offerings are erected, grave sites are decorated with gorgeous wreaths and flowers, and in many villages, marigold petals are scattered along paths from the graves to the altars so the dead souls can find their way.

Two weeks before the holiday, markets are filled with handmade objects devoted to death. The imagery is wild and animated, satiric and humorous, including sugar skulls and skeletons from all walks of life. These little figures are made to decorate altars and for children.

Plate 76
Funeral Scene
Oaxaca, Oaxaca
1978
Paper, earthenware, cardboard, cotton, fabric, and paint; figures: height, 4″; dead body: 3½ × 6½″. SAMA

This small funeral is a traditional Day of the Dead scene from Oaxaca. Ironically, the mourners look like skeletons while the dead person looks very much alive. The old mestizas are wearing traditional Spanish mantillas and reading newspaper bibles. In any rural cemetery in Mexico you could find a similarly arranged tombstone. The small cups on the side would be filled with the favorite drinks of the deceased, and marigolds, wildflowers, and burning candles would fill the pots or tin cans at each corner of the grave.

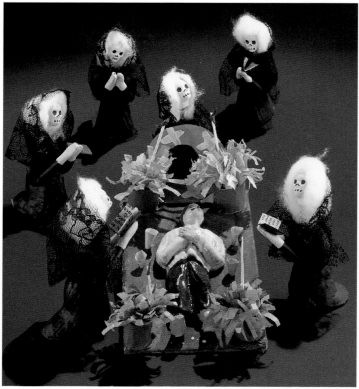

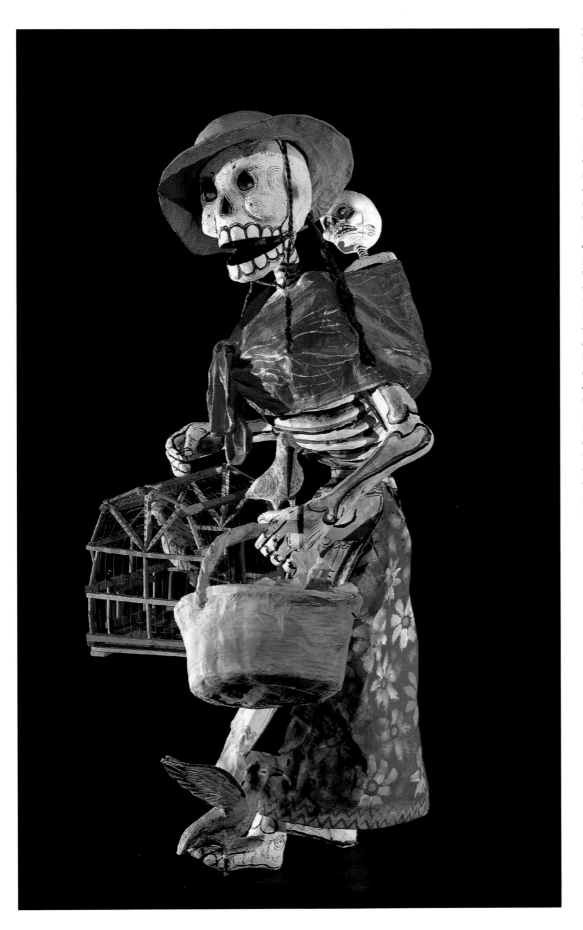

Plate 77
Miguel Linares
Skeleton Vendor
Mexico, D.F.
Mid-1970s
Paper, wood, wire, and paint,
36 × 19 × 14". SAMA

In bygone days an astonishing array of vendors sold their wares in the streets of Mexico City. A cacophony could be heard from daybreak to sundown. This lady, disguised as a skeleton, with her baby bundled up in a rebozo, represents a *chichtuilotera*, a traditional street peddler who sold small birds from the lake areas that originally surrounded the city. This piece was part of a Day of the Dead exhibit made by Miguel Linares honoring these disappearing regional characters. The series was inspired by a series of Posada metal engravings portraying a cast of *calaveras* (literally "skulls," but the term embraces all skeleton and skull imagery). Posada engraved a satiric broadside of *calaveras* that was dedicated to women and men at work: making tortillas and tamales, selling chickens, and performing all the other daily work activities peculiar to turn-of-the-century Mexico.

Plate 78
Santiago
State of Guanajuato
1930s
Carved, gessoed, and painted wood,
gold leaf, and sisal, $17 \times 14 \times 10''$.
SAMA

Santiago, or Saint James, one of
Spain's most important saints, always
appears on a rearing white steed.
His spiritual aid to the Spaniards in
their victorious battle against the
Moors in A.D. 834 established him
in a symbolic role as patron saint of
soldiers and of Spain. He was
introduced to Mexico at the time of
the Conquest. In Mexico he led a
double life, first aiding the
Spaniards in defeating the Indians
and, later, aiding the Mexicans in
defeating the Spaniards.

The Santiago dance is popular
throughout Mexico, and a dancer
often attaches a carved wooden horse
to the front of his body to enact
Santiago fighting the heathens. This
variation of the battle between the
Moors and the Christians recounts
the victory of Christianity in New
Spain. This carving depicts the
soldier Santiago almost as large as
his horse, which is rearing in
victory. His metal sword is missing,
and his costume blends the pilgrim's
cape and hat with the soldier's tunic.

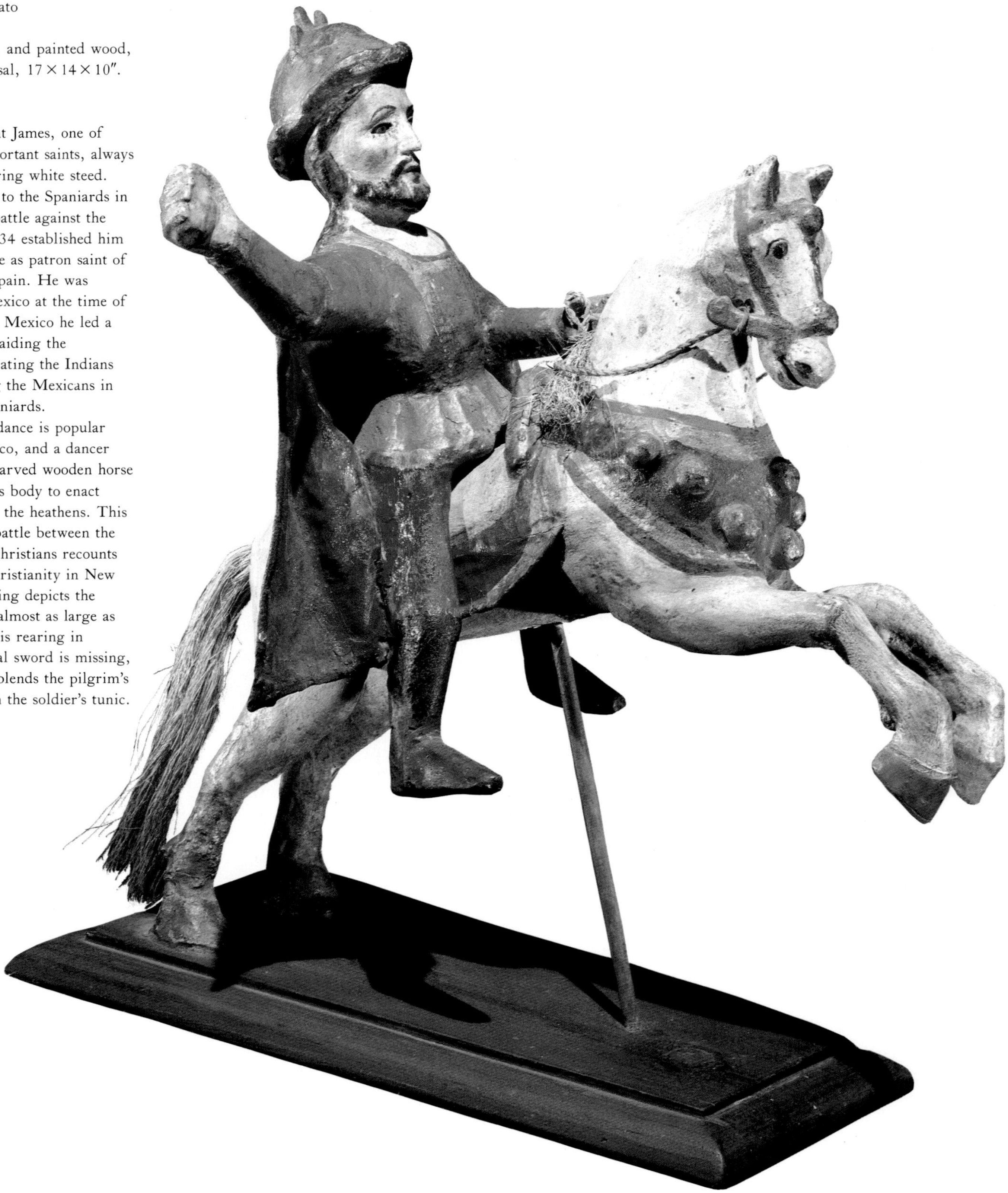

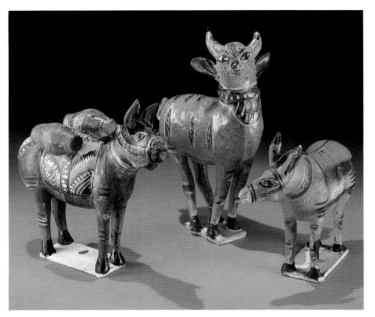

Plate 79
Julio Acero
Animal Banks
Santa Cruz de las Huertas, Jalisco
1930s
Mold-made, painted, and varnished earthenware, maximum height, 10″.
MM and SAMA

In a town well known for its production of piggy banks and ceramic toys, Julio Acero emerged as its most famous toy-maker. Acero, himself a son of toy-makers, produced a menagerie of animal banks unrivaled in Mexico. These animals, which were used as savings banks or toys, were part of Acero's large repertoire, which he sold in the nearby markets of Guadalajara and Tlaquepaque. Acero used an unusual decorative spatter technique in which he blew on the paint-filled brush to cover the surface of the piece with a misting of dots. Few of these banks have survived; the need for money meant that his art was often short-lived.

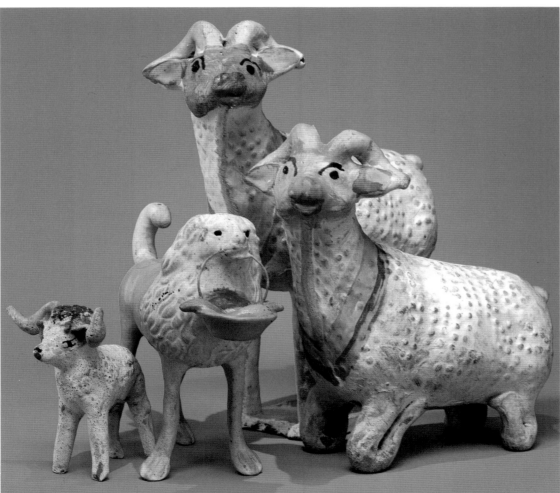

Plate 80
Toy Banks
Metepec, State of Mexico
Early 20th century
Molded, single-fired, and painted earthenware, 8¼ × 13″. MM and SAMA

These wonderful animal banks are antique Metepec pieces made for Day of the Dead altars. Time has faded the once brightly painted faces, and the clay peeks through the whitewash of calcium carbonate. These mold-made animals might have been models for the *alfeñique* artists who covered their sweet fantasies with a profusion of sugar and potato starch daubs, or is it the other way around? After their stay on the altar, these banks are used to save hard-earned centavos. Very few of these banks have survived.

Plate 81
Julio Acero
Dog Banks
Santa Cruz de las Huertas, Jalisco
1930s
Mold-made, painted, and varnished
earthenware; left to right: heights,
9″, 10″, 9″. MM and SAMA

These mold-made canines,
whimsically painted and spattered,
have animated personalities achieved
by Acero's skill at capturing the
playful or pugnacious essence of an
animal. Using antique molds, he
always managed to transform these
banks into unique and vibrant

pieces. Since the turn of the century,
ceramic banks were named
according to their cost per dozen in
centavos. These banks would be
called "trenta y seis" (thirty-six).

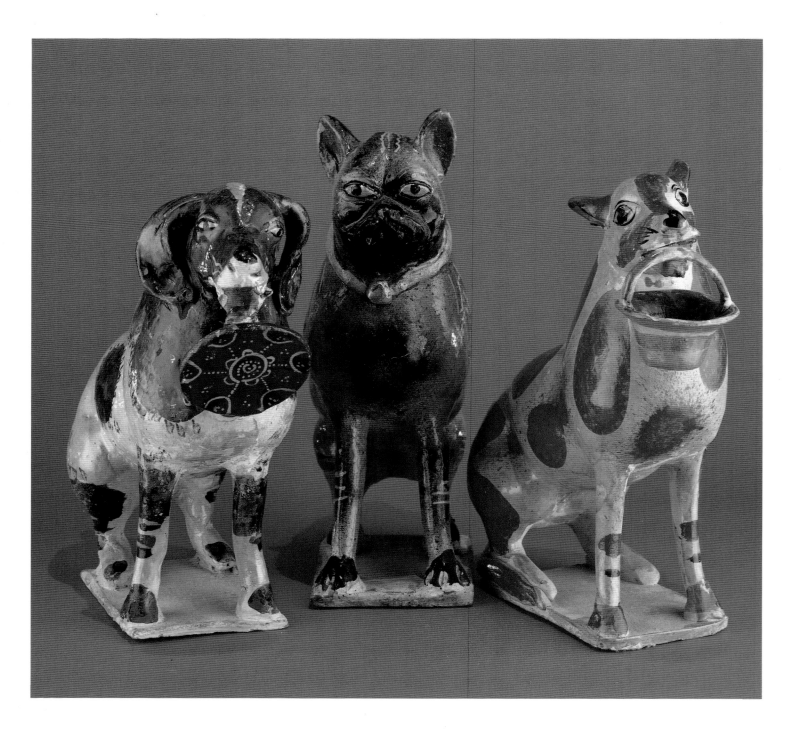

Plate 82
Julio Acero
Lion Banks
Santa Cruz de las Huertas, Jalisco
1930s
Single-fired, painted, and varnished
earthenware, 9½×9″. MM

These stately, ferocious, but friendly lions, almost Chinese in feeling, are Julio Acero's finest and most stylized animal banks. Using the antique molds that had been passed down in his family, he created brightly painted, varnished banks in highly imaginative color combinations. Simply by adding pinched strips of clay, he has given the lion an impressive mane and with delicate brushstrokes captured its leonine essence. These banks are painted with anilines and varnished.

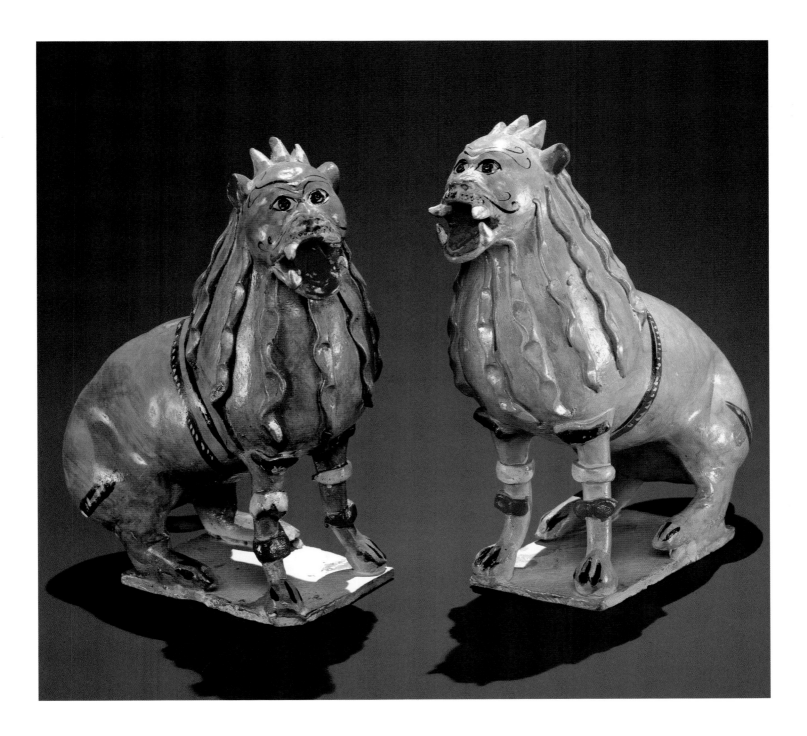

Plate 83
Marcelino Vicente
Devil Whistle
Ocumicho, Michoacán
1930s
Single-fired earthenware, paint, and
varnish, 9½ × 6 × 6″. SAMA

This unusually benign representation
of a devil, whose nose is longer than
its arms, is cleverly sculpted so that
the devil's tail supports its body and
also serves as the whistle. It is
certainly one of the seminal pieces in
the wildly creative outpouring of
Ocumicho polychromed ceramics.
The small whistles that were once
made in Ocumicho have been
abandoned in favor of a bizarre
world of hand-built devils, demons,
beasts, and religious tableaux often
combined with folk interpretations
of creation, birth, and death.

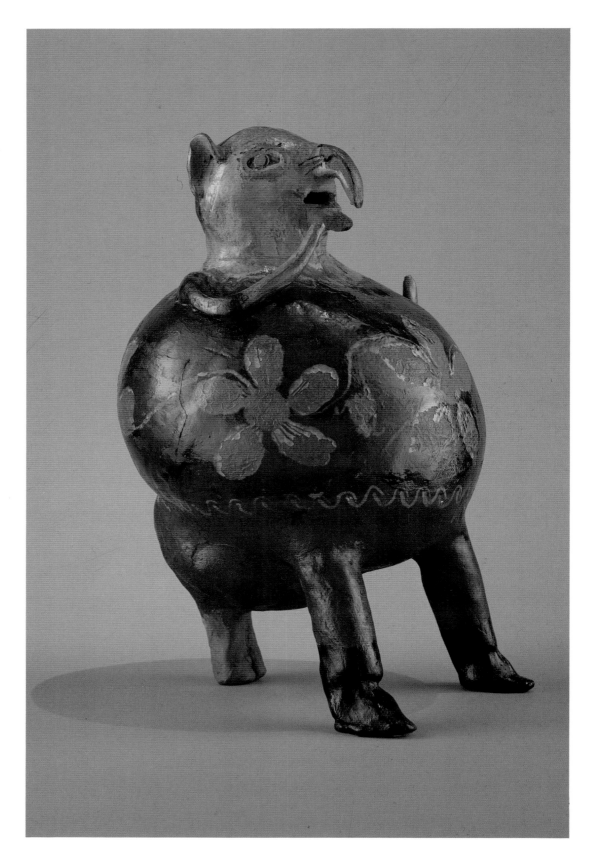

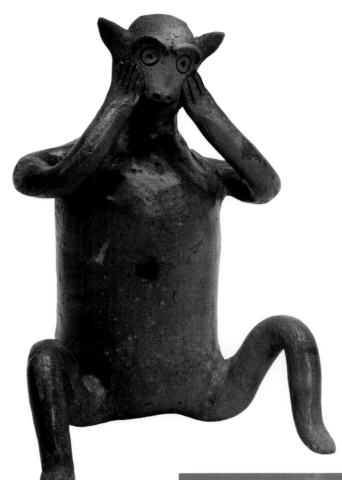

Plate 84
Monkey Whistle
San Bartolo Coyotepec, Oaxaca
1930s
Burnished, single-fired earthenware,
6⅞ × 4¾″. SAMA

Long-legged, leaping monkeys were
often represented in pre-Hispanic
relief work, paintings, and flat
stamps and were particularly popular
with the ancient Mixtec culture.
Monkeys are often associated with
the ancient god of pulque and
inebriation. The shape of this
whistle derives from the traditional
Coyotepec black clay monkey bottles
that are used to hold mescal.
Coyotepec artisans produced
enchanting whistles in the earlier
part of the century. This small
monkey whistle is a sculptural gem
reminiscent of the highly stylized
pre-Hispanic "caricature" ceramics
from Ixtlan, Nayarit.

Plate 85
Corn Husk Dolls
Santa Ana Acatlán, Jalisco
1930s
Corn husk, sisal, bamboo, wood,
and grasses, approximately
8½ × 3½″. MM and SAMA

Corn, the staple of Mexican life, is
grown all over the country. Indians
in the most remote villages prize
their *milpa* (corn patch), even if it is
miles from home on a precipitous
mountainside. No wonder the supply
of corn husks is so plentiful and put
to so many decorative uses. To make
these dolls, artisans wrap the husks
around bunched grasses, a corncob,
or bamboo. After being assembled,
the pieces are brightly painted with
aniline dyes. A tumpline runs
around the forehead of the
campesino and is attached to *huacales*
(cargo carriers) made of bamboo
or reeds.

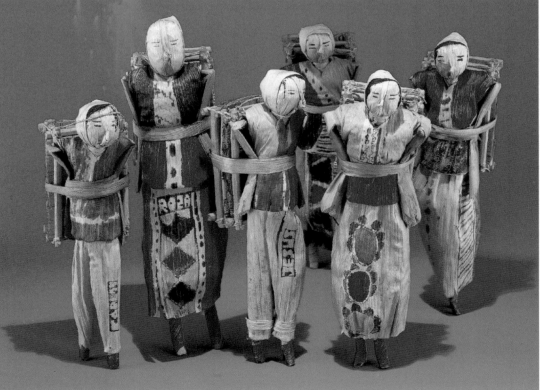

Plate 86
Teodora Blanco
Animal Band
Santa María Atzompa, Oaxaca
1978
Single-fired and glazed earthenware,
7½ × 3½″. MM and SAMA

These little musicians are zoomorphic representations of a village band. Music is a key element in Mexican celebrations, and local bands incorporate the gamut of musicians, from horn players and guitarists to cellists, flautists, and percussionists. Since participation is often a religious obligation, the musical output can vary from the melodious to the ragtag, from the practiced to the unschooled. Religious ceremonies, dance dramas, and local fiestas all call for musical

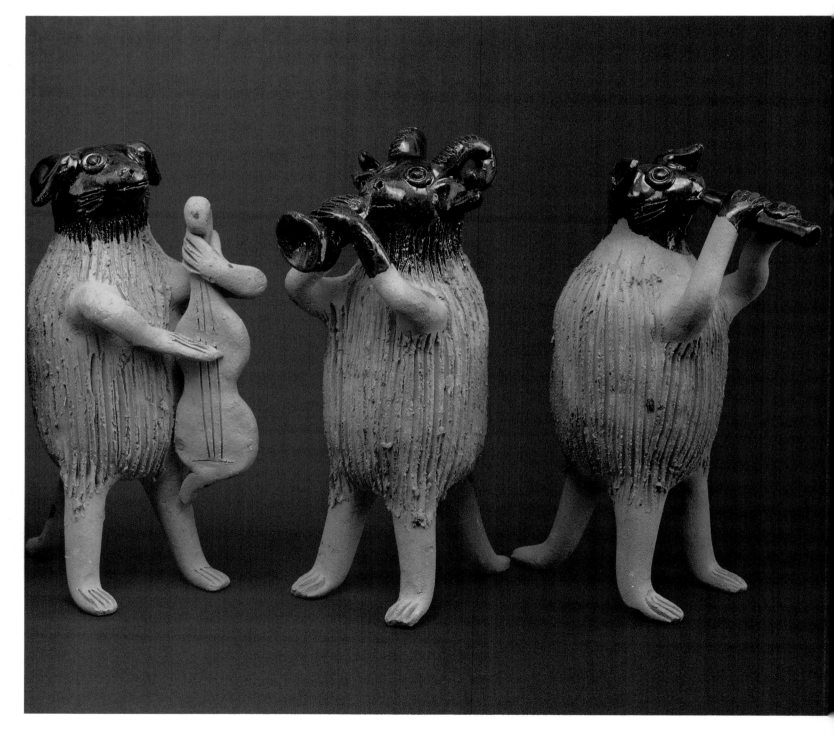

accompaniment, and watching and listening to a band in action are captivating, regardless of the performance, since musicians are above all serious and intense.

These whimsical musicians are a village band disguised as dogs, elephants, deer, and frogs. Their scored, striated bodies can be seeded with chia, and if watered they become a band in bloom.

As a teenager, Teodora Blanco invented this veritable carnival of animals in her creative interpretation of everyday life. They have been adapted by other Atzompans and are now part of the large ceramic repertoire from that village.

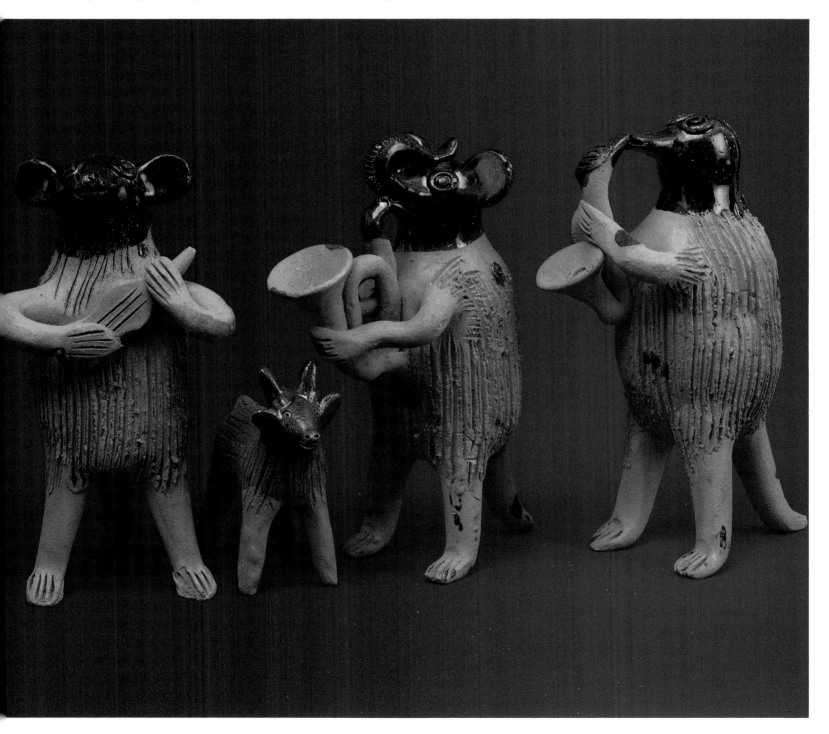

Plate 87
Aurelio Flores
Vaqueros (Cowboys)
Izúcar de Matamoros, Puebla
1930s
Earthenware, gesso, paint, and
varnish, 5½ × 3 × 5¾″. SAMA

Antique clay toys made by Aurelio
Flores are rarely seen anymore.

Although the Flores family
continues to make trees of life and
incense burners, the small figures of
men and women and horses and
riders made by Aurelio's father at
the turn of the century have almost
disappeared. These small figures,
partially mold-made, are covered
with thick, creamy gesso (a mixture
of "Spanish white" and zinc) and

painted with aniline dyes thinned
with alcohol. They are coated with a
natural varnish made with prickly
pear juice and a local tree resin.
Because the anilines are dissolved,
the painted pieces appear stained or
saturated. The thick, lustrous
varnish imparts a deep and glossy
finish.

Horses and riders are common

themes with folk artists. These
rather amusing variations show a
well-heeled and booted *charro* sitting
sidesaddle on a *macho* or burro
instead of on an elegant horse. The
mustached rider is sitting on a
saddled, black-spotted red bull, an
unlikely occurrence anywhere.

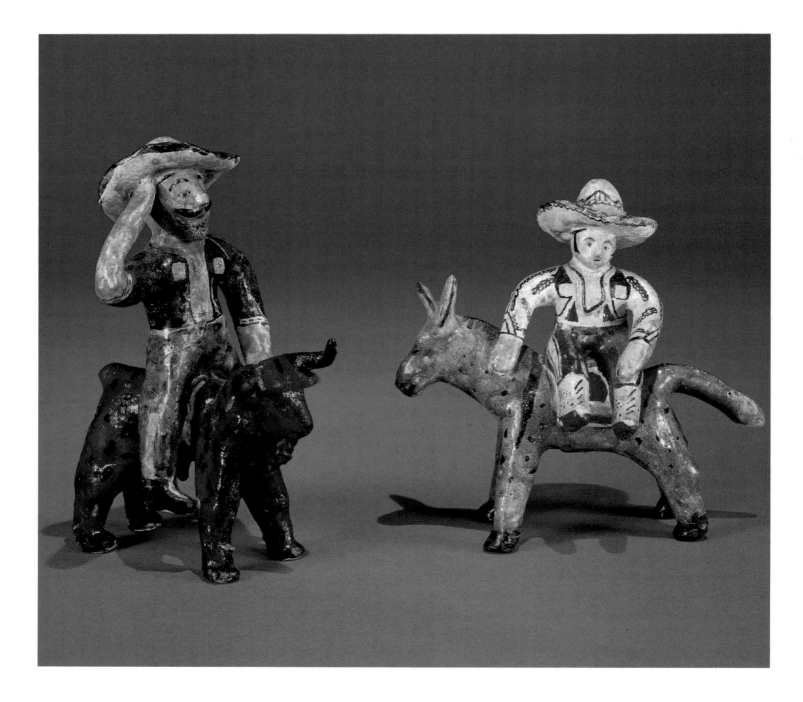

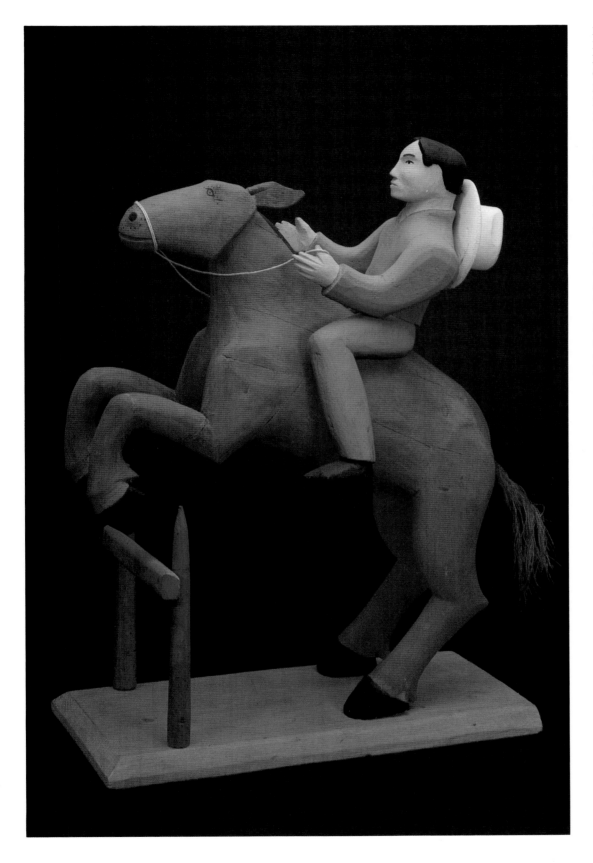

Plate 88
David Villafáñez
Horse and Rider
Oaxaca, Oaxaca
Late 1960s
Painted and carved wood,
15 × 11½ × 8″. SAMA

David Villafáñez, master woodcarver, is renowned for his unique and stylized sculptural carvings of religious and popular Mexican subjects. His fluid carving and sensual modeling are achieved through an economy and purity of style. Villafáñez' palette is always bright and crisp. His work has had a profound influence on contemporary wood carving in the Oaxaca valley. The horse-and-rider theme is popular among Mexican folk artists; many of the heroes and saints of Mexico, including Zapata and Santiago, are portrayed on horseback.

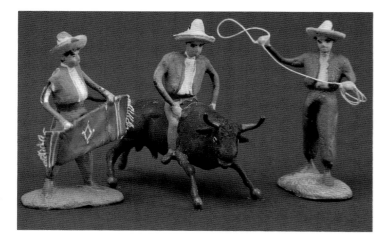

Plates 89 and 90
Angel Carranza
Miniatures
San Pedro Tlaquepaque, Jalisco
1930s
Mold-made, painted earthenware
and wire, ½″ to 1½″. SAMA

Mexico has an obsession with miniaturization. Angel Carranza, born in Tlaquepaque in 1901, was the acknowledged master of miniatures. On his tiny figures, he lavished details that only a magnifying glass reveals. His multiple-figure sets included weddings, baptisms, market scenes, and Nativities. These bullfight and *charreada* figures, typical of his miniatures, are perfectly painted with anilines and coated with a mixture of egg yolk and the resin of the mesquite tree to give them a brilliant finish. The figures depicted below come from a variety of Carranza sets. At left, we see a paunchy bullfighter trying to attract a bull with his colorful sarape, a *charro* riding a frisky bull during a *charreada*, and a *charro* demonstrating his roping skills.

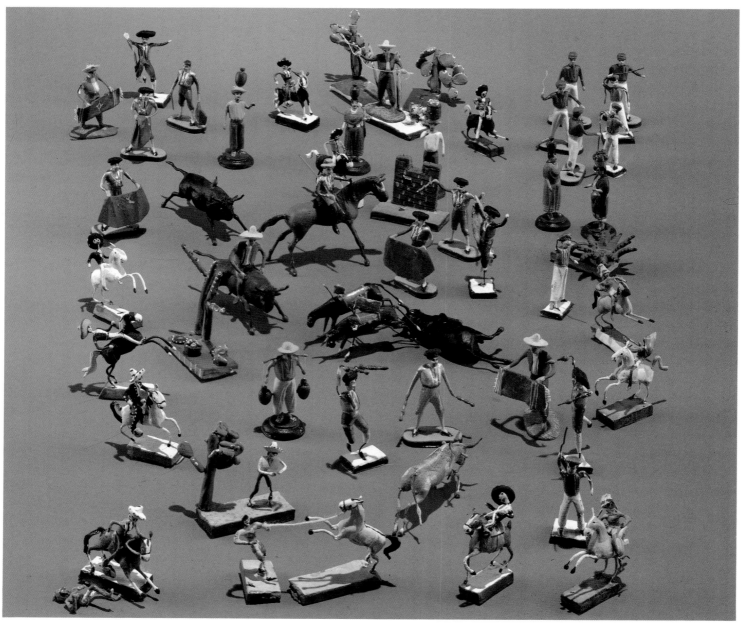

Plate 91
Miniatures and Toy Whistles
Various states
1930s
Glazed earthenware, painted
earthenware, hand-hammered
copper, and wood, ⅜″ to 3″. MM
and SAMA

To enter the universe of Mexican
miniatures and toys is to become lost
in a world of imagination, humor,
color, and sound. It is an endless
journey of starry-eyed fulfillment
and hands-on involvement for
children and for adults who are
children at heart. There are few
countries in the world with such an
extensive inventory of simple
pleasures. Toys are often vehicles of
socialization. In this photograph, the
miniatures of utilitarian pottery
allow a young girl to play with
cazuelas, cántaros, bean pots, and
chocolate beaters long before she is
ready to help out at home.

Children often begin to learn
ceramic modeling techniques by
making miniatures or pieces
requiring very small hands. The
painted earthenware whistles are
turn-of-the-century toys from
Ocumicho. The whistle is cleverly
disguised in the *cántaro* on the
woman's shoulder and the birds
perched on their heads. The wooden
toys are delicately turned on a lathe
and the copper utensils are hand-
hammered.

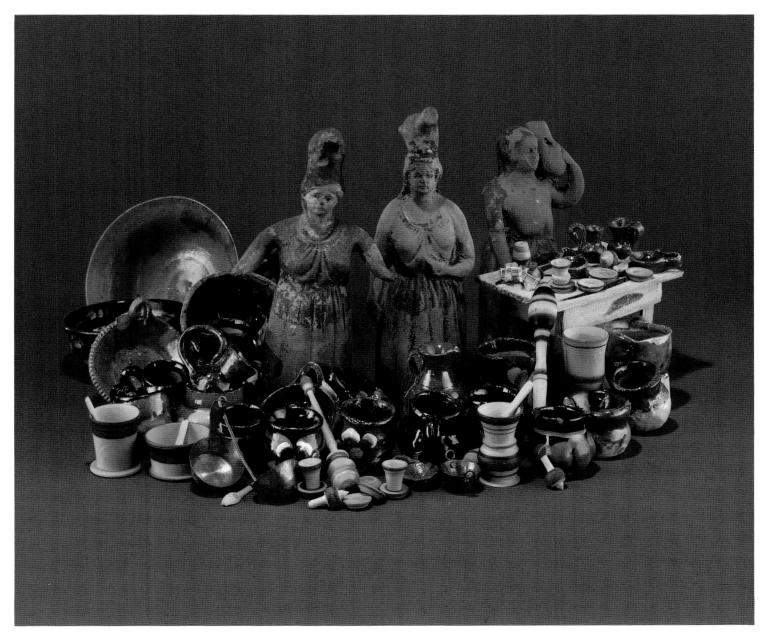

Plate 92
Conchero Pull Toys
State of Guanajuato
1930s
Wood, painted earthenware,
feathers, cloth, cardboard, bottle
caps, paper, and fur, maximum
height, 20″. SAMA

The lavish and spectacular costumes
of the popular *conchero* dancers were
the inspiration for these exuberant,
articulated toys. They exemplify a
toy-maker's ingenuity in the
combination of scrap materials to
produce realistic *concheros*, with
cardboard *conchas* with pencil-line
strings, bottle-top instruments, and
feathered and furred costumes.
Their painted pink faces with
Spanish features reinforce a bearing
befitting dancers of the Conquest.
With a pull of a string, they can
stamp their feet just as the lively
brotherhoods of *concheros* do at
fiestas throughout Mexico.

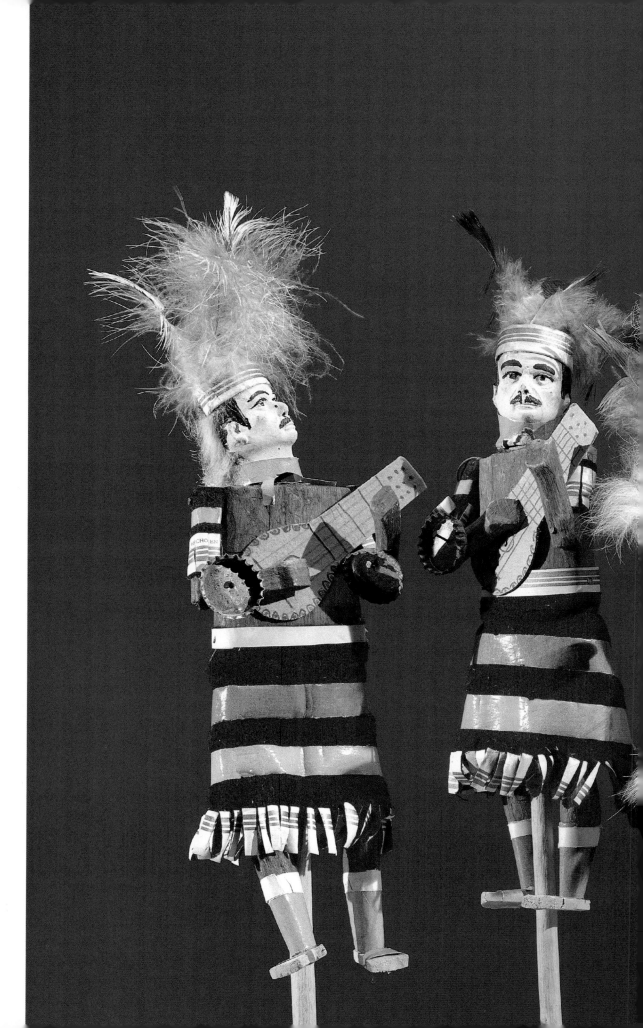

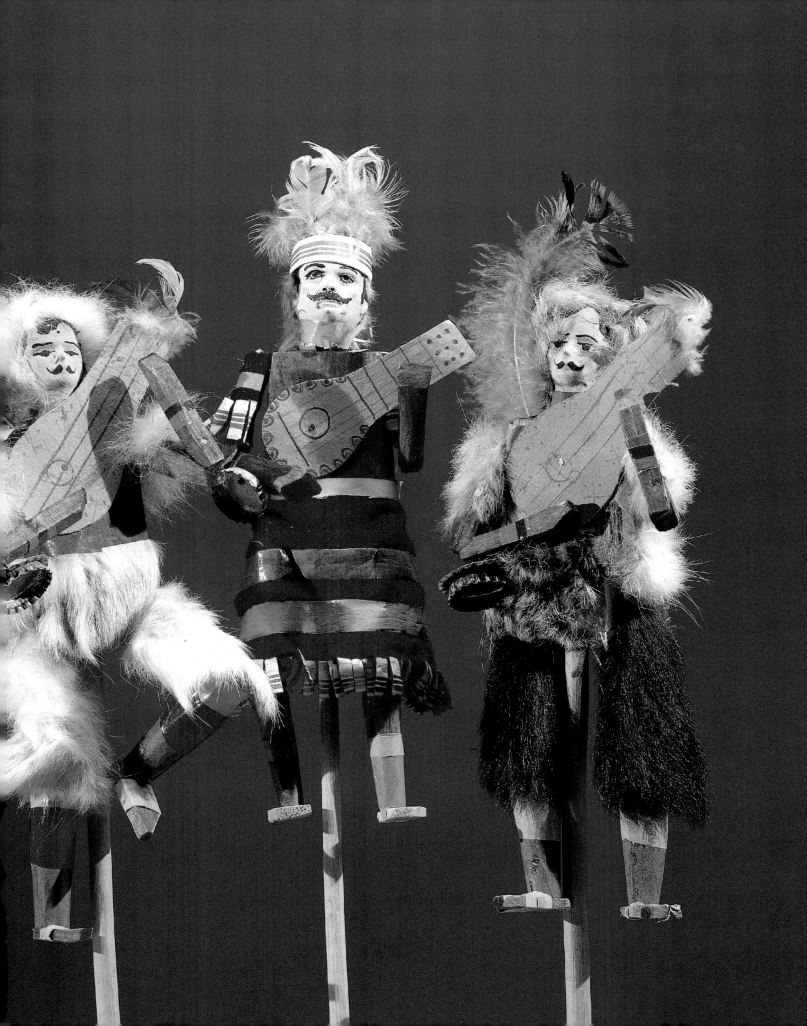

Plate 93
Pull Toy
North central Mexico
1930s
Painted wood and string,
9⅜ × 1 × 9½″. SAMA

The spirit of Mexican invention has endless play in the realm of toys. Children and toy-makers are intrigued by movement, and Mexican toys are made to pull, to push, to fly, to flutter, to leap and tumble, to hit, to terrify, to laugh at, and to teach and learn from. Toys are made of humble materials with basic tools and with simple and unconcealed mechanisms. Toy-makers know that toys are often ephemeral—that their life expectancy may be a day or a year. But this never diminishes the effort or energy that goes into making these handmade treasures.

A whole cast of characters is used for push and pull toys, from skeletons and bandits to *charros* and animals. This brightly dressed, pistol-toting *charro*, atop a vivid red horse, is a traditional wooden pull toy made of very light wood and assembled with cord. When the string is pulled, the horse starts riding—fast or slow, depending on how fast or slow the string is pulled.

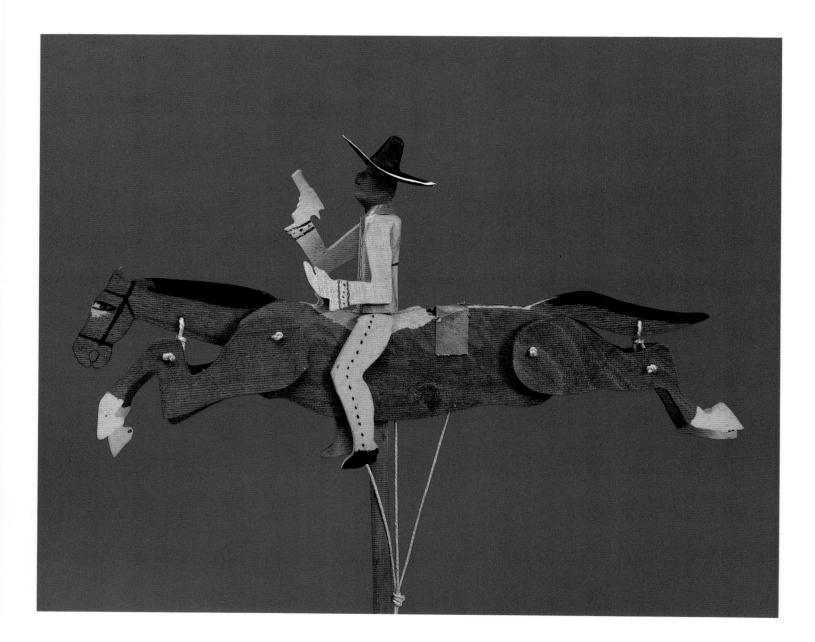

Plate 94
Push Toy
North central Mexico
1930s
Painted wood, wire, and nails,
13½ × 4 × 27″. SAMA

This traditional wooden push toy has
a long handle for a child to hold. As
the toy is pushed along the street or
floor, the wheel, attached to the
charro by wire, turns and pulls the
rod, giving the *charro* a thrilling
and bumpy ride. The horse is
painted with great gusto.

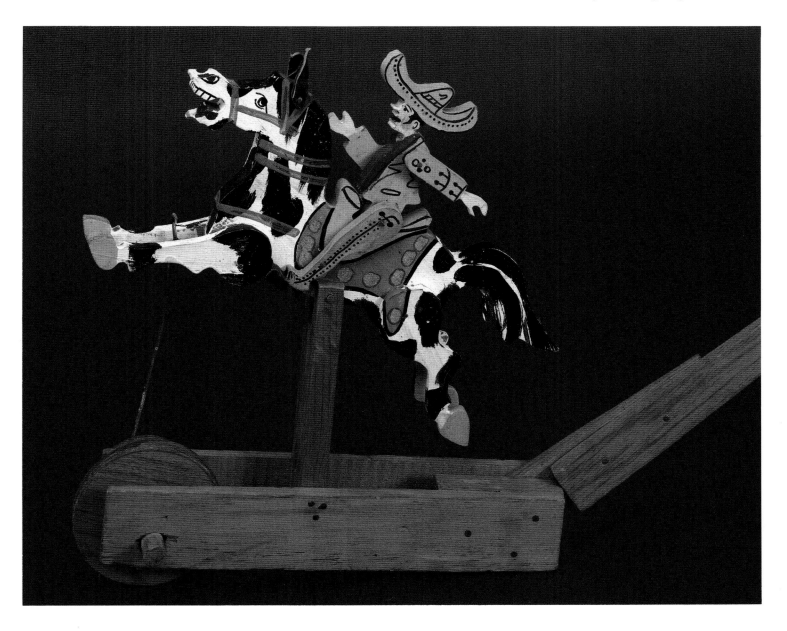

Plate 95
Aguilar family
Mothers and Children
Ocotlán de Morelos, Oaxaca
1960s
Painted earthenware, 10″ to 12″.
SAMA

These ceramic dolls were probably among the first made by the Aguilar family in its departure from the traditional Ocotlán figures. The women appear to be Trique Indians from the Sierra Madre wearing their heavy woven tube skirts, which have three pleats on either side of the front and are held up by long, embroidered sashes. Many of the first figures made by the Aguilar family in this genre were women with large nursing children. The faces lack the detail of the Aguilars' later pieces. Mouths are rarely more than incised lines or pinched folds, and eyes are painted in simple hollows. These pieces might have been made by the late Jesús Aguilar. They are certainly the prototypes for the creations of his daughters.

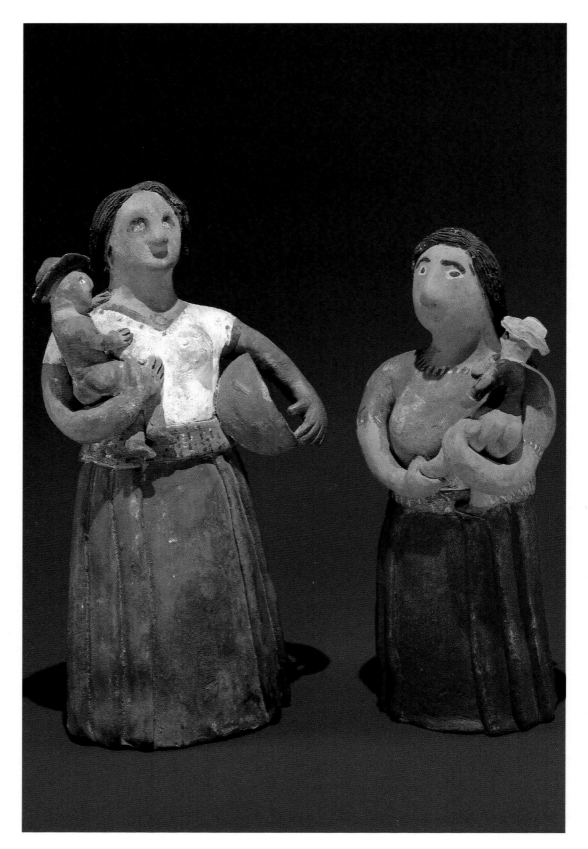

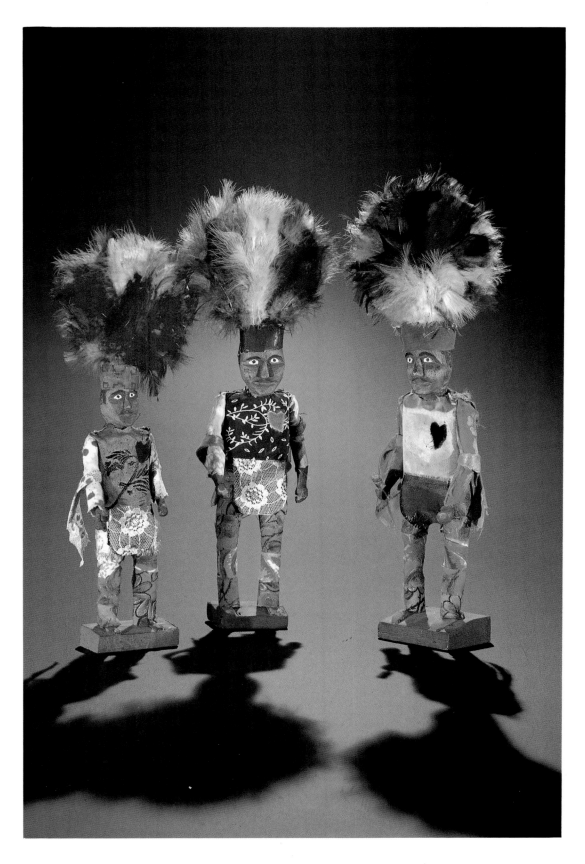

Plate 96
Plumed Dancers
Teotitlán del Valle, Oaxaca
Late 1960s
Dyed feathers, carved, painted
wood, fabric, and paper, maximum
height, 16″. SAMA

Feather dancers who perform La
Danza de las Plumas recreate the
tragic story of the Conquest. This
historical dance is the Indians'
perspective of the Conquest that
ends happily and ironically, when
the Indians all become
Christianized. The splendid
costumes they wear allow the
Indians to look upon their past with
great pride. Scraps of bright
brocade, shiny rayon, imitation lace,
vibrantly dyed feathers, and small
rattles were used by this artisan to
portray the elaborately adorned,
plumed dancers famous throughout
the Valley of Oaxaca.

Plate 97
Marionettes
Puebla, Puebla
1960s
Painted, single-fired earthenware,
fabric, wood, and thread, 7″ to
8″ × 3″. MM and SAMA

Mexicans' fascination with
marionettes goes back to colonial
times. After Mexico achieved
independence from Spain,
European-influenced toys were soon
seen all over Mexico. Cloth dolls
with porcelain heads and hands were
extremely coveted by young girls
and were immediately copied and
Mexicanized. In many towns,
itinerant puppeteers presented
puppet theaters for local fairs and
fiestas; miniature home puppet
theaters became popular.
Nineteenth- and early-twentieth-
century printers sold broadsides with
scripts for home puppet shows.
Marionettes were also used for
teaching Catholic doctrines in an
entertaining format.

In the nineteenth century, Puebla
was known for puppetry and for
puppet makers. In a country of toy
lovers intrigued with movement,
making puppets was a natural
outgrowth for the already skilled
doll makers. These twentieth-
century marionettes are a
continuation of a colonial tradition
with a new cast of international and
national characters. Left to right,
they depict a devil, Popeye, Charlie
Chaplin, Cantinflas, and a soldier.
Fine sewing thread is attached to the
ceramic hands, cloth pants, and hat.
The figures can be manipulated into
stylized, mimelike postures.

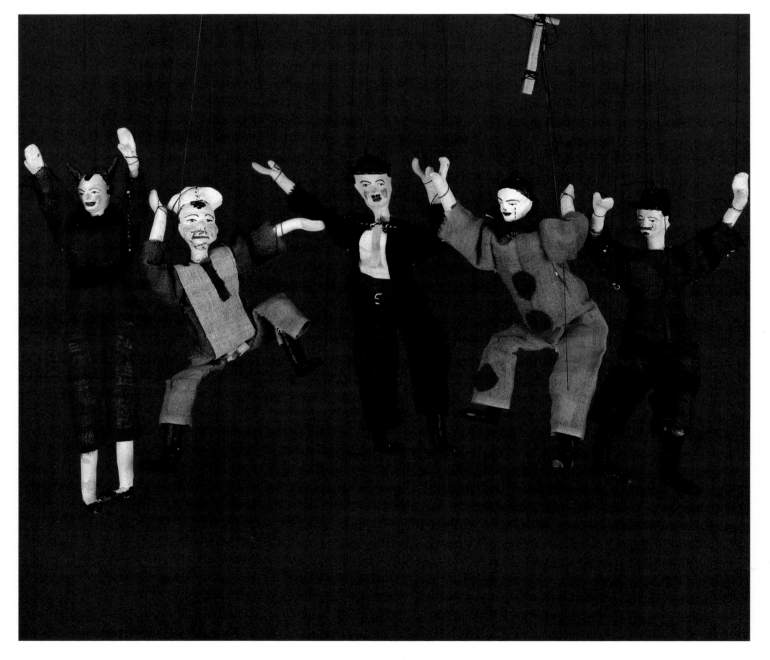

OBJECTS OF PLAY AND FANTASY

A third, large and important category in the Rockefeller collection is made up of objects whose primary function is to entertain and amuse. Consisting mainly of toys—some of which originated in pre-Columbian and colonial times—this folk art is made and used all over Mexico, in cities and villages, by old and young alike. Here, Mexican artists are at their best, being free to respond to the world around them both in traditional and in often delightfully spontaneous ways. A quickly whittled twig becomes a lurching iguana, a deftly pinched lump of clay changes a figure's facial expression, and a string transforms a bundle of cloth into a dancing rag doll. Charlene Cerny, director of the Museum of International Folk Art in Santa Fe, New Mexico, observes:

> *The Mexican craftsman seems to give full play to all creative impulses in the production of toys. Perhaps this is because toy making is not regarded with the same degree of seriousness, as, say, weaving or pottery making, or that a certain whimsy is not only encouraged but expected. Or perhaps it is because the prototypes of many toys still made today were inspired by affection for a particular child.* [16]

The objects of fantasy and play in the collection are often significant at levels far beyond that of entertainment and frequently reveal important elements in a society's social and psychological makeup. The widely used *lotería*, for example, is pure entertainment on one level, but when analyzed further, the devils, drunks, scorpions, dandies, and hearts found on Mexican lottery boards can also be seen as the embodiment of the players' hopes, fears, and loves. Popular all over Mexico, buffoon masks are integral parts of many dance dramas. Often used in scandalous skits, they mock and belittle that which is sacred and good in a community, thereby reinforcing positive mores through contrary behavior. Toys of all sorts encourage Mexican children to prepare themselves for adulthood through play. Little girls nurse rag dolls just as they have seen their mother do with younger siblings. Dramas of everyday life are played out with toys in a child's private world, not unlike that of the parents.

Mexican toys are also often rich in ethnographic information. Minia-

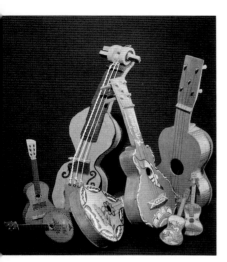

Plate 98
Manuel Jiménez and unknown
artists
Toy Musical Instruments
San Cristobal de las Casas, Chiapas;
Paracho, Michoacán; Arrazola,
Oaxaca; Mexico, D.F.
1930s to 1970s
Wood, wire, cord, and broomstraw,
5″ to 16″. MM and SAMA

Stringed instruments of all sorts are
strummed, plucked, and fiddled by
Mexican musicians. Even in remote
villages it is possible to find a
guitarist or a fiddler. Some of these
vibrantly painted toy instruments are
for the shelf, and others make tinny
and discordant sounds pleasing only
the player. The six-stringed guitar
and four-stringed banjo were
lovingly crafted in the 1930s. The
three-stringed instrument was
carved by Manuel Jiménez to
accompany a musician since
disappeared. The red and pink
scrap-wood guitars are from Chiapas
and are designed with elaborate
rosettes around the sound holes.
Names or designs take the place of
frets or position marks, but the toy-
makers are faithful with the bridge
and the heels. The simple guitar on
the right is from Paracho,
Michoacán, where Mexico's finest
guitars are crafted. The bodies of
the miniature guitars on the lower
right are decorated with elaborate
broomstraw landscapes and
geometric motifs.

ture market scenes, similar to those made by the Aguilar family in Ocotlán, Oaxaca, and ceramic bands from Michoacán and Guerrero are often models of real-life equivalents, thereby making them invaluable tools for a better understanding of Mexican culture.

The Rockefeller collection of toys is large and varied. Pull toys (also called trundle toys) from the 1920s and 1930s, earthenware animal bands from the 1970s, miniature bullfighting scenes, animal banks, puppets, and papier-mâché and rag dolls all are represented by excellent examples.

Of central importance is a set of articulated *conchero* pull toys made in the 1930s (pl. 92). These lively performers have faces of clay and torsos and limbs of wood, cardboard, feathers, fur, and tinfoil. The instruments they play are bottle caps. Although the provenance of this group is uncertain, similar examples were made and sold in San Juan de los Lagos, Jalisco, and Salamanca, Guanajuato, some decades ago.[17]

In the late 1960s Rockefeller obtained a similar set of figures (pl. 96) from the State of Oaxaca—they are plumed dancers, named after one of the many conquest dances for which the region is famous. Other important kinetic toys in the collection include a horse and rider made during the 1930s in North central Mexico, and a larger equestrian set from the same period (pls. 93, 94).

The collection also includes dozens of miniature sets of painted clay and wire figures. Miniatures of this kind are legendary in Mexico and can still be found in astonishing variety all over the country. The best of these were made by Angel Carranza of Tlaquepaque, Jalisco. Perhaps the most splendid example of his work is a tiny bullfight scene—charging *toros*, elegant matadors, daring banderilleros, crusty old picadores—all stationary but with form and color that give them movement and life (pls. 89, 90). Carranza's *charreada* also seems alive with prancing horses, ladies riding sidesaddle, and cowboys roping or wrestling ferocious bulls. Miniature scenes of daily life and death from the city of Puebla are also represented, providing humorous and charming tableaux of the city before the turn of the century.

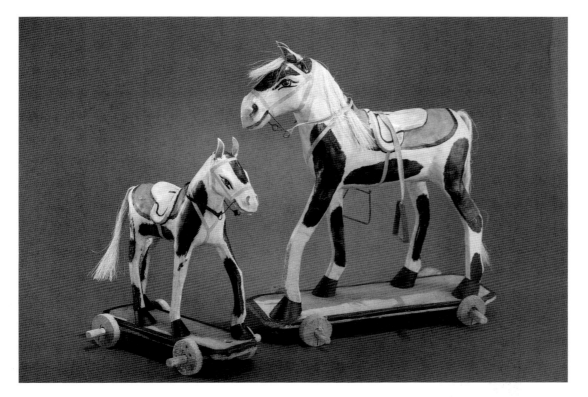

Plate 99
Toy Horses
Celaya, Guanajuato
1930s
Mold-made papier-mâché, wood, leather, metal, and sisal; left: 16 × 19 × 7½″; right: 27 × 24 × 12″. MM and SAMA

These delightful horses can be pulled or ridden. They are mold-made and mounted on wooden legs to give them extra strength. The clay or plaster molds are made in at least two pieces. Wet paper saturated with wheat paste is pressed into the molds in multiple layers and left to dry. When almost dry, the pieces are taken out and patched together with more of the paper and wheat-paste mixture. *Cartoneros* (papier-mâché artisans) like to recycle brown paper bags, heavy wrapping paper, old cement bags, and newspapers. The stronger the paper, the more durable the piece. The sisal tail, mane, and ears are put on before the pieces are joined. The piece acquires its real character when the painter bestows it with individual and spontaneous touches.

The earliest pre-Conquest ceramic toys were animals on wheels. For some reason, wheels were first used for toys, not for their more far-reaching applications.

The collection has a large selection of painted earthenware animal banks from Tlaquepaque and Santa Cruz de las Huertas, Jalisco. The elegant lions made by Julio Acero of Santa Cruz de las Huertas (pl. 82) represent the height of his art. Of similar elegance are the barrel-laden mules from Tlaquepaque made by an unknown artist during the 1930s.

Toy whistles and bells from various parts of Mexico are also to be found in the collection. From a historical point of view, the most important whistle is a bulbous figure acquired during the 1930s from the now-famous Tarascan village of Ocumicho, Michoacán. Representing a fantastic devil-animal, this piece (pl. 83) is one of the earliest surviving examples of figural ceramics from Ocumicho. A similarly shaped whistle can be seen in Montenegro's 1948 book on Mexican folk art and is invaluable for comparative purposes.[18]

Whimsical animal bands from Atzompa, Oaxaca, heavily varnished polychromed figures from Izúcar de Matamoros, Puebla, and hundreds of other objects that must go unmentioned, some old, some new, provide additional charm and serve as a reminder of the infinite variety of the folk art of Mexico.

Plate 100
Ceramic Doll
Ocotlán de Morelos, Oaxaca
1960s
Painted, single-fired earthenware,
3½ × 2″. SAMA

Charming ceramic dolls such as this
one are produced throughout
Oaxaca. These hollow, hand-built
Ocotlán dolls bear close resemblance
to their relatives on the Isthmus.
The pinched and flattened faces,
wide-eyed stares, dignified postures,
and floral decorations of the Ocotlán
dolls, the San Blas Atempa water
cooler bases, and Teodora Blanco's
dolls exhibit the transmission and
adaptation of regional styles. Many
of these figures are made for the
January 6 celebration, El Día de los
Reyes (Epiphany)—the day children
receive gifts and toys.

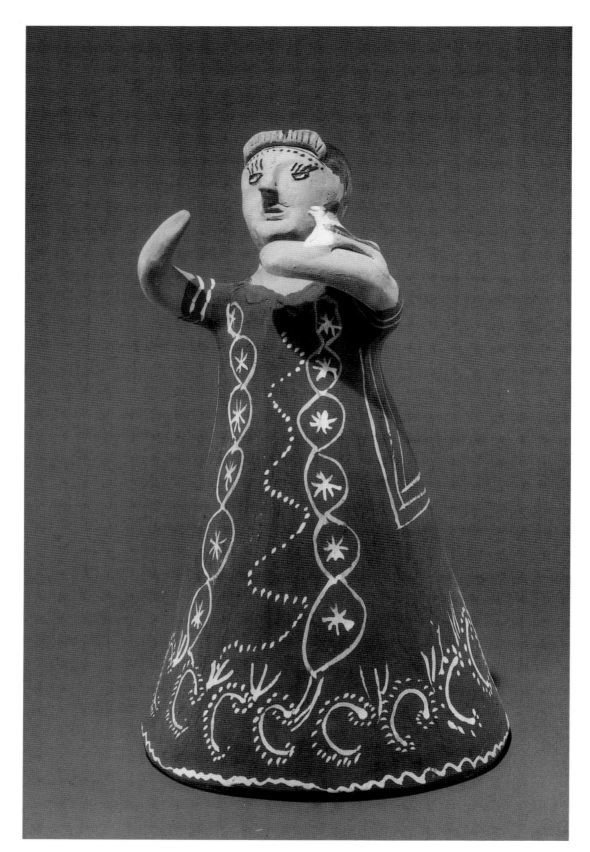

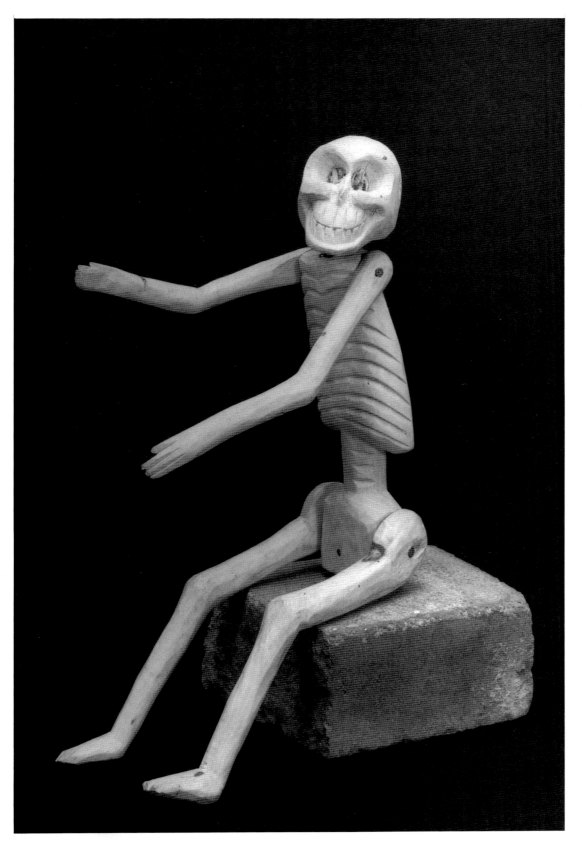

Plate 101
Day of the Dead Skeleton
San Martín Tilcajete, Oaxaca
1978
Carved wood, height, 15″. SAMA

This leering, long-limbed,
articulated skeleton is another in the
abundant production of Day of the
Dead objects. San Martín carvers
have recently added skeletons to
their repertoire. Left unpainted, the
piece's white wood accentuates the
skeleton's lack of life and color. This
expressive, wide-eyed skeleton can
be manipulated into an amusing
variety of relaxed, deathlike
postures. He looks identical to his
pre-Hispanic ancestors, who were
often attached to Mixtec tripod
bowls.

Plate 102
Wax Dolls
San Cristobal de las Casas, Chiapas
1930s
Beeswax, wool, cotton, string, sisal,
and animal hair, heights, 4″. MM
and SAMA

A set of regional wax dolls from
remote Chiapas represents a curious
and by-now-disappeared folk art.
Wax dolls have a long European
history; the most exquisite ones were
made in the nineteenth century. In
Mexico, mid-nineteenth-century
delicately modeled wax genre
figures, sculpted over a wooden
framework and dressed in regional
costumes, were fashionable for the
wealthy to collect. In the nineteenth
century, Puebla crèche figures were
fashioned of solid beeswax.
Although beekeepers are found even
in the remote mountains, beeswax is
now only occasionally used.

Viewing this assemblage of figures
is like visiting the market in San
Cristobal de las Casas, where a great
diversity of regional costumes can
be observed and many local dialects
heard. This area, so rich in
contemporary Mayan textiles, is one
of the few places in Mexico where
weaving still plays a central role in
the lives of women. This group of
dolls represents Indians from
Chamula, Zinacantan, Tenejapa, and
Santa Magdalena, with their variety
of layered garments, sisal bags,
headware, jewelry, and sashes. The
heavy, handwoven wool is necessary
in the Mayan highlands where
mountain weather is chilling. The
handwoven cotton *quechquémitls* and
embroidered blouses are faithful
replicas of women's clothing.

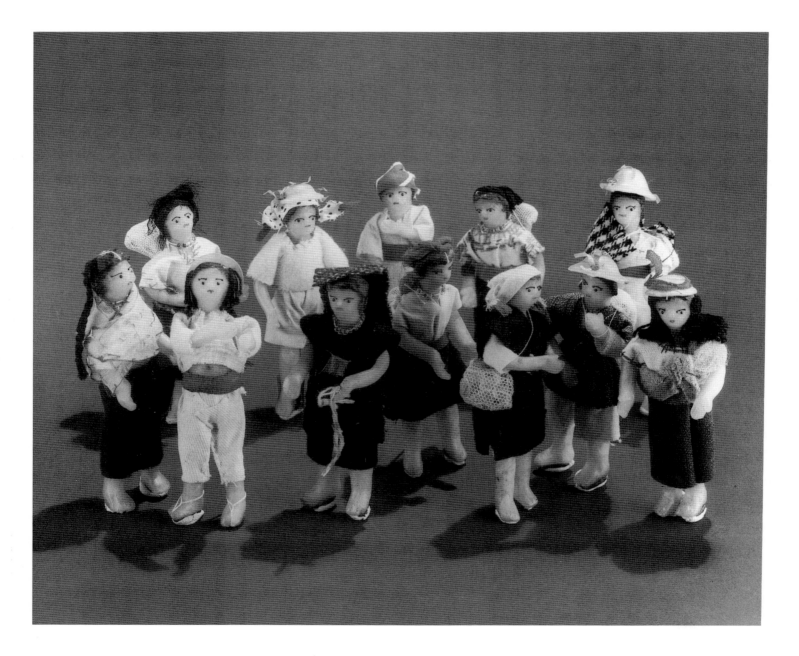

Plate 103
Palm Leaf Figures
Santa María Chicmecatitlán, Puebla
1930s
Woven and dyed palm leaves and
bamboo, maximum height, 6″.
MM and SAMA

This group of small people, in town
for a patriotic fiesta, is made of
woven palm leaves. The colors of
the Mexican flag are reflected in
their clothing.

The ingenuity of the Mexican
artisan is at its height when he or
she is working with nature's
offerings. Giant palm leaves,
bamboo, broomstraw, wheat straw,
maguey, grasses, rush, and willow
branches are all part of the Indians'
palette of materials. Palm is
particularly versatile; it is durable,
waterproof, and when green and wet
lends itself to almost any kind of
manipulation—it can be woven,
twisted, braided, folded, joined, and
dyed. This collection of figures
incorporates each of these
techniques. Since the palm is
worked when damp, it is easy to
shape the clothing, the curve of the
arms, and the stylish rake of the
sombreros. Hundreds of thin strands
can be made from one enormous
palm leaf. *Petates,* rain covers,
walls, sombreros, rattles, offerings,
miniatures, and toys such as these
are all created from the magnificent
palm.

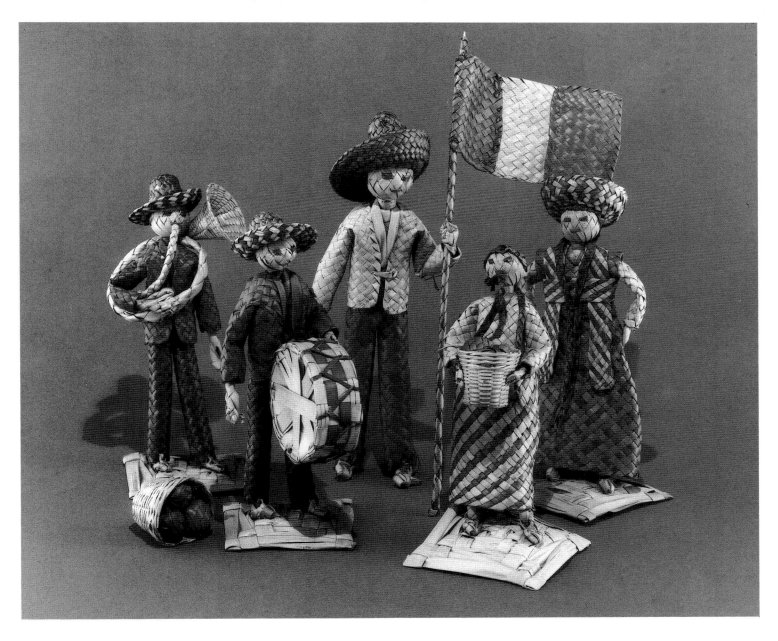

DECORATIVE OBJECTS

The decorative portion of the Rockefeller collection is small and comprises objects that do not fit easily into any of the preceding categories. Created as objects of beauty, their main function is to adorn the home or some other place. In contrast to the objects in other categories, their form is not related to their function, and in this respect they resemble much of fine art except that these objects are grounded in and bound by the traditions of the artisans' culture. Practically all of the decorative objects in the Rockefeller collection, it should be noted, were made to be sold, mainly to customers from outside the community in which they were made.

Among the most impressive pieces are several large jars and platters from Tonalá, Jalisco. A tall, exquisitely painted and burnished jar (pl. 105) is among the most outstanding examples of Tonalá ceramics from the 1930s to have survived. Its intensively decorated surface reflects the Art Nouveau style favored by potters of Tonalá during the 1920s and 1930s, shortly after the village had become an active exporter of decorative pottery. There are many other fine examples from the same period and place. Stereotypical and romantic images of rural Mexico were often conveyed in this style of pottery; some of the images, however, are less than complimentary. Peasants covered by large sombreros, sitting lazily beneath large cacti, formed a favorite theme.

Another splendid decorative piece is a crane gourd. Too fragile to be a toy, this piece (pl. 125) is among the most beautiful objects in the collection. Edward Weston, who, like Rockefeller, was impressed by these elegantly painted and lacquered gourds from Olinalá, Guerrero, wrote enthusiastically about them in his *Daybooks*:

> *Again to write down admiration for the Indian in his sense of balance, knowledge of anatomy, —for in painting and amplifying upon the gourd, actually recreate. The perfect placing of the legs upon the round gourd's body, —slightly straighter or more sharply angled, and the fine continuity of line would not have been achieved. As it stands, I cannot imagine a great sculptor anywhere creating more sensitively.* [19]

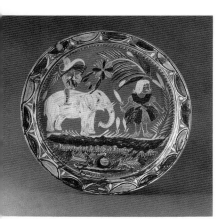

Plate 104
Plate
Metepec, State of Mexico
Late 1930s
Painted and glazed earthenware,
diameter, 17½". SAMA

Charros did not court their señoritas atop white elephants in Metepec. The fact that no elephants exist in Mexico outside of zoos did not deter this artisan from painting a very amusing, or perhaps satiric, takeoff on a traditional theme. The elephant is even smaller than the young *charra* to whom the *charro* is tipping his sombrero. Although its pictorial details are unusual, this plate is a traditional form from a renowned pottery village that produces both *loza corriente* (utilitarian pottery) and *barro de cocina* (cooking ware), along with the famed polychromed trees of life, toys, and ceremonial figures. Metepec has been producing pottery since the sixteenth century, and the old Metepec market displayed a staggering array of ceramics. The color of fine-particled, rich red clay that is used can be seen through the glaze. The message on this souvenir plate reads "Un Recuerdo de la Villa de Metepec Charritos," meaning, "A Remembrance of Metepec's Little Charros."

Plate 105
Burnished Jar
Tonalá, Jalisco
1930s
Single-fired, painted earthenware,
20 × 17″. SAMA

This large, burnished pot collected in Tonalá in the 1930s is covered with wonderfully stylized and intricately painted flowers and leaves. The sophisticated colors used on this pot are not typical of those used by Tonalá painters today. The raised bands circling the piece pick up the dominant colors for an unusual decorative effect.

The surface of this pot is almost completely covered with decorative brushwork. It is said that many Tonaltecans have a fear of leaving any part of a piece undesigned. Although not traditional, this piece is an example of the exquisite brushwork that had developed in Tonalá by the 1930s.

Tonalá pottery is usually a collaborative family effort, from clay gathering to final burnishing. A piece may be signed by the male head of the family, concealing the participation of women and children. Families in Tonalá have distinct styles, and many collectors covet pieces by the Galván and Jimón families, both of which are represented in the Rockefeller collection. Many of the pieces are made in molds that are passed down through the generations to become hallmarks of a particular family. The burnishing tools used to finish the unglazed pieces are family treasures and are surrounded by some superstition since artisans often feel that the technical skill required to produce a high or low luster not only requires years of practice but also depends on particular burnishing stones.

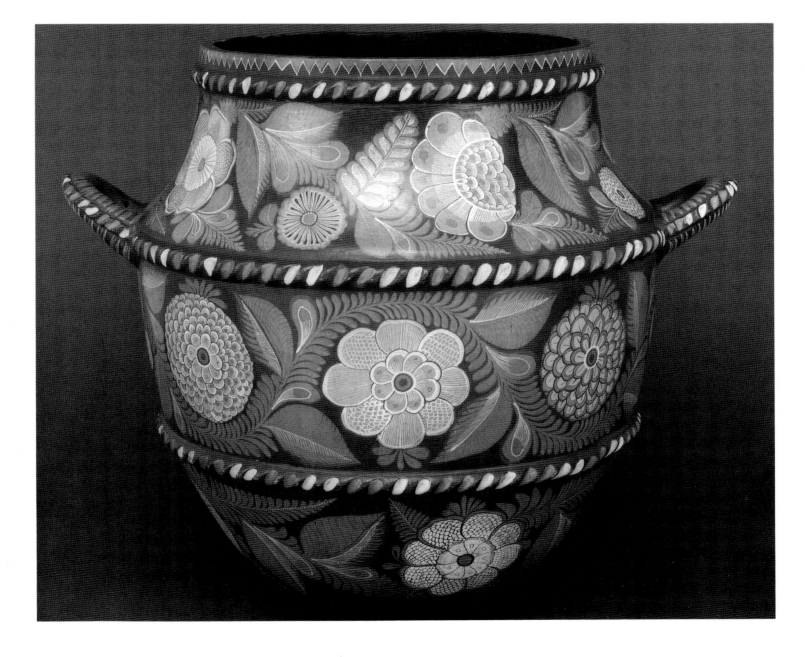

Plate 106
Lion and Deer Carving
Temalacasingo, Guerrero
1976
Carved wood, 9½ × 10 × 3¾".
SAMA

An Indian couple walked many hours in the rugged Guerrero mountains to carry these two carvings to the Olinalá market. This sculpture is small in size but monumental in power and concept. Temalacasingo has traditionally supplied Olinalá with a variety of carvings—fruit, deer, lions, and toys. In recent years, the artisans have been decorating their pieces with oil-based paints, forgoing the complicated process involved in lacquering. Often the piece's finish detracts from the underlying sculptural forms, which are graceful and carved with an economy of knife, machete, and chisel work.

No lions of this sort live in Mexico, but deer inhabit the surrounding mountains. Perhaps this is a reinterpretation of the pre-Hispanic "jaguar eating man" theme, with the head already inside the mouth and the legs extended.

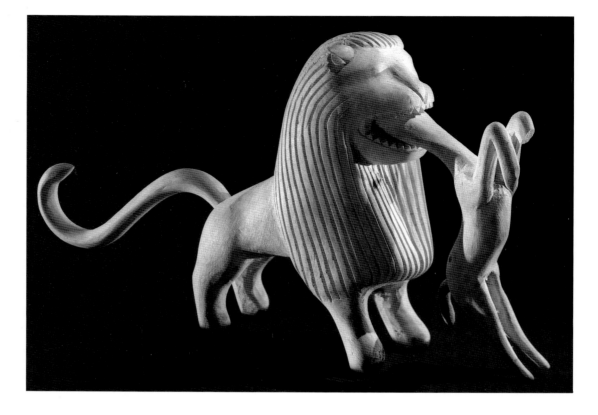

The large, fantastic earthenware sculptures by Doña Teodora Blanco are also decorative (pls. 108, 115). The basic forms of the figures and others like them were inspired by water-cooler supports from the Isthmus of Tehuantepec but did not retain their utilitarian function. Instead, they became purely decorative objects. Rooted in the legends of Atzompa, Oaxaca, these exotic sculptures depict Zapotec women going to and from market, animals holding other animals and sometimes suckling them, street vendors, and a host of other intriguing, often bizarre scenes. Rockefeller purchased dozens of these pieces from Doña Teodora during his last trip to Mexico, and they were among his favorite objects in the collection. They range in size from small pieces of just under six inches to life-size sculptures more than five feet tall.

Rockefeller collected three *alebriges* by Pedro Linares in the late 1960s, when the wild and fantastic imagery of Linares' flying creatures (pl. 129) was just being developed. "Alebrige" is a word created by Linares himself to represent these images. They may have been inspired by those depicted in a

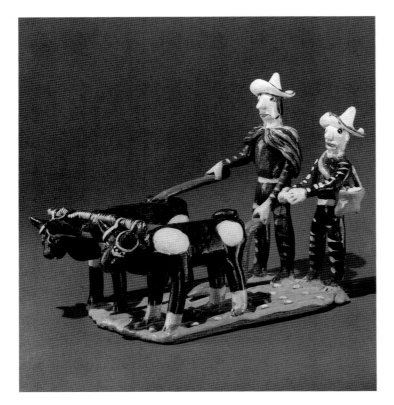

Plate 107
Farmers with Oxen
Ocumicho, Michoacán
1978
Single-fired, painted, and varnished
earthenware, 12 × 8″. MM

Ocumicho's inimitable repertoire of
figural ceramics includes bizarre
devils, Last Supper watermelon
feasts, wild and macabre Day of the
Dead sculptures, and tableaux of
campesino life. Ocumicho work is
stylistically faddish and easily
influenced by outside demands.
These campesinos are planting their
cornfield in the primitive and labor-
intensive method common to peasant
societies. While the father guides
the wooden plow, his son seeds the
field with oversize kernels of corn.
The folk artist who created this
piece faithfully portrayed an
important event of the agricultural
cycle. While Ocumicho pieces are
crude and primitive, it is this very
naïveté and lack of inhibition that
make these painted and varnished
pieces coveted by collectors.

Plate 108
Teodora Blanco
Ceramic Doll
Santa María Atzompa, Oaxaca
1978
Single-fired earthenware,
36 × 14 × 14″. SAMA

This large ceramic doll has curious
details rooted in Teodora Blanco's
fascination with witchcraft. This
piece illustrates her belief in
nahuales, an ancient concept that
each person has a particular animal
counterpart that from birth protects
and befriends that person. In this
piece, the projecting animal heads
are the protective *nahuales*, and if
they die, the baby animals are there
to continue their work. Teodora's art
is full of this type of imagery. Her
preoccupation with nurturing and
the intermingling of animal and
human spirits were dominant themes
in her later pieces—pieces that
displayed a baroque flair for
decoration.

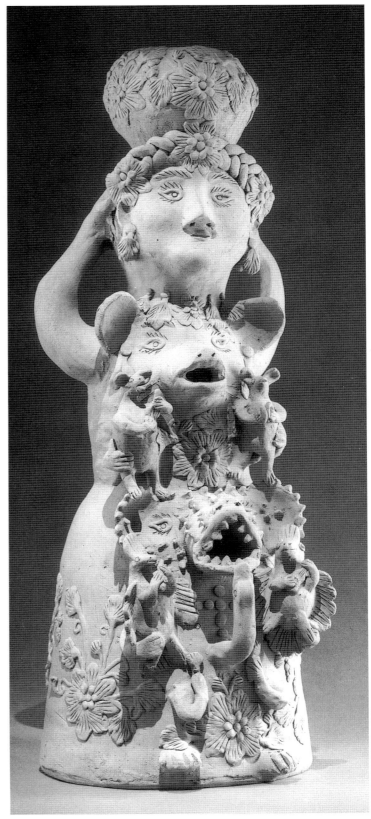

woodcut by José Guadalupe Posada, but their origin is still not clearly understood.

There are a number of important decorative paintings in the collection. Two still-life paintings (pls. 118, 119) are significant primarily because they are excellent examples of popular still-life representations of the nineteenth century. They are among only a small handful of similar paintings to have survived.

The collection has three canvas oil paintings depicting scenes associated with *charro* activities. Painted during the 1930s, these canvases (pls. 109, 110) reveal the strong influence exercised by Ernesto Icaza, the great *charro* painter of a slightly earlier period.

Among the most delicate and rare decorative paintings in the collection are two small lacquered and painted octagonal dishes from the Lake Pátzcuaro region of Michoacán. Made during the nineteenth century, these dishes are unrivaled in quality and charm (pl. 116). Another unusual decorative object of considerable importance is a half-lacquered and half-painted plaque (pl. 117). This Olinalá painting depicts scenes typical of provincial life in Mexico City. The composition is very reminiscent of domestic scenes painted on Olinalá chests and documented by Jorge Enciso and others.[20]

Plate 109
Charro Painting
North central Mexico
20th century
Oil on canvas, 34 × 24½″. SAMA

Nineteenth-century provincial life was well documented by anonymous painters. *Ranchero charros*, a new class of wealthy Mexican landholders, emulated the Spanish penchant for fine horses and riding. With money to spend, they indulged themselves in the splendor of exquisitely decorated costumes, bridles, and saddles. These mestizo ranchers were the original *charros*.

This very energetic painting depicts the branding and roping skills of Mexico's early *charros*. In the midst of all the activity, a campesino dressed in white is running toward a *charro*, imploring him to leave his cows alone. The two snow-covered peaks in the background are the majestic Popocatépetl and the sleeping beauty Ixtaccíhuatl.

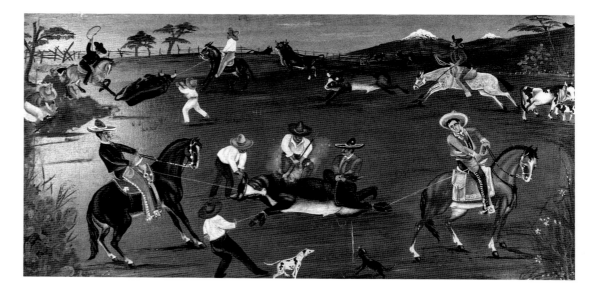

The collection also contains four exceptionally fine broomstraw mosaics, executed by the late Felipe Olay of Mexico City, who carried the form further than any other artist of his time. The portrait of a Huichol Indian (pl. 120) clearly demonstrates the excellent quality of Olay's work and shows how far the technique could be taken.

Other significant decorative objects in the collection include a dozen nineteenth-century samplers from central Mexico, candelabra and picture frames made of tin, nineteenth-century coconut shells carved by prisoners from Veracruz, and other intriguing objects.

The process of putting together this vast and varied collection gave Nelson Rockefeller immense pleasure. It is a vital reminder of his eclectic taste and of his enthusiasm for art independent of its market value. Now, through this collection, the viewer may share in the joy of discovering Mexican folk art at its exuberant best.

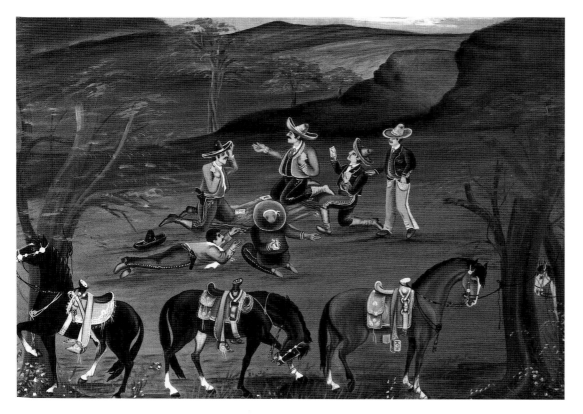

Plate 110
Charro Painting
North central Mexico
20th century
Oil on canvas, 34 × 24½". SAMA

This painting reveals everything about *charros'* taste in horses and costumes, from heavy felt sombreros to silver inlaid pommels and carved and ornamented saddles. These six *charros* are enjoying a game of cards during a ride in the verdant foothills. No two *charros* wear the same outfit, and the elegant horses are also each outfitted differently. Popular painters were not academy trained but were technically inventive. A clue to the location of this landscape is the strong wind that is portrayed, not unlike the violent winds described by early visitors to the mining districts of north central Mexico.

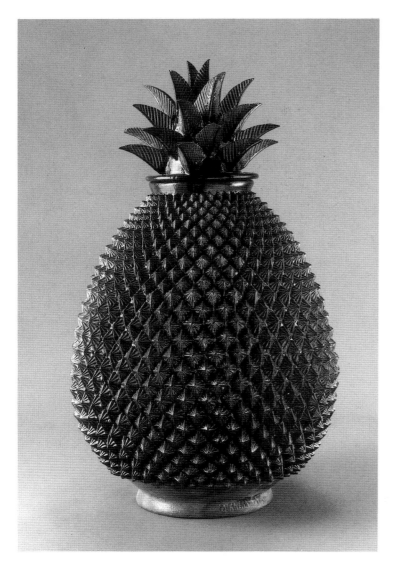

Plate 111
Water Jar
Patamban, Michoacán
1960s
Glazed earthenware, 32½ × 19½″.
SAMA

This heroic pineapple jar is a type of deluxe water container called a *piña*. These jars are mold-made, with daubs of clay applied by hand. These numerous protrusions vary from crude lumps to carefully appliquéd pieces that can be hand-formed but are generally mold-made. In the past fifteen years, the *piñas* have become increasingly complex, with hundreds of modeled leaves covering larger and larger jars. The spiked crown of the pineapple is the lid of the jar.

The origin of the use of these pineapple motifs is not known, although in western Mexico in pre-Conquest time, covered jars with similar decoration were produced.

Piñas can store water or, at times, *tepache*, one of Mexico's regional drinks made from pineapple, pulque, water, and cloves.

Plate 112
Pulque Pitcher
Barrio de la Luz, Puebla
1930s
Mold-made, drip-glazed earthenware, 19 × 10¾″. SAMA

Barrio de la Luz, an area in the city of Puebla where many potteries were established in the eighteenth century, produces highly glazed utilitarian ware. The deep red earthenware is streaked with spatters, splotches, and drips of a runny black glaze in a glazing style known as *chorreado*. This large, amusing piece with double spouts is used for serving pulque. Pulque was the national drink of Mexico until the introduction of beer in the late nineteenth century. Written on the front of this pitcher are the words, "María de la Gloria, de Puebla. A todos les boi a serbir a esta umilde reunion. Agosto 22 año 1936 un recuerdo de A. Alonso." María de la Gloria, of Puebla, is the young woman depicted on the pitcher; the rest of the artist's message translates as follows, "I will serve everyone at this humble reunion. August 22, 1936. A memento from A. Alonso."

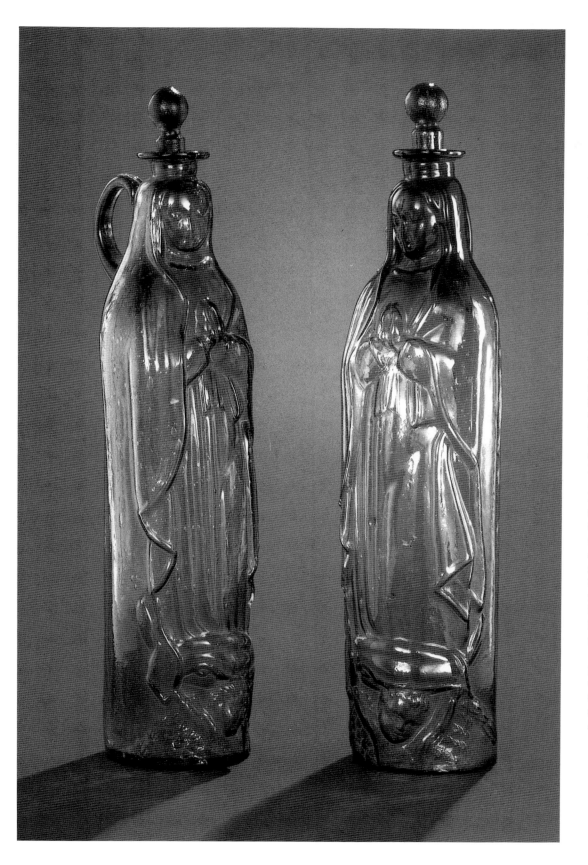

Plate 113
Bottles
Mexico, D.F.
1930s
Hand-blown glass, heights, 13½".
MM and SAMA

Spaniards brought the craft of glassblowing to Mexico, where it was quickly adopted. The first glassblowers settled in Puebla and from there moved on to set up factories in Mexico, D.F., Guadalajara, and Texcoco. Pressed glass is made primarily in Puebla.

The variety of glassware in Mexico extends beyond the utilitarian to highly decorative miniatures and toys. The beauty of some Mexican glassware derives from the unusual quality of the glass, often characterized by random patterns of air bubbles that create a sparkle and luster, making each piece unique. Often the coloration is gradated, and the uneven saturation gives the glass a rich, handmade appearance. This commemorative Guadalupe bottle might have been used for celebratory drinks or carried away from a great fiesta in Mexico City as a souvenir.

The Virgin of Guadalupe, Mexico's patroness and most beloved and popular saint, is lovingly crafted and molded in every imaginable material. The legend of the miraculous apparition of the dark-skinned Indian Virgin followed the Spanish denial of cult worship after the Conquest. Her shrine is the holiest in Mexico, and her fiesta on December 12 is one of the Catholics' most holy days.

These bottles were undoubtedly production pieces. Similar bottles were exhibited in the famous 1921 exhibition of folk art in Mexico City and also at the Museum of Modern Art in 1940.

Plate 114
Adam and Eve
San Pedro Tlaquepaque, Jalisco
1930s
Painted and varnished earthenware,
7 × 4 × 2″. SAMA

The Spaniards brought Catholicism
to Mexico along with all the
participants of Judeo-Christian
mythology. Adam and Eve are
popular figures with ceramic artists,
who place them at the bases of trees
of life and in elaborate Nativity
crèches. This depiction of Adam and
Eve, missing their apple tree, was
made for a crèche. The mold-made
figures are identical, except for
Adam's beard. Mexican Nativities
include a staggering cast of biblical
characters in a rural Mexican
setting and are not complete without
these visitors from the Garden of
Eden.

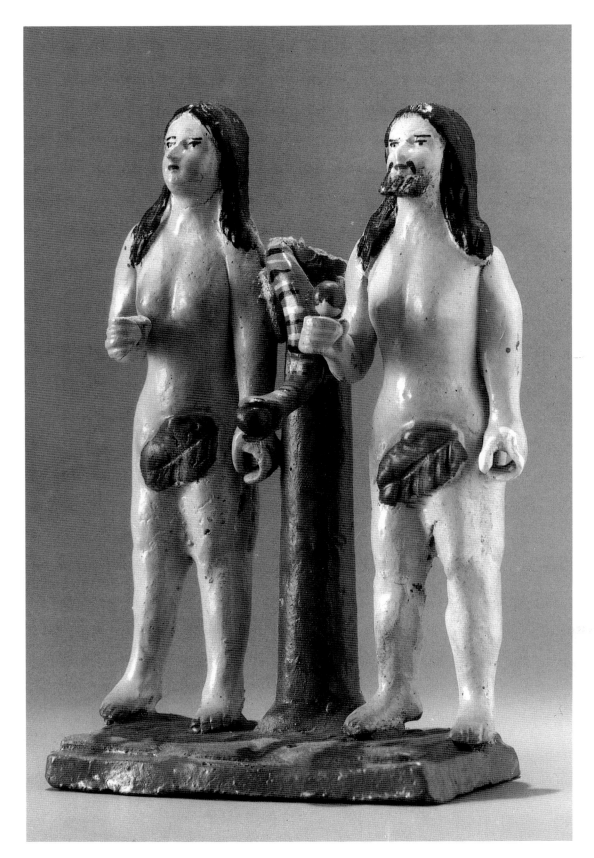

Plate 115
Teodora Blanco
Ceramic Figures
Santa María Atzompa, Oaxaca
1978
Single-fired earthenware, average
height, 14″. MM and SAMA

Teodora Blanco, one of the most
creative and vital folk artists in
Mexico, died in 1981, leaving
behind a history of unique invention
that set her apart from other potters
in Santa María Atzompa. Her
parents were successful farmers.

Although they were also traditional
potters, it was not necessary to push
Teodora into commercial pottery. As
a child she visited archaeological
museums in Oaxaca and was
inspired by animal and figural
ceramics. Her innovations began as
a teenager, when she formed animal
musicians. She then started attaching
wings and tails to pitchers, whose
spouts became animal heads. If she
was working on a traditional shape,
she would always add animal
appendages. In her late twenties she
began making her legendary figures

of women, such as those seen in this
photograph. Her figures constantly
evolved and changed as she
experimented with various
combinations of women, animals,
and mythical creatures. Beasts poked
out of abdomens, breasts became
animal heads, and animals and
babies tugged at shoulders and
skirts. Teodora's impulse for surface
adornment was intense, and by the
late 1970s her figures were covered
with appliquéd coils, animals
emerging from the bodies, and arms
typically engaged in holding or

carrying children, animals, or
market baskets. In spite of all this
sculptural abandon, her women are
always dignified and elegant. For
Teodora, the only reason to live was
to make pottery.

Rockefeller was truly captivated
by Teodora's artistic energy, humor,
and dedication to her personal
vision. He started collecting her
work in the late 1960s. During his
final visit to her house in 1978, he
bought every ceramic doll she had.

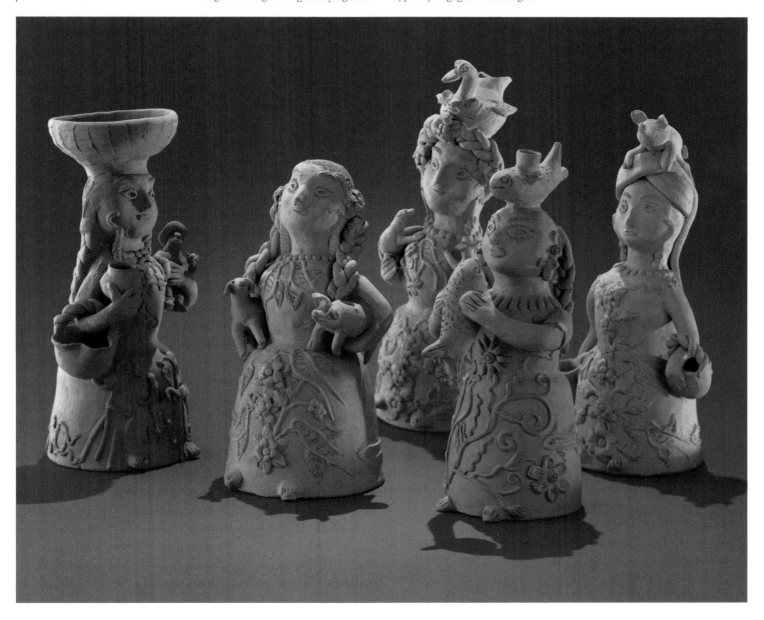

Plate 116
Lacquered Dish
Pátzcuaro, Michoacán
19th century
Lacquered wood and gold leaf,
diameter, 7½". SAMA

Michoacán has a great and ancient
tradition of lacquerware dating back
to the sixteenth century. This
exquisite piece, acquired in the
1930s, was made in the middle to
late nineteenth century. The portrait
of the young woman is delicate and
stylized. The rose, held in an almost
Hindu pose, seems to symbolize the
blush and ripeness of her youth. The
rosy hue of the flower is reflected on
her face. The feathery brushstrokes
in the surrounding motif
complement her femininity. The
colors are all natural pigments
ground by hand on a metate
according to guild traditions.
Formulas for making pigments and
lacquer are often well-guarded
family secrets. This is one of the
rarest pieces in the Rockefeller
collection, as very few of these
fragile dishes have survived.

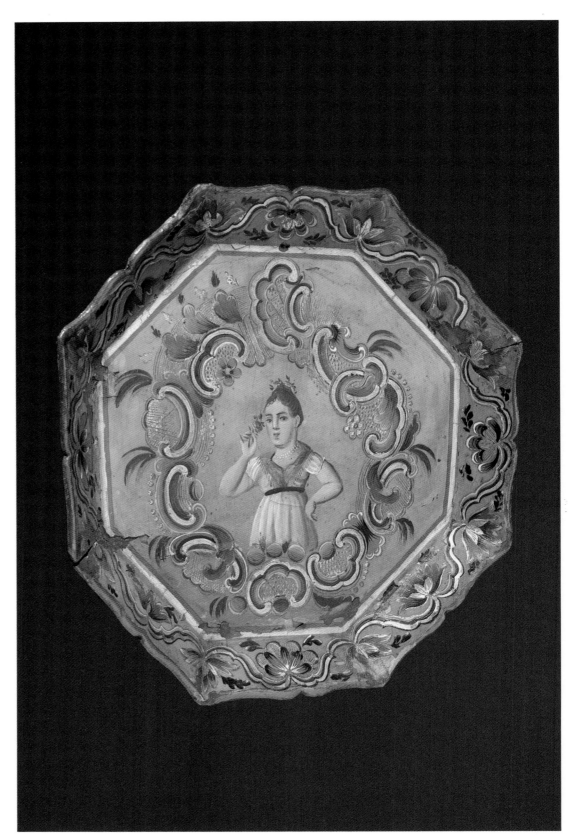

Plate 117
Lacquered Plaque
Olinalá, Guerrero
Early 20th century
Lacquered and painted wood,
9½ × 6½". SAMA

This unusual plaque is a curious mix of portraiture and ironic social commentary on nineteenth-century life. The *funcionario* (bureaucrat)

with quilled pens and a small ink jar, ready to sign away someone's land, is loyally attended by two barefoot women in European dress and holding parrots. This scene was not indigenous to Olinalá but was probably copied from a book or a postcard. The plaque is executed in the *rayado* (incised) technique. After the first coats of lacquer and pigment have been applied and polished,

another coat is applied. While this coat is still damp, the artist incises the design with a thorn. The areas of the undercoat to be exposed are revealed by the delicate removal of the sections of the outer layer within the incised lines. Each time-consuming step is performed by a different specialist. In this piece, the three figures were painted on after the lacquerwork was completed.

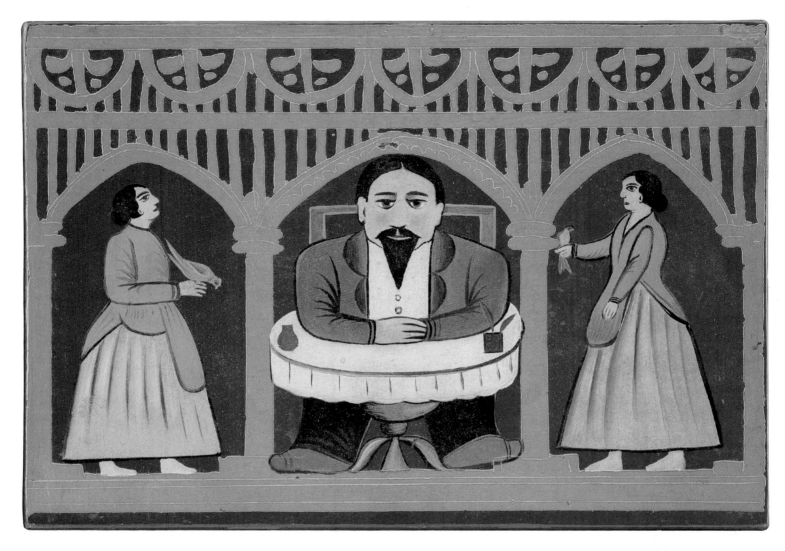

Plate 118
Still Life
State of Puebla
Mid-19th century
Oil on canvas, 22 × 30". SAMA

Nineteenth-century popular
painting—portraits, still lifes, and
landscapes—reveals much about day-
to-day life in colonial Mexico.

This charming painting of a fiesta
table depicts an assortment of the
wondrous sweet breads available
from Mexican *panaderías* (bakeries),
where breads and rolls of every
shape and size are part of daily life.
This mound of goodies might
include "cat's ears," "butterflies,"
"partridge eyes," "neckties," or any
other of the three hundred varieties
of breads available in Mexico.
Artfully arranged on a Talavera
platter, the breads are adorned with
papel picado (punched foil and tissue
paper) decorative flags that are made
in San Salvador Huixcolotla,
Puebla. The elegant decanters and
heavy, silver filigreed jar holder are
clues to the wealth of the owners.

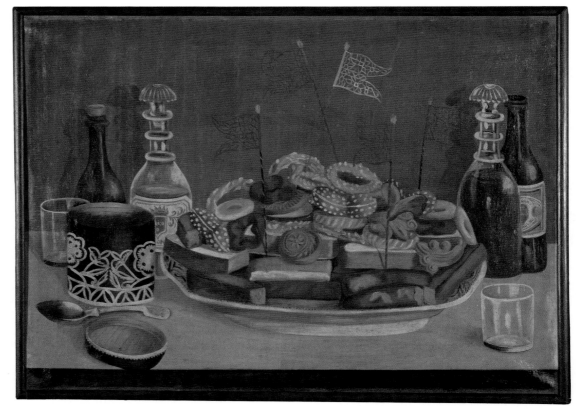

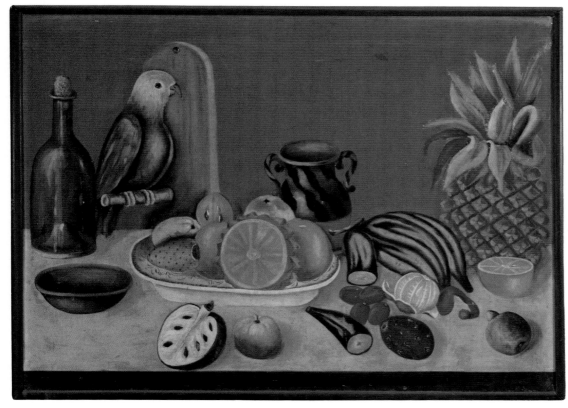

Plate 119
Still Life
State of Puebla
Mid-19th century
Oil on canvas, 22 × 30". SAMA

This still life depicts a parrot and a
Talavera platter overflowing with
Mexican fruits—*zapote blanco*, *piña*
(pineapple), *tuna* (fruit of the
prickly pear cactus), mangoes,
limes, and apples, bananas, and
grapefruits. Parrots were often pets
of upper-class families, and the
small pitcher from Barrio de la Luz
is a clue to a Puebla locale.

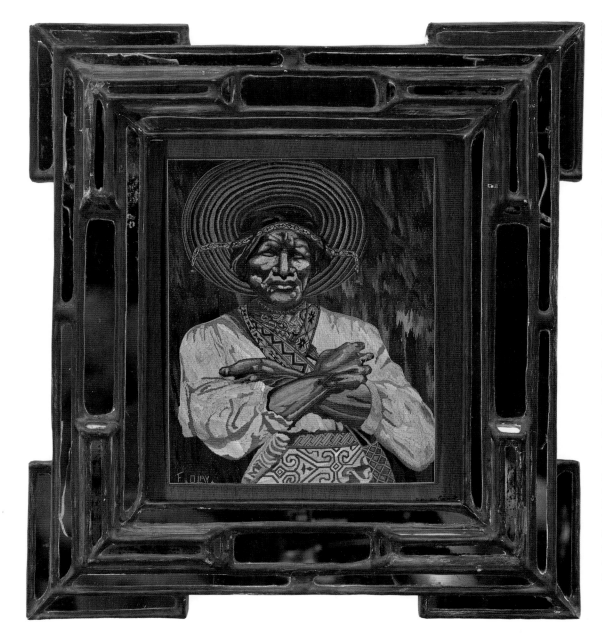

Plate 120
Felipe Olay
Portrait
Mexico, D.F.
1930s
Broomstraw, wax, and aniline dyes;
gold-leaf frame; 10 × 8″. SAMA

Felipe Olay's faithful portrait of a
Huichol Indian from the Sierra de
Nayarit is a most unusual example of
the disappearing art of *popote*.
Popoteros were not uncommon in the
late 1800s, but today only a few
craftsmen are working in Mexico
City. Olay was considered Mexico's
finest practitioner of this art.

These intricate mosaics of hollow
broomstraw require many tiny pieces
to be precisely inlaid on a thin layer
of wax that overlays a drawing. The
artist tints the *popote* with vegetable
or aniline dyes mixed with boiling
water. Once dry, it is cut into
thousands of small pieces according
to the design. Seen at a distance, this
portrait appears to be a painting.
Up close, the intricate mosaic of
broomstraw leaves you in awe of the
imagination and skill that pieced it
together.

The Huichol Indian portrayed in
this piece is accurate in every
regional nuance. The detail in his
hat makes it appear to be
handwoven. The sinews of his arms
and the lines in his face impart the
nobility, fortitude, and strength
necessary to survive in the remote
mountains.

Plate 121
Jar
Tonalá, Jalisco
1930s
Single-fired, painted, and burnished
earthenware, 31×21″. SAMA

Tonaltecan pottery dating back at
least to the seventeenth century is
famous for its exquisite brush
painting and for its aromatic clay.
Loza del Olor (aromatic ceramic
ware) is famous throughout Mexico
for the flavor it imparts to the water
stored within. In the early twentieth
century, some Tonalá pottery was
elaborately painted with very fine
and feathery brushstrokes almost
Chinese or Persian in the attention
to detail and style. Tonaltecan
pottery is burnished before it is
fired. This piece epitomizes the
fabulous artistic experimentation and
a subtle departure from traditional
color and design. The allover floral
motifs are painted with natural
pigments mined in the Tonalá
vicinity.

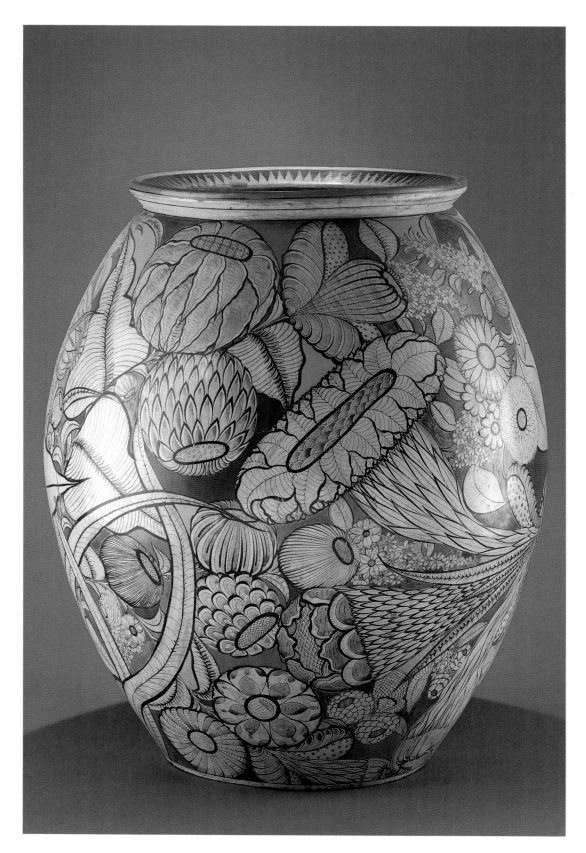

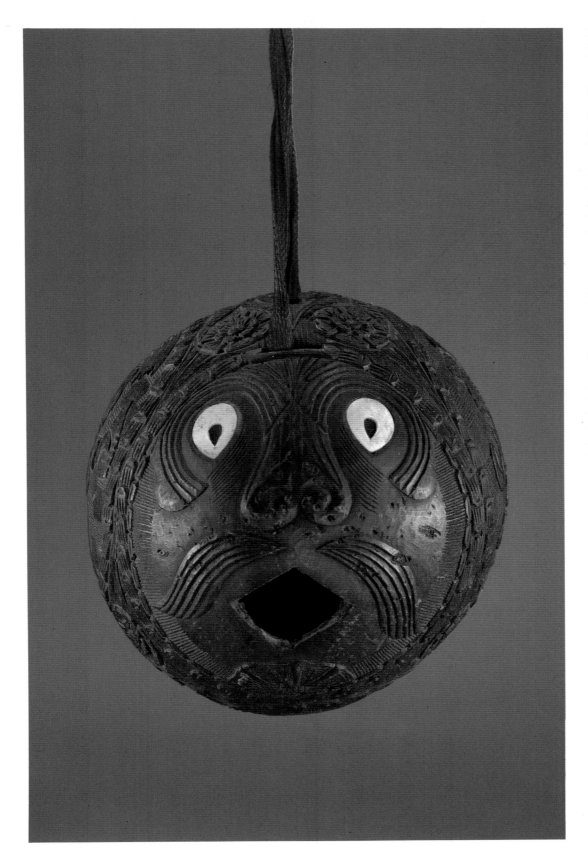

Plate 122
Carved Coconut Bank
Veracruz, Veracruz
Late 19th century
Carved coconut, 6 × 5″. SAMA

Coconuts, mamey pits, and walnut
shells have all intrigued carvers.
This coconut shell representing a
mustached feline has inlaid mother-
of-pearl eyes. The head is framed
with a motif of pre-Hispanic hands,
and the remaining coconut is carved
with a man holding a mug or bottle
on one side and on the other a
patriotic eagle and serpent. These
pieces were made in the San Juan de
Ulúa jail in Veracruz or regional
jails in Tabasco. Mexican inmates
often spend hours each day engaged
in a craft that can be sold by their
relatives to supplement the family
income or by the prisoner to
supplement his food allowance. It is
not unusual for the prisoner to
discover a new talent while doing
time. Prisoners often used the items
they made as ex-votos: the carver
would depict his crime on one side
of the piece and, on the other side,
the saint to whom he was asking
forgiveness.

Plate 123
Josefina Aguilar
Ceramic Figures
Ocotlán de Morelos, Oaxaca
1970s
Hand-formed, single-fired painted
earthenware, average height, 22″.
SAMA

These large ceramic figures by
Josefina Aguilar are from the set
that had been displayed on the
Aguilar picket fence and which
Rockefeller bought in its entirety
during his 1978 trip to Oaxaca.
They are part of a cast of regional
dolls that she enjoyed making and
that lent themselves to various
techniques in hand-forming and
modeling. The woman on the left is
probably from the Mixteca Alta of
Oaxaca, evidenced by the wrapping
and pleating of her tube skirt worn
with an embroidered belt. She is
wearing a large necklace and
earrings representative of the
filigreed gold jewelry popular in
Oaxaca and often included in a
Zapotec woman's dowry in
Tehuantepec. A rosary is draped in
her hand and a rebozo over her
shoulder. She combines many of
Oaxaca's regional details. The man,
wearing traditional cotton pants and
huaraches, is proudly holding his
cobija (blanket). He might be from
San Sebastián Peñoles, Oaxaca,
where the blanket borders typically
are colored orange, red, and dark
brown. Aguilar molded for him a
belt and a scarf that is tied around
his neck. She painted his face a dark
color. Is he from the coast of
Oaxaca or nearby? These figures
were ceramic samplers for Aguilar's
experimentation with the wealth of
regional differences she observed in
her market town. Most important,
she instilled these figures with great
dignity and character.

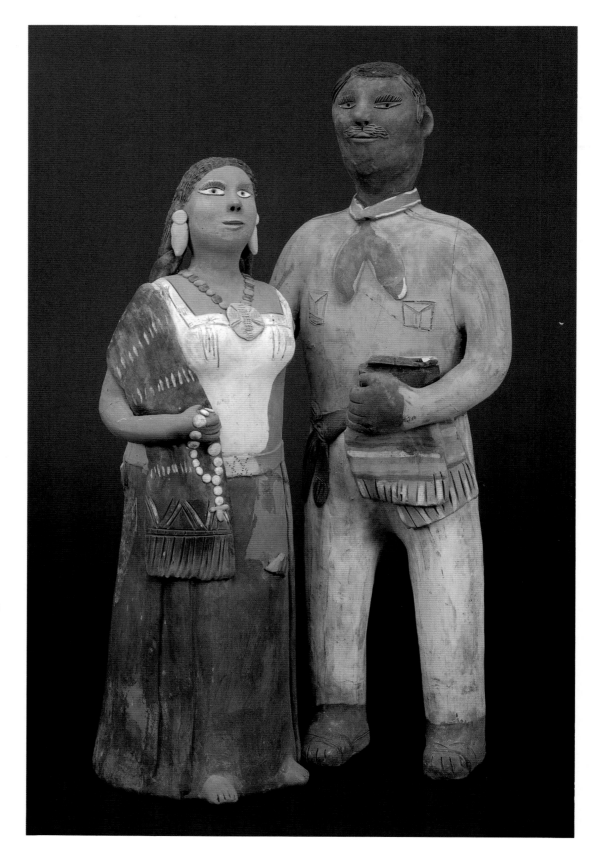

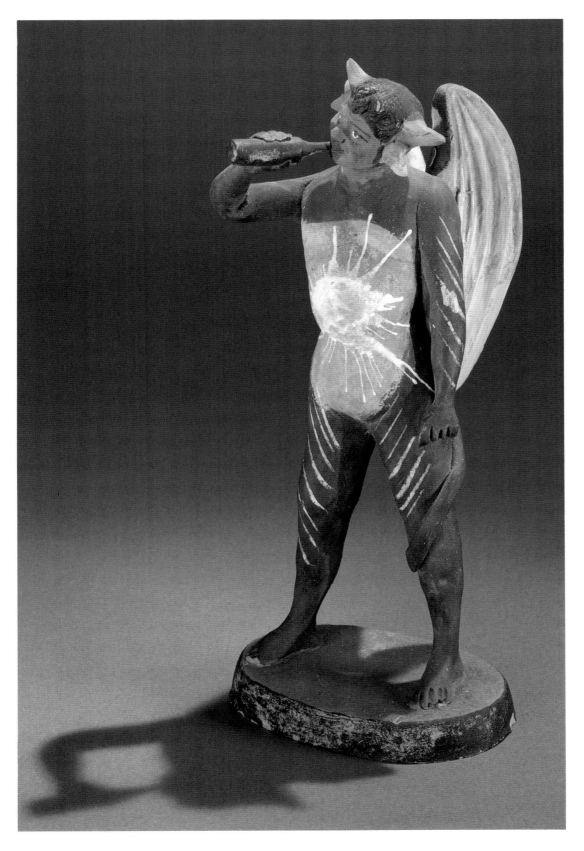

Plate 124
Devil
San Pedro Tlaquepaque, Jalisco
1930s
Painted earthenware, 11 × 3″.
SAMA

Mold-made devils from
Tlaquepaque are fashioned for
crèches and represent the evils of
temptation. They are painted in
lurid colors and often have
prominent ribs, clenched fists, and a
tail wrapping around the leg and
ending beneath the knee. Set off to
one side, lurking in the moss-
covered crèche, the devils'
outrageous and wonderful color
combinations vibrate visually in
contrast to the more serious subject
of the Nativity. This devil with his
spontaneous splotch of paint has the
additional vice of drink.

Plate 125
Lacquered Crane
Olinalá, Guerrero
Collected in the 1930s
Lacquered and painted gourd;
wooden legs and base; $22 \times 15 \times 6''$.
SAMA

This perfectly balanced, graceful
crane was one of Nelson
Rockefeller's favorite pieces. Made
of a lacquered gourd, its spindly,
reed-thin legs are carved of wood.
With all of its fragility this crane
has survived a long migration and a
variety of owners, beginning in the
mid-1920s. The early luminaries of
the Mexican popular arts renaissance
treasured this piece, which was first
shown at the Metropolitan Museum
in New York at the 1930 *Mexican
Arts* exhibition, designed by René
d'Harnoncourt.

Gourds have been used by artisans
throughout Mexican history. Their
multitude of shapes has produced an
equal variety of uses, from the most
logical and enduring water vessels
and bowls to storage containers,
hats, rattles, and decorative objects.
Lacquering is one of Mexico's oldest
arts, and fragments of colored
gourds have been found in ancient
tombs. Gourds are still used in
many parts of Mexico as canteens
and, when cut into bowl shapes, to
hold hot drinks and gruel.

Preparing a gourd so that it is
dry and smooth enough to hold
lacquer is a long and time-
consuming process. The base coat,
usually made with chia seed oil, is
covered by powdered dolomite and
burnished. Then the ground
pigments are applied and burnished
to a brilliant sheen. The layer can be
thin, or it can be built up to
produce a thick coat. Burnishing a
gourd is extremely difficult because
of its curved surface.

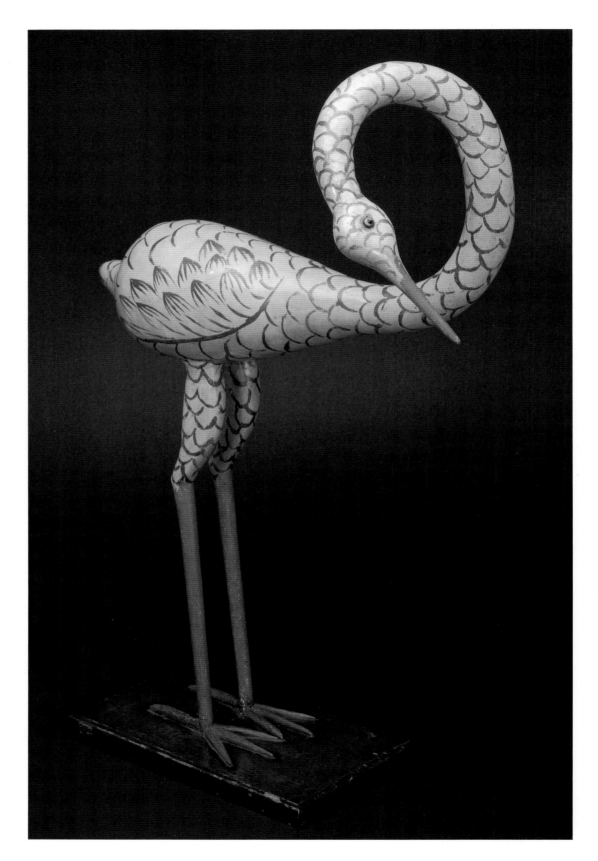

Plate 126
Manuel Jiménez
Wood Animals
Arrazola, Oaxaca
Late 1960
Painted wood, maximum height, 8″.
Destroyed by insects while in
storage in the early 1980s

These brightly painted wood animals
were made by a former adobe mason
and bracero cane cutter, who started
carving for his own pleasure.
Jiménez recalls that as a small boy
he loved tending animals. When he
was out in the fields he would often
fashion small figures from
streambed mud. He sees these small
toys he made as a boy as the
beginning of his art. When he
began carving wood, there was little
call for his work, aside from an
occasional need for a mask or a *santo*
(saint) in his village. He brought his
earliest pieces to a vendor in the
Oaxaca market and was soon
discovered by tourist shops. Jiménez
uses a *tsompanclé* wood, from a tree
found in the surrounding mountains.
He carves the pieces when the wood
is green and soft enough to work.
He uses a machete for roughing out
the animal and a knife for fine
carving. Legs, arms, and ears are
carved separately and nailed on.
Jiménez now uses chisels, awls,
rasps, and drills, but his early pieces
were simply carved. His animals are
always captivating. Their
expressions are imploring, and the
curves of their bodies suggest subtle
and interesting movement. With an
economy of machete strokes he
managed to transform a branch into
an engaging animal with an
abundance of energy. He painted
these animals with bright and
primary aniline colors. These pieces
are typical of his favorite palette in
the late 1960s. In addition to
animals, he carved large Nativity
scenes, sirens, Madonnas, and
devils. His highly acclaimed
carvings are collected
internationally.

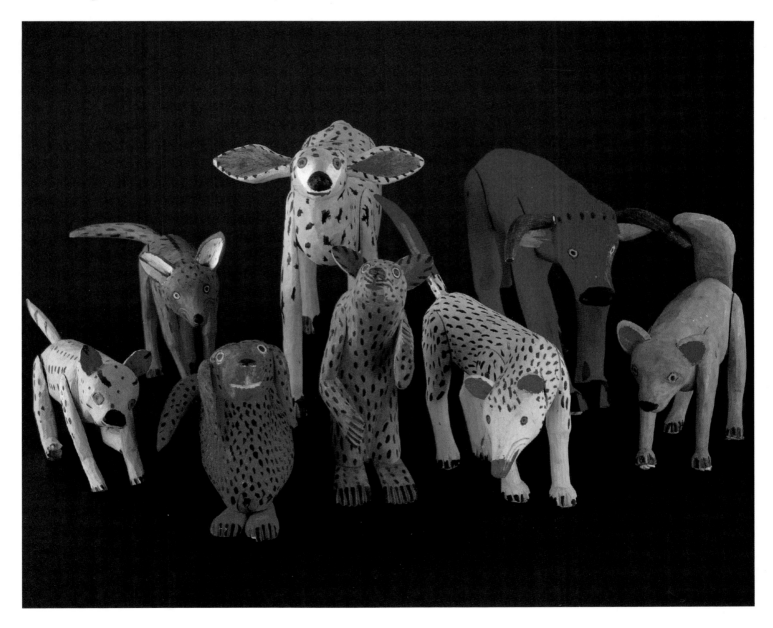

Plate 127
Panduro family
Fruit and Market Vendors
San Pedro Tlaquepaque, Jalisco
1930s
Single-fired, mold-made
earthenware, painted and varnished,
6¾ × 5 × 4″. MM and SAMA

In elaborate crèches, every aspect of traditional Mexican life is represented. Mexican families pride themselves on the size of their crèches, which frequently have over one hundred figures. Market vendors such as these are often present in Nativity scenes. Tlaquepaque artisans work all year to make these figures for the Christmas rush, and during November they bring their wares to markets throughout Mexico.

The Panduro family molds have been used for generations. The finer the original mold, the more intricate the figures. The painting of mold-made objects often determines their quality, and the Panduros are noted for their careful brushwork and attention to detail. Aniline dyes fixed with egg yolk were used as paint.

Today many artisans prefer airbrushing their figures with commercial oil-based or vinyl paint. The ceramic fruit banks in the foreground of this arrangement can be strung up on altars or used to save centavos. These vividly painted banks are made in every variety of delectable tropical and regional fruit.

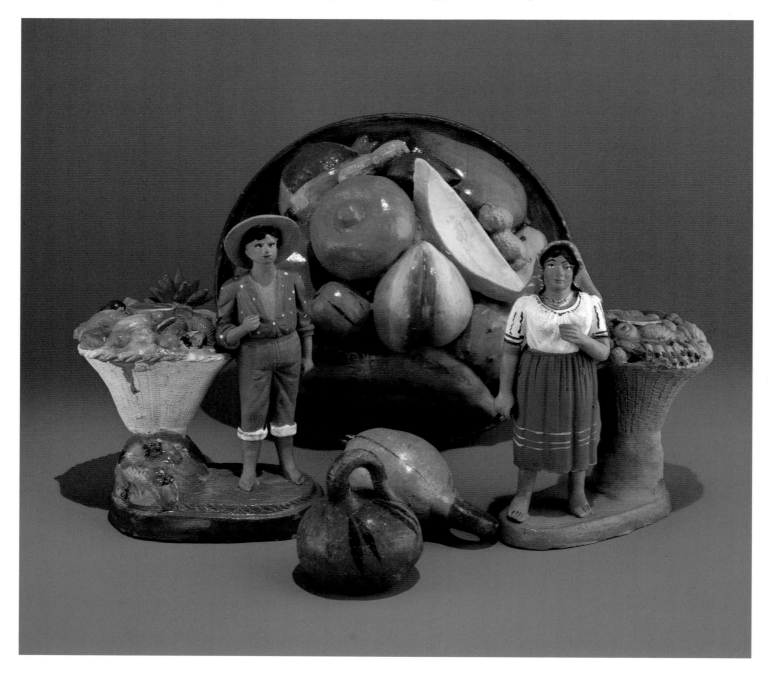

Plate 128
Wooden Containers
San Antonio de la Isla, State of
Mexico
1930s
Turned and incised wood, carved
bone handles and feet; left to right:
4¼ × 4″, 6 × 4″, 4¾ × 3½″. MM
and SAMA

These delicate polished and chiseled
wooden boxes are made in a small
village near Toluca. San Antonio de
la Isla has many craft traditions:
carving cattle-horn combs, turning
molinillos (chocolate beaters), and
making wooden boxes incised with
flowers, animals, and geometric
designs.

In the early part of the century,
these boxes were turned on primitive
foot-powered lathes and then incised
with chisels. The tops were inlaid,
and the bone knobs were whimsically
carved with birds, animals, and
faces. Today more sophisticated tools
have replaced much of the hand
carving, but the small boxes with
their tight-fitting lids are still used
to store modest treasures and
powders.

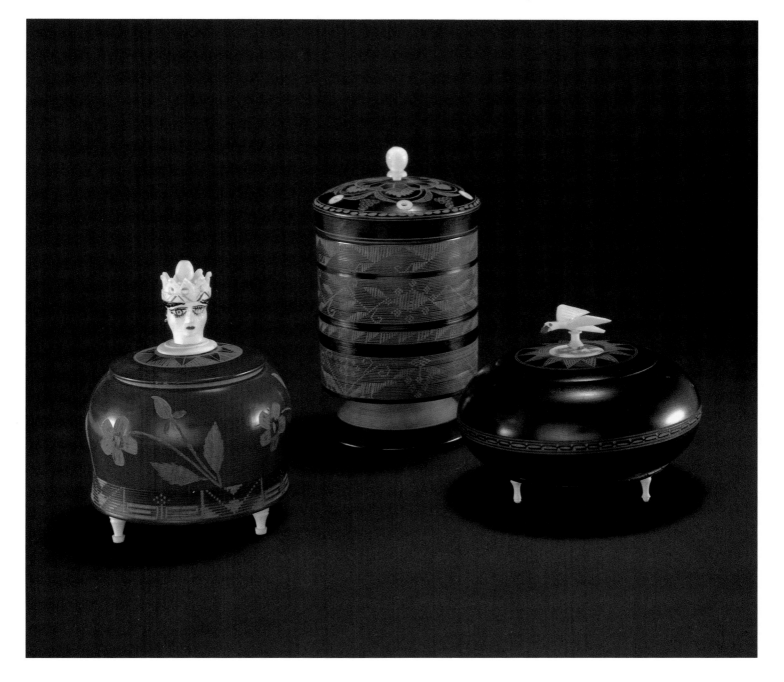

Plate 129
Pedro Linares
Alebriges
Mexico, D.F.
1968
Papier-mâché, paint, and varnish,
approximately 17 × 14 × 19″.
SAMA

Pedro Linares, Mexico's foremost
legendary *cartonero*, created
alebriges: flying dragons, winged
lizards, and mythical creatures that
leap and soar in a world of ultimate
fantasy. As a gravely ill young man,
Linares had a vision in which he
saw ugly and frightening things—
ominous clouds in the shape of
dragons with sharp teeth and
protruding eyes hurling themselves
at him. From this trip into eternity
alebriges were born. He transformed
his vision into exuberant paper
monsters that were intricately
painted and wildly outlandish. It is
more likely that Linares, a *cartonero*
by trade, saw a turn-of-the-century
Posada engraving portraying the
seven deadly sins as flying winged
creatures attacking a rich man who
reputedly died as a victim of his
own vices. Linares was fascinated
with the endless artistic potential of
this subject and probably needed a
change from his seasonal production
of *piñatas,* Judas figures, devils,
demons, and skeletons. With various
molds used interchangeably he
creates a large cast of fabulous flying
sculptures—each piece is unique.
The three *alebriges* that Rockefeller
owned, made in 1968, are very
early examples of these fantastic
Linares works.

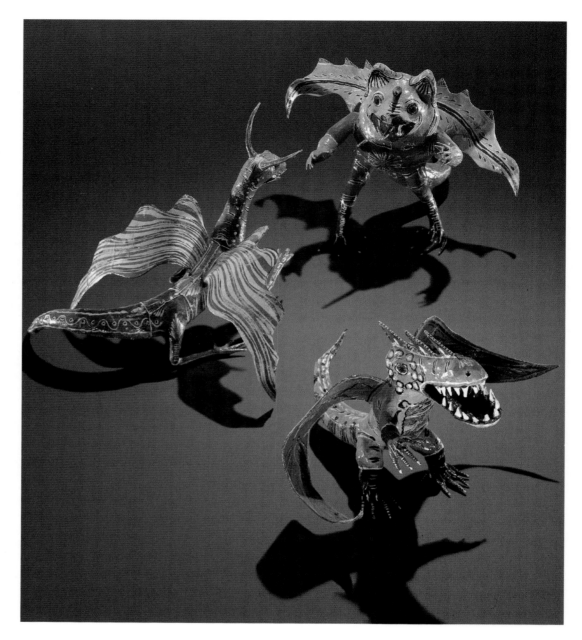

Plate 130
Cart and Animals
San Martín Tilcajete, Oaxaca
1970s
Painted wood and sisal; cart:
17 × 10 × 11″; oxen: 11 × 7″; tiger:
13 × 5 × 6″. SAMA

Driving through the Valley of
Oaxaca, one always sees carts pulled
by teams of oxen. They carry
enormous loads of wheat, corn, and
other crops to the pueblos from the
fields.

This miniature version of the cart
is quite realistic with the exception
of the cargo: two oversize men
restraining a tiger placed there to
make a humorous photograph. The
carts always appear to be enormous
hand-built toys with very basic
construction and joinery making
them easy to load and unload. The
oxen yoke is a miniature of one
Rockefeller bought in the Ocotlán
market, where beasts of burden and
other animals are sold and bartered.

San Martín Tilcajete has become
an important center for carvers in
the Oaxaca valley. They developed
this craft following the success of
Manuel Jiménez.

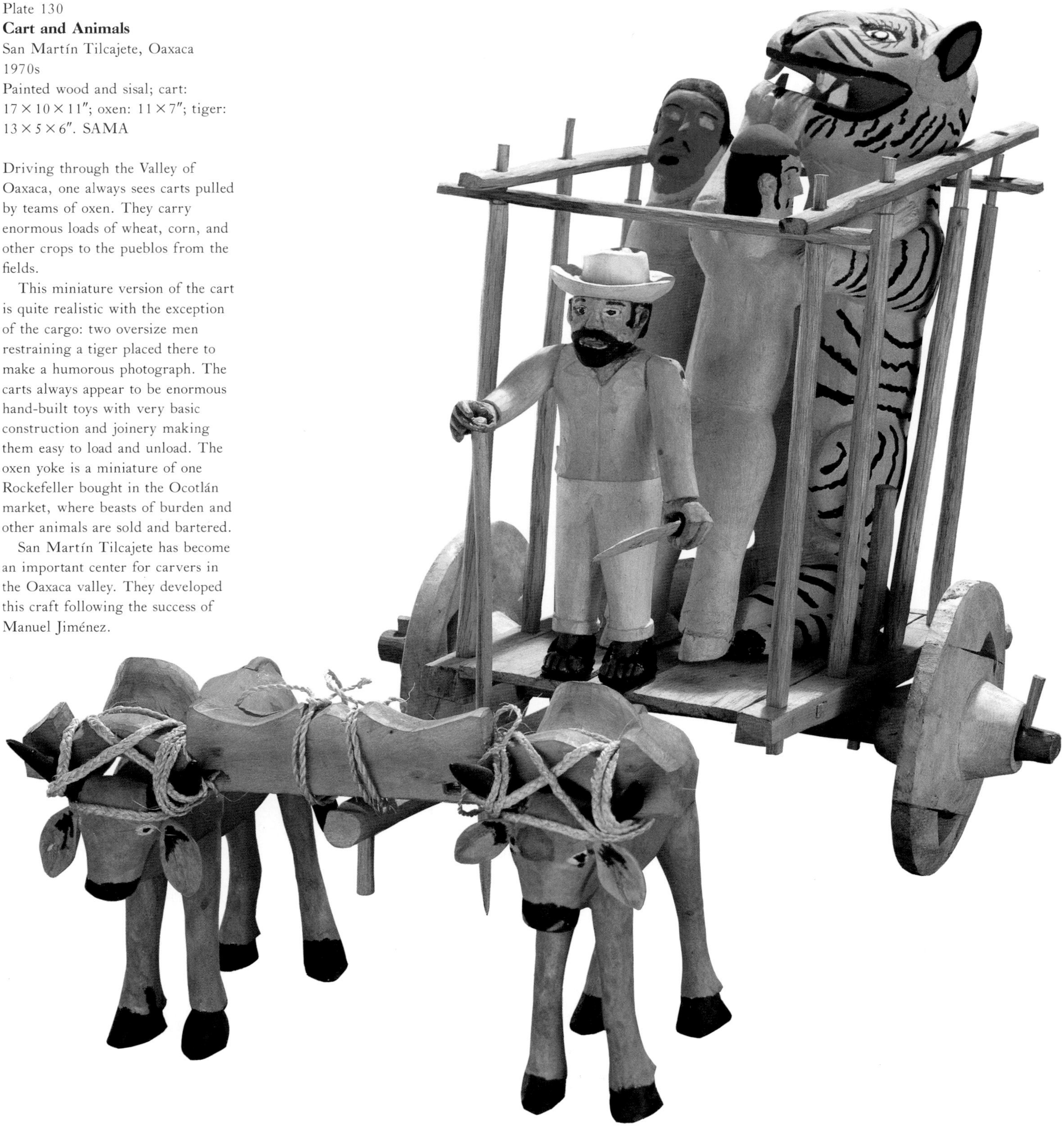

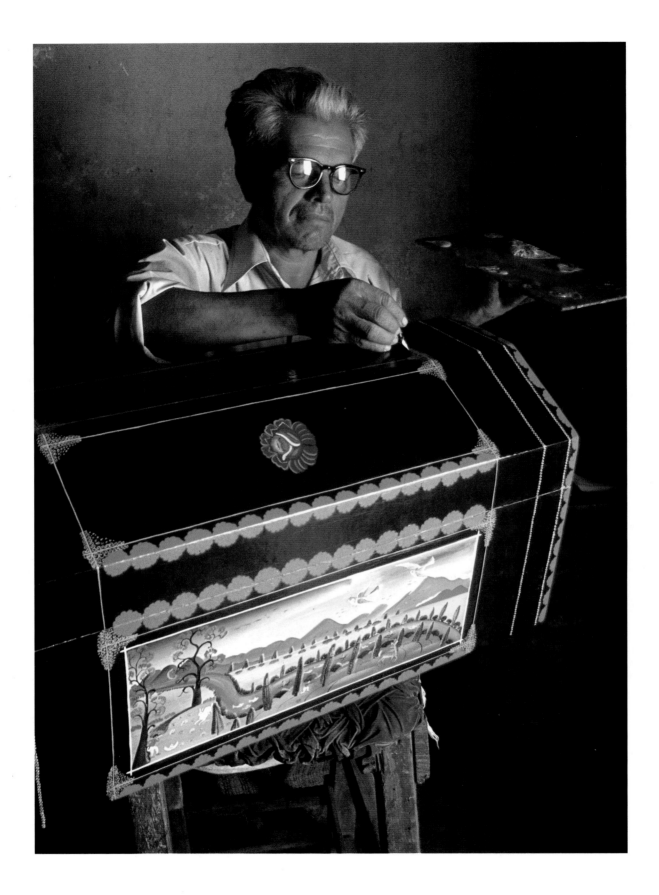

The Mexican Folk Artist

Their hands model the face of Mexico.
　　　　—Rafael Carillo Aspeitia[1]

From his first trip to Mexico in 1933 to his last visit in 1978, Rockefeller always was profoundly moved by the creativity of the folk artists he encountered. He never lost sight of the human hand and social history involved in each piece that he collected. His photographic recall of pieces he had discovered nearly fifty years earlier brought back a wealth of memories of remote villages, marketplaces, and artisans.

Folk artists are still found all over Mexico. They live and work in the bustling cities, regional market towns, and in thousands of small peasant villages throughout the republic. They are young and old, male and female, mestizo and Indian. They are almost always desperately poor. Despite their low economic status, these artists frequently are shown great respect, mainly because they are recognized as vital links between the past and the present and are able to fit important traditional customs into contemporary settings.[2] For the outside world, folk artists are "brokers" of Mexican culture and are largely responsible for presenting images of Mexico as varied as the country itself.

Since Mexican folk artists play to many different audiences and respond to a wide variety of needs, their art is enormously diverse, ranging from the mundane to the exotic, from the ephemeral to the enduring. It is eaten, paraded, broken intentionally, worshiped, adorned, cursed, and burned. "Their objects elicit fear, loathing, love, humor, anger, hate, envy, and a host of other feelings. They always demand and usually receive strong emotional

Alfonso Jiménez, contemporary Olinalá lacquerware artist, decorating a chest. The stylized pastoral landscape shows a fish-filled river surrounded by rabbits and deer (now mainly hunted out). Doves fly overhead as men work and rest nearby; the rugged mountains surrounding Olinalá are seen in the distance. It takes an artist several weeks to decorate a chest such as this one. Olinalá, Guerrero, 1976

participation."[3] Although incorrectly described as being detached from their work aesthetically, Mexican folk artists, like all artists, place strong value on their art and are concerned with its effect on others.

Dr. Atl, a pioneer in the study of Mexican folk art and himself a painter, describes some of the anguish of creation in the life of the potter Zacarias Jimón:

Ascetic, with large bones, strong hands, and jutting jaw, with a wide mouth and features that express continuous concentration. He tells me "I paint because there is something inside that makes me produce in travail . . . my own wish is that I could give away the pots I decorate instead of selling them. One's hands are tied when a piece is commissioned. This thing that is a painting should remain a thing meant for one only, so that whoever likes what has been done may carry it away free."[4]

Since most folk artists live in close-knit communities, amid those who buy and use their products, they are constantly subject to local criticism. Just as the work of Aztec folk artists reflected upon their moral lives and reputations within the community, the same judgments are often levied upon contemporary folk artists. A weaver whose cloth is loose and uneven will be judged as having a disorganized life. A potter who makes objects that are not balanced is likely to be out of balance in other ways. By contrast, a good folk artist is someone who is in harmony with himself and the surrounding world.

Anxieties over "doing the job right" are also commonly vented by folk artists in Mexico. Consider a traditional artisan from Patamban, Michoacán, who makes paper-thin wax floral arrangements for the church:

As the day approaches, and as I am getting behind in my work, I start worrying and can't sleep. In the middle of the night I think up an arch. Should the top be pointed or squared off? Should the circles on the sides be larger or smaller? In my mind I make the changes, then I go back to my original design, and then I start making changes all over again.[5]

Most folk artists in Mexico today are part-time specialists who spend most of their time carrying out duties not related directly to folk art production. Many are peasant farmers who spend their days in the fields. Some are herdsmen, housewives, carpenters, brick masons, and other tradesmen. Mask-maker Javier Olivares, for example, works as postmaster in the small Nahuatl-speaking village of Atliaca, Guerrero, and from time to time he picks up extra money working in a nearby brick factory. For these part-time specialists, folk art offers an escape from a tedious and monotonous life-style and an opportunity to express devotion to a saint, to vent frustrations, and to supplement meager incomes. More important, it is a way for people of modest incomes to participate in the ceremonial and ritual life of the community through traditionally accepted means. Most often, these artists produce objects for local consumption and frequently for no cost. Their motivation derives from the desire to please a village saint or to satisfy the wishes of their children and the needs of their community. For the most part very conservative artistically, these artists adhere closely to traditional forms and generally work within the boundaries of acceptability established by the community.[6]

Other Mexican folk artists are full-time specialists who use their craft as a main source of financial support for themselves and their families. Herón Martínez, the famous potter from Acatlán, Puebla, is a good example of this type of artist. In some cases, these artists evolved from part-time specialists primarily for economic reasons. Generally, they have a broader world view than their part-time relatives. Their motivation is largely economic, and their artistic response is mainly to a market outside their local area. In the Valley of Oaxaca, folk artists who once responded almost exclusively to local needs are now producing items almost exclusively for outsiders. It is highly probable that folk artists such as woodcarver Manuel Jiménez and the Aguilar family of ceramists have not made folk art for Mexican consumption in years, much less for use in their own small communities. Instead, their highly original objects are sold to foreign visitors or shipped to shops all over the world.

Both of these groups are folk artists, although they are working for different reasons and motivated in different ways. For the first group, motivation is local, strongly traditional, and accurately reflects the values and standards of the community in which they live and work. The second group is motivated to a great extent by external economic forces and have more readily

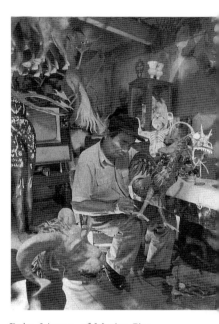

Pedro Linares, of Mexico City, decorating one of his *alebriges*, 1976. Finished and unfinished paper figures in every corner and on every surface give the room a fantastical aura, reflecting the full range of Linares' creativity

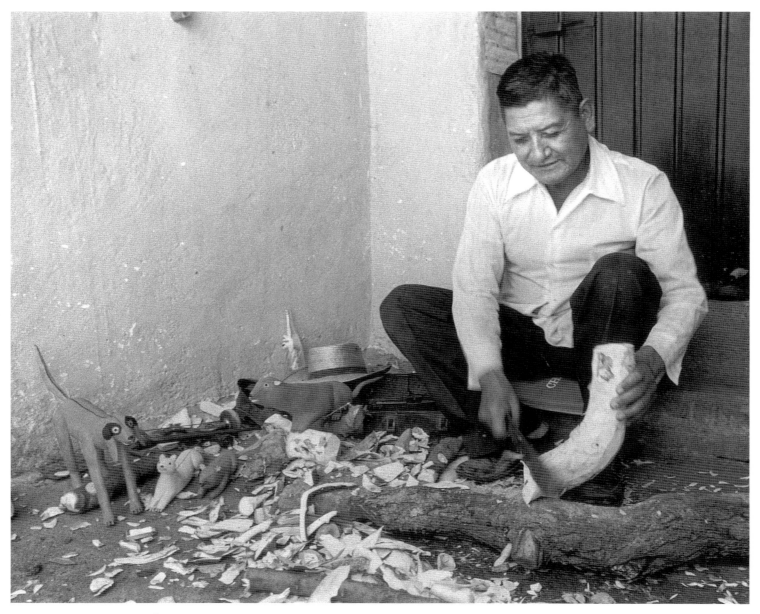

Manuel Jiménez, woodcarver of
Arrazola in the Valley of Oaxaca,
carving one of his wooden animals,
1977. After carving the animals out
of poplar or cedar wood, Jiménez
paints them with vivid dyes.
Rockefeller collected many of his
pieces, which unfortunately were
destroyed by insects while in storage

adapted their work to meet outside demands. Both groups exemplify how folk art is used as a mechanism to cope with social, religious, and economic conditions and pressures inside and outside the community.[7]

Folk artists draw their inspiration from the world around them and therefore can provide insightful clues to the nonmaterial culture of the area. Candelario Medrano, the late eccentric figural ceramist from Jalisco, explained:

> *The animals come from stories that my grandmother and grandfather told me when I was an esquincle (small child). The yellow animal with the lumpy mane and metates (grinding stones) and petates (mats) sticking to its side is a bad nahual (spirit). During the day it is a person, but at night it turns into a witch and steals things from peoples' kitchens.[8]*

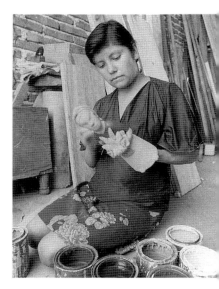

Josefina Aguilar of Ocotlán painting one of her clay dolls, 1977

Josefina Aguilar of Ocotlán de Morelos, Oaxaca, and her family draw inspiration from the rites of passage in their small village to create the colorful ceramic weddings, religious processions, and funerals for which they are now famous worldwide.

Frequently, there is a strong division of labor among folk artists, especially in Indian Mexico. Women who care for children and maintain the household while their husbands work in the fields often engage in folk art activities such as pottery production and weaving, both of which can be done within a family's courtyard. Traditionally, women have always woven on back-strap looms, but in communities where Spanish upright looms are used, weaving is done more frequently by men. In the Nahua community of Zacualpa, Guerrero, pottery production is shared by both sexes, but certain steps of production are performed exclusively by either men or women. Zacualpan men gather the clay and wood for firing, and the women do the actual forming, burnishing, and firing. Both men and women take pottery to market to sell.[9]

Mexican folk artists learn their art and skills from a variety of sources. Some folk artists are self-taught, but the incidence of this seems to be rare. In more traditional communities, folk art skills are passed on from mother to daughter, father to son. Children begin to learn the crafts of their parents early, sometimes making practice pieces as soon as they can manipulate the medium. Unlike our own society, in which children's activities differ greatly in kind from those of their parents, in rural Mexico, the difference is mainly one of degree. A child who is learning a craft is not expected to do adult-level production but is expected to engage in the same activity. As the child grows older, expectations rise. One weaver from the Tzotzil village of San Pedro Chenalho, Chiapas, recalls her own socialization as a folk artist:

> *When I was about fifteen, I began to use the spindle. . . . "Do it this way," my mother would say. "Don't make it too soft or too hard." When my spindle didn't turn right she would hit me with it. . . . My mother would say, "Where did you come from, woman, that you don't know how to handle your spindle? Women have to learn. You'll probably have a strict mother-in-law who knows how to weave very well and she'll scold you. She'll hit you on the head with the spindle and whorl if you don't know how to use them."[10]*

In other cases, folk art socialization takes place through lengthy apprenticeship. Candelario Medrano credits his folk skills to his tutelage with folk artist Julio Acero:

> *When I was a little boy I was adopted by Julio Acero, the best toy maker in Santa Cruz. The Señor taught me to make toy whistles, animals and roosters. Before dawn during the month before big holidays, I would take the Señor's burro to get the clay nearby. When I returned, I would spread the clay on the street in front of the Señor's house. In this way, with one day's street traffic, the clay would be broken down enough that by the next morning it could be sifted and mixed with water for the day's clay supply. To this day some potters still place their fresh clay from nearby mines in the street to be broken down by cars and trucks, as well as by foot and cart traffic.*
>
> *The wet clay I mixed first with my bare feet and worked in small sections by kneading it with my hands. The Señor taught me to form the figures of people and animals by hand. The faces we made with old molds which the Señor's father had used before him. When we finished making the figures, we put them inside to dry slowly in the shade. We used to use* leña *(firewood) and* ocote *(highly resinous pine chips that burn clean) for fueling the kiln, but now we use dried cow manure and old rubber tires to fire the clay for one or two hours. Yes, the wood is very scarce and expensive now.[11]*

An important and unexplored area of folk art socialization is that which takes place through regional jails. All over Mexico, prisoners must pay for a

An Aguilar child at work on a small figure, Ocotlán, 1977. Children of artisans begin working as soon as they can manipulate the material comfortably

large portion of their own keep and often do so through the production of folk art, an activity that is learned within the jail from other inmates. Prisoners in Tlapa, Guerrero, make baskets and rush-covered bottles; those in jail in Tehuantepec, Oaxaca, weave hammocks in a style made famous in that area. As early as the late nineteenth century, prisoners in the colonial jail of San Juan de Ulúa, Veracruz, were expertly carving finely detailed scenes on coconut shells. Often these magnificent objects were used as ex-votos depicting the prisoner's crime and showing an appeal to a saint or the Virgin for forgiveness. In some cases, artistic knowledge acquired while in jail is taken back to one's village, where it is introduced and becomes a significant factor in the local folk art scene and economy.

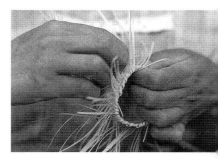

The hands of a Tlaxiaco woman weaving a basket, October 1978

Folk art is often called "anonymous" art, since most traditional folk artists prefer not to sign their names to their work, either because they simply cannot do so or, more likely, because it is not customary. Members of an artist's community, however, easily pick out the work of individual artists by the way facial features are executed, the formation of handles on the sides of a pot, or the manner in which paint is applied to the surface of a gourd. Although no written signatures are usually present, pieces are signed in other ways, allowing them to be identified community-wide as the work of a particular artist.[12]

Although the Mexican folk artist is under constant siege by an increasingly industrialized society that belches forth mass-produced, impersonal objects twenty-four hours a day, he has been amazingly tenacious. While plastics replace clay, synthetic fibers are woven instead of natural ones, and tinsel sequins instead of berries and seeds are applied to costumes, folk artists in Mexico continue to interact vigorously with the society in which they live and in their own unique ways chronicle their time for us to enjoy. Perhaps more than any other group, they mold, carve, and paint the face of Mexico.

Notes

ROCKEFELLER THE COLLECTOR

1. Douglas Newton, *Masterpieces in Primitive Art* (New York: Alfred A. Knopf, 1978), p. 20.

2. Joe Alex Morris, *Nelson Rockefeller: A Biography* (New York: Harper and Row, 1960), p. 75.

3. Nelson A. Rockefeller, "The Governor Lectures on Art," *The New York Times Magazine*, 9 April 1967.

4. *Masterpieces of Modern Art* (New York: Hudson Hills Press, 1981), p. 13.

5. Bland Blackford, *Bassett Hall, the Williamsburg Home of the Rockefeller Family* (Williamsburg: The Colonial Williamsburg Foundation, 1984), p. 24.

6. Morris, *Rockefeller: A Biography,* p. 73.

7. Abby Aldrich Rockefeller to Nelson A. Rockefeller, 1928, Rockefeller Archive Center, North Tarrytown, N.Y.

8. Mexican Arts Association, Inc., Certificate of Incorporation, Rockefeller Archive Center, North Tarrytown, N.Y.

9. Ibid.

10. *Masterpieces of Modern Art,* p. 5.

11. Francine du Plessix, "Anatomy of a Collector: Nelson Rockefeller," *Art in America* 2 (1965), p. 44.

12. Ibid.

13. Bertram D. Wolfe, *The Fabulous Life of Diego Rivera* (New York: Stein and Day, 1969), p. 302.

14. Ibid., p. 311.

15. Ibid., p. 323.

16. Nelson A. Rockefeller to Diego Rivera, April 1933, Rockefeller Archive Center, North Tarrytown, N.Y.

17. Wolfe, *Fabulous Life of Diego Rivera*, p. 322.

18. Rockefeller, "The Governor Lectures on Art."

19. Rockefeller to Rivera, April 1933, Rockefeller Archive Center.

20. Amy Conger, *Edward Weston in Mexico, 1923–26* (Albuquerque: University of New Mexico Press, 1983), p. 21.

21. Edward Weston, *The Daybooks*, ed. Nancy Newhall, 2 vols. (Millerton, N.Y.: Aperture, 1973), Vol. I, p. 187.

22. Daniel Rubín de la Borbolla, *Arte Popular Mexicano* (Mexico: Fondo de Cultura Económica, 1974), p. 274.

23. Frances Toor, *Mexican Popular Arts* (Mexico: Frances Toor Studios, 1939), p. 11.

24. Weston, *Daybooks*, Vol. I, p. 130.

25. Telephone interview with Sarah d'Harnoncourt, 25 March 1987.

26. Weston, *Daybooks*, Vol. I, p. 172.

27. Jean Charlot, *The Mexican Mural Renaissance, 1920–1921* (New Haven: Yale University Press, 1963), p. 29.

28. René d'Harnoncourt, *Mexican Arts* (Portland, Maine: Southworth Press, 1930), p. XI.

29. Interview with Mildred Constantine, April 1987, New York.

30. Ibid.

31. Charles R. Richards to Thomas B. Appleget, 23 May 1928, Rockefeller Archive Center, North Tarrytown, N.Y.

32. Newton, *Masterpieces in Primitive Art*, p. 20.

33. Essay by Rockefeller, November 1978, Rockefeller Archive Center, North Tarrytown, N.Y. Previously unpublished, this essay now appears in its entirety as the Foreword of this book, pp. 13–19.

34. Ibid.

35. Ibid.

36. William Spratling, *File on Spratling: An Autobiography* (Boston: Little, Brown, 1967).

37. Carlos Espejel, *The Nelson A. Rockefeller Collection of Mexican Folk Art* (San Francisco: Chronicle Books and the Mexican Museum, 1986), p. 3.

38. Ibid.

39. Interview with Mary C. Rockefeller, New York, April 1987.

40. Espejel, *Rockefeller Collection of Mexican Folk Art*, p. 3.

41. Carl Fox, *The Nelson A. Rockefeller Collection of Mexican Folk Art* (New York: The Museum of Primitive Art, 1969).

42. Wolfe, *Fabulous Life of Diego Rivera*, p. 377.

43. Essay by Rockefeller, November 1978. See note 32.

44. Ibid.

45. Ibid.

46. Du Plessix, "Anatomy of a Collector," p. 27.

47. Rockefeller to Rivera, April 1933, Rockefeller Archive Center.

48. Ibid.

49. Newton, *Masterpieces in Primitive Art*, p. 19.

50. James R. Mellow, "Rocky as a Collector," *The New York Times Magazine*, 18 May 1969.

51. Interview with Laurance Rockefeller, New York, April 1987.

52. Du Plessix, "Anatomy of a Collector," p. 27.

53. Ibid., p. 46.

54. Ibid., p. 27.

55. Malcolm N. Carter, "Nelson Rockefeller: 'I know exactly what I like,'" *ARTnews*, May 1978, p. 115.

56. Espejel, *Rockefeller Collection of Mexican Folk Art*, p. 4.

THE COLLECTION

1. Katherine Anne Porter, *Outline of Mexican Arts and Crafts* (Los Angeles: Young and McCallister, 1922), p. 4.

2. Nelson A. Rockefeller to Robert C. Smith, 6 July 1942, Rockefeller Archive Center, North Tarrytown, N.Y.

3. Interview with Susan Herter, Santa Fe, Spring 1987.

4. *20 Centuries of Mexican Art* (New York: The Museum of Modern Art and the Instituto Nacional de Antropología e Historia, 1940); Carl Fox, *The Nelson A. Rockefeller Collection of Mexican Folk Art* (New York: The Museum of Primitive Art, 1969); Annie O'Neill and Charlene Cerny, *Mexican Folk Art from the Collection of Nelson A. Rockefeller* (New York: Center for Inter-American Relations, 1984); Carlos Espejel, *The Nelson A. Rockefeller Collection of Mexican Folk Art* (San Francisco: Chronicle Books and the Mexican Museum, 1986); and Marion Oettinger, Jr., *Con Cariño: Mexican Folk Art from the Collection of the San Antonio Museum Association* (San Antonio: San Antonio Museum Association, 1986).

5. Frances Toor's 1939 catalogue, *Mexican Popular Arts*, has a photograph of Tulimán pottery taken by Manuel Alvarez Bravo, p. 64.

6. The Robert K. Winn collection of Mexican folk art in San Antonio contains a similar object. Unfortunately, it, too, is without certain provenance.

7. For a good discussion of Mexican furniture, see *El Mueble Mexicano: Historia, Evolución e Influencia* by Carmen Aguilera et al. (Mexico: Fomento Cultural Banamex, 1985).

8. Leopoldo Méndez et al., *The Ephemeral and the Eternal of Mexican Folk Art*, 2 vols. (Mexico: Fondo Editorial de la Plástica Mexicana, 1971), Vol. I, p. 335.

9. An excellent discussion of the history, description, and use of the sarape can be found in Ramón Mena's article "El Zarape," *Mexican Magazine* 4, Vol. II (September 1926).

10. James Jeter and Paula Marie Juelke, *The Saltillo Sarape* (Santa Barbara: New World Arts, 1978).

11. Chloë Sayer, *Costumes of Mexico* (Austin: The University of Texas Press, 1985), p. 51.

12. Méndez et al., *Ephemeral and Eternal*, Vol. II, p. 738.

13. Ibid., p. 739.

14. Annie O'Neill and Charlene Cerny, *Mexican Folk Art from the Collection of Nelson A. Rockefeller* (New York: Center for Inter-American Relations, 1984), p. 13.

15. Méndez et al., *Ephemeral and Eternal*, Vol. I, p. 337.

16. O'Neill and Cerny, *Mexican Folk Art*, p. 29.

17. Francisco Javier Hernández, *El Juguete Popular en México: Estudio de Interpretación* (Mexico: Ediciones Mexicanas, 1950).

18. Roberto Montenegro, *Museo de Artes Populares* (Mexico: Ediciones de Arte, 1948), p. 29.

19. Weston, *Daybooks*, Vol. I, pp. 172–73.

20. Jorge Enciso, "Painting on Wood in Michoacán and Guerrero," *Mexican Folkways* 1, Vol. VIII (1933), pp. 4–34.

THE MEXICAN FOLK ARTIST

1. Méndez et al., *Ephemeral and Eternal*, Vol. I, p. 10.

2. Marion Oettinger, Jr., *Con Cariño: Mexican Folk Art from the Collection of the San Antonio Museum Association* (San Antonio: San Antonio Museum Association, 1986), p. 27.

3. Ibid.

4. Charlot, *Mexican Mural Renaissance*, p. 28.

5. Fernando Horcasitas, "Mexican Folk Art," *National Geographic* 5, vol. 153, p. 654.

6. Oettinger, Jr., *Con Cariño*, p. 27.

7. Ibid., p. 28.

8. Lenore Hoag Mulryan, *Mexican Figural Ceramicists and Their Works* (Los Angeles: Museum of Cultural History, UCLA, 1982), p. 19.

9. Marion Oettinger, Jr., and Ted Warmbold, *Zacualpa Ceramics: Traditional Pottery from Southern Mexico* (San Antonio: San Antonio Museum Association, 1986).

10. Sayer, *Costumes of Mexico*, pp. 130–31.

11. Mulryan, *Mexican Figural Ceramicists*, pp. 17–18.

12. Oettinger, Jr., *Con Cariño*, p. 28.

Chronology

1908	Nelson A. Rockefeller born in Bar Harbor, Maine, on July 8, the third of five children, to John Davison Rockefeller, Jr., and Abby Aldrich Rockefeller.
1918–26	Attends Lincoln School, New York City.
1926–30	Attends Dartmouth College, graduating with a degree in economics. Elected to Phi Beta Kappa.
1930	Returns to New York to enter family businesses.
1930–31	Travels around the world. Meets Rosa and Miguel Covarrubias in Bali. Develops an interest in primitive and popular art and collects his first objects.
1932	Elected to Board of Trustees at the Metropolitan Museum of Art. Takes an active role in the Museum of Modern Art. Diego Rivera's Rockefeller Center mural project begins and is terminated.
1933	First trip to Mexico to buy paintings for the Museum of Modern Art generates what will become a lifelong interest in Mexican popular and pre-Hispanic art. While there, visits archaeological sites and the remote countryside; is introduced to Roberto Montenegro, William Spratling, Fred Davis, Frances Flynn Paine, and David Alfaro Siqueiros; and buys twenty-six cases of popular and pre-Hispanic art.
Mid-1930s	Meets René d'Harnoncourt, who becomes his mentor in collecting.
1935	Becomes a director of Creole Petroleum, a Venezuelan-based oil company.
1937	Takes first trip to Peru; brings back a planeload of weavings and artifacts. Takes a twenty-nation tour of Latin America to study economic, social, and political conditions.
1938	Made president of Rockefeller Center.
1939	Travels again in Latin America. Elected president of Museum of Modern Art; begins planning the first major show of Mexican culture in the United States.
1940	Helps organize a major exhibition, *20 Centuries of Mexican Art,* at the Museum of Modern Art. Becomes coordinator of the Office of Inter-American Affairs, which he established at the request of President Roosevelt. Resigns his directorship in Creole Petroleum. Organizes Rockefeller Brothers Fund, with his four brothers. Serves as American co-chairman of the Mexican-American Development Commission.
1944	Appointed Assistant Secretary of State for American Republic Affairs by President Roosevelt.

1945 Initiates the first Inter-American Conference of Problems of War and Peace, known as the Chapultepec Conference, held in Mexico City. Resigns as Assistant Secretary of State for American Republic Affairs. Active in the establishment of the United Nations.

1946 Becomes chairman of the board of Rockefeller Center. Receives Order of the Aztec Eagle from the Mexican government. Rockefeller Brothers establishes the American International Association for Economic and Social Development (AIA), which finances many nonprofit health, educational, agricultural, and social projects in Latin America.

1947 Organizes International Basic Economy Corporation (IBEC) to help raise living standards in foreign countries through new economic enterprises, concentrating initially in Latin America.

1948 Travels to Mexico in June with his family; Roberto Montenegro accompanies Rockefellers.

1954 Founds Museum of Primitive Art in New York with René d'Harnoncourt. (The museum opened in 1957.)

1959 Becomes governor of New York State. Is eventually elected to four four-year terms.

1960 Creates the nation's first State Council on the Arts.

1969 Exhibition of Rockefeller's Mexican folk art collection opens at the Museum of Primitive Art, New York. This is the first time the material has been shown in twenty-five years.

1973 Resigns as governor of New York State.

1974–77 Holds office of vice president of the United States under President Gerald R. Ford.

1977 Returns to Rockefeller family office in New York City.

1978 Embarks on a series of five art books on his major collections. Begins Nelson Rockefeller Collections, a business to reproduce major works from his collections. Travels to Oaxaca, Mexico, to reacquaint himself with Mexico and its folk art. Begins work on book about his Mexican folk art collection.

1979 Dies January 27, of a heart attack.

Glossary

Abrazo.   An embrace between males in Latin America. A form of greeting

Alebriges.   Fantastic papier-mâché figures made by the family of Pedro Linares. Probably inspired by a woodcut by José Guadalupe Posada

Ambiente.   Physical or spiritual environment in which a thing is found

Banderillero.   One who sticks *banderillas* (darts) into a bull's nape prior to the kill

Barrio.   A distinct ward or neighborhood of a city or town

Bolsa.   Bag or purse

Calavera.   Skull

Campesino.   A peasant or one who lives in the *campo* (countryside) and works the land

Cántaro.   Water jug

Cargador.   Porter or person who carries things

Charreada.   Mexican rodeo in which *charros* perform

Charro.   Mexican horseback riders who perform cowboy stunts

Colonias.   Ward or barrio of a town

Concha.   Guitar used by *conchero* dancers. Back of most of these guitars is made of armadillo shell

Conchero.   Dancer who dresses in romantic Aztec attire and usually performs at major pilgrimage sites and on feast days

Copal.   Incense made from pine resin, used in religious ceremonies throughout Mexico

Esquincle.   Derived from the Nahuatl word for "dog," used as a term of endearment for children

Estofado.   Technique of decorating sculpture whereby the carving is covered with plaster and painted and adorned with gold leaf

Ex-voto.   A votive offering, most frequently in the form of a painting placed on an altar to commemorate recovery from a grave illness or escape from serious danger. Very popular in nineteenth-century Mexico

Faja.   A belt or sash

Hacienda.   Large rural estate

Huipil.	A straight, sleeveless, and shapeless blouse of pre-Hispanic origin still worn by Indian women in some parts of Mexico
Huitzilopochtli.	Aztec god of war
Ikat.	A method of textile decoration in which select threads are wrapped and thereby separated prior to dyeing
Ixtle.	Fiber from the maguey plant, used primarily to make bags and nets
Juguete.	Toy
Leña.	Firewood
Lináloe.	A scented wood, rare today, used in lacquerware of Olinalá, Guerrero
Lotería.	Lottery game similar to Bingo
Matador.	Bullfighter
Matraca.	Noisemaker frequently used during Carnival and on Saturday of Glory during Holy Week
Mercado.	Marketplace, as well as the activities occurring there
Mestizo.	A person of mixed blood, usually Spanish and Indian. Also a cultural indicator
Metate.	Grinding stone
Milagro.	Miracle. Also name of miniature objects in silver, tin, and gold pinned on or near a religious image as an offering for a favor, such as miniature eyes for problems of sight, ears for hearing difficulties, and countless other forms, still used in churches throughout Mexico
Morral.	Bag
Nahual.	One's spiritual counterpart. Often an animal and frequently mischievous
Ocote.	Resinous wood used to start fires and make torches
Olla.	A clay cooking pot
Petate.	A woven palm mat used for sleeping
Picador.	Horseman who spears bull in nape to lower the head in a bullfight
Popote.	Mexican straw used for making brooms
Portal.	Portico
Promesa.	A religious pledge
Pulque.	A slightly alcoholic drink, made from the maguey plant, whose use dates to pre-Hispanic times
Pulquería.	A place where pulque is sold and consumed, frequently decorated with murals, altars, and other forms of folk expression

Quechquémitl.	A triangular shoulder garment of pre-Hispanic origin, still worn by Indian women in some parts of Mexico
Raffia.	A type of palm fiber used in the weaving of mats and baskets
Rebozo.	A multipurpose shawl worn by women in rural Mexico
Retablo.	A religious screen behind the altar. Also, paintings of saints and other religious figures placed behind church and household altars. Frequently painted on tin or copper
Sarape.	A rectangular garment with slit opening for head. Worn mainly by males
Sombrero.	A large hat
Tabla.	A board, or when used in reference to Huichol art, a large panel
Tastoane.	Masked dancer (and dance) related to Santiago (Saint James) and historical battles between Christians and Moors. Found in State of Jalisco
Tequitqui.	Works of art during the Spanish colonial period, which continued to show survivals of indigenous style
Tlaloc.	Aztec god of rain
Toro.	Bull
Tortilla.	A round flat bread made of corn or, less frequently, of flour. Basic diet of rural Mexico
Velación.	Vigil

Bibliography

Aguilera, Carmen, et al. *El Mueble Mexicano: Historia, Evolución e Influencia*. Mexico: Fomento Cultural Banamex, 1985.

Atl, Dr. [Gerardo Murillo]. *Las Artes Populares en México*. 2 vols. Mexico: Editorial Cultura, 1921.

Blackford, Bland. *Bassett Hall, the Williamsburg Home of the Rockefeller Family*. Williamsburg: The Colonial Williamsburg Foundation, 1984.

Bullock, William. *Six Months' Residence and Travels in Mexico*. London: John Murray, 1824.

Calderón de la Barca, Frances. *Life in Mexico: The Letters of Fanny Calderón de la Barca*. Garden City: Doubleday, 1966.

Carter, Malcolm N. "Nelson Rockefeller: 'I know exactly what I like.'" *ARTnews*, May 1978.

Cerny, Charlene. "Everyday Masterpieces." *The New York Times*, n.d.

Charlot, Jean. *The Mexican Mural Renaissance, 1920–1921*. New Haven: Yale University Press, 1963.

Codex Mendoza. Mexico: 1979.

Collier, Peter, and David Horowitz. *The Rockefellers: An American Dynasty*. New York: Holt, Rinehart and Winston, 1976.

Conger, Amy. *Edward Weston in Mexico, 1923–26*. Albuquerque: University of New Mexico Press, 1983.

Decaen (ed. pub.). *México y sus alrededores: Colección de vistas, trajes y monumentos*. Mexico, 1855–56.

Du Plessix, Francine. "Anatomy of a Collector: Nelson Rockefeller." *Art in America* 2 (1965).

Durán, Fray Diego. *Book of the Gods and Rite of the Ancient Calendar*. Norman: The University of Oklahoma Press, 1971.

Eche, Tseng Yu-Ho. *Chinese Folk Art in American Collections*. The Chinese Institute of America, 1976.

Enciso, Jorge. "Painting on Wood in Michoacán and Guerrero." *Mexican Folkways* 1, vol. VIII (1933).

Erb, Charles. *Nelson A. Rockefeller and Latin America*. N.d.

Espejel, Carlos. *Mexican Folk Crafts*. Barcelona: Editorial Blume, 1978.

———. *Mexican Popular Ceramics*. Barcelona: Editorial Blume, 1975.

———. *The Nelson A. Rockefeller Collection of Mexican Folk Art.* San Francisco: Chronicle Books and the Mexican Museum, 1986.

———. *Olinalá.* Mexico, D.F.: SEP-INI, Museo Nacional de Artes e Industrias Populares, 1976.

Esser, Janet Brody. *Máscaras Ceremoniales de los Tarascos de la Sierra de Michoacán.* Mexico City: Instituto Nacional Indigenista, 1984.

———. "The Persistent Memory: New Directions in Folk Art Studies." *Arte Vivo: Living Traditions in Mexican Folk Art.* Memphis: Memphis State University Gallery, 1984.

Fomento Cultural Banamex. *Mexico: XIX Century People and Landscapes.* Mexico: Fomento Cultural Banamex, 1981.

Fox, Carl. *The Nelson A. Rockefeller Collection of Mexican Folk Art.* New York: The Museum of Primitive Art, 1969.

Harnoncourt, René d'. *Mexican Arts.* Portland, Maine: Southworth Press, 1930.

Hernández, Francisco Javier. *El Juguete Popular en México: Estudio de Interpretación.* Mexico: Ediciones Mexicanas, 1950.

Herrera, Hayden. *Frida.* New York: Harper and Row, 1983.

Horcasitas, Fernando. "Mexican Folk Art." *National Geographic* 5, vol. 153 (1978).

Jeter, James, and Paula Marie Juelke. *The Saltillo Sarape.* Santa Barbara: New World Arts, 1978.

Kelemen, Pál. *Vanishing Art of the Americas.* New York: Walker and Company, 1977.

Linati, Claudis. *Costumes civils, militaires et religieux du Mexique.* Brussels, 1828.

Masterpieces of Modern Art. New York: Hudson Hills Press, 1981.

Mellow, James R. "Rocky as a Collector." *The New York Times Magazine,* 18 May 1969.

Mena, Ramón. "El Zarape." *Mexican Magazine* 4, vol. II (September 1926).

Méndez, Leopoldo, et al. *The Ephemeral and the Eternal of Mexican Folk Art.* 2 vols. Mexico: Fondo Editorial de la Plástica Mexicana, 1971.

Montenegro, Roberto. *Museo de Artes Populares.* Mexico: Ediciones de Arte, 1948.

Morris, Joe Alex. *Nelson Rockefeller: A Biography.* New York: Harper and Row, 1960.

Mulryan, Lenore Hoag. *Mexican Figural Ceramicists and Their Works.* Los Angeles: Museum of Cultural History, UCLA, 1982.

Navarrete, Carlos. "Prohibición de la danza del tigre." *Tlalocan,* vol. VI, no. 4 (1971).

Nebel, Carlos. *Voyage pittoresque et archeologique dans la partie la plus interéssante du Mexique.* Paris, 1836.

Newton, Douglas. *Masterpieces in Primitive Art.* New York: Alfred A. Knopf, 1978.

Oettinger, Marion, Jr. *Con Cariño: Mexican Folk Art from the Collection of the San Antonio Museum Association*. San Antonio: San Antonio Museum Association, 1986.

———. *Dancing Faces: Mexican Masks in a Cultural Context*. Washington, D.C.: Meridian House International, 1985.

———, and Ted Warmbold. *Zacualpa Ceramics: Traditional Pottery from Southern Mexico*. San Antonio: San Antonio Museum Association, 1986.

O'Neill, Annie. "Nelson A. Rockefeller: The Collector." In Carlos Espejel, *The Nelson A. Rockefeller Collection of Mexican Folk Art*. San Francisco: Chronicle Books and the Mexican Museum, 1986.

———, and Charlene Cerny. *Mexican Folk Art from the Collection of Nelson A. Rockefeller*. New York: Center for Inter-American Relations, 1984.

Porter, Katherine Anne. *Outline of Mexican Arts and Crafts*. Los Angeles: Young and McCallister, 1922.

Redfield, Robert. *Peasant Society and Culture*. Chicago: The University of Chicago Press, 1956.

Richard, Paul. "Gentle Strokes from Gentle Folks." *The Washington Post*, 19 November 1981.

Rockefeller, Nelson A. "The Governor Lectures on Art." *The New York Times Magazine*, 9 April 1967.

Rockefeller Report on the Americas. Chicago: Quadrangle Books, 1969.

Rubín de la Borbolla, Daniel. *Arte Popular Mexicano*. Mexico: Fondo de Cultura Económica, 1974.

Saarinen, Aline. *The Proud Possessors*. New York: Random House, 1958.

Sahagún, Fray Bernardino de. *General History of the Things of New Spain (Florentine Codex)*, Book 10. Santa Fe: The School of American Research, 1961.

Sayer, Chloë. *Costumes of Mexico*. Austin: The University of Texas Press, 1985.

Spratling, William. *File on Spratling: An Autobiography*. Boston: Little, Brown, 1967.

Starr, Frederick. *Catalogue of a Collection of Objects Illustrating the Folklore of Mexico*. London: The Folk-lore Society, 1898.

Teshe, Robert T. "What Is Folk Art?" *El Palacio*, vol. 88 (1982–83).

Toor, Frances. *Mexican Popular Arts*. Mexico: Frances Toor Studios, 1939.

———. *A Treasury of Mexican Folkways*. New York: Crown, 1947.

20 Centuries of Mexican Art. New York: The Museum of Modern Art and the Instituto Nacional de Antropología e Historia, 1940.

Walz, W. G. *Illustrated Catalogue of Mexican Art Goods and Curiosities*. Philadelphia: Edward Stern, 1888.

Ward, H. G. *Mexico in 1827*. 2 vols. London, 1828.

Weismann, Elizabeth Wilder. *Art and Time in Mexico*. New York: Harper and Row, 1985.

Weston, Edward. *The Daybooks*. 2 vols. Edited and introduced by Nancy Newhall. Millerton, N.Y.: Aperture, 1973.

Wolf, Eric. *Sons of the Shaking Earth*. Chicago: The University of Chicago Press, n.d.

Wolfe, Bertram D. *The Fabulous Life of Diego Rivera*. New York: Stein and Day, 1969.

Index

Photograph Credits

The photographs of the objects (which are designated as plates) were taken by Lee Boltin, unless otherwise noted below:
John Dyer: plates 7, 9–11, 13, 14, 37, 40, 52, 54, 60, 65–69, 74, 84, 86, 88, 89, 93, 94, 97, 101, 105, 110, 119, 120, 123, 125; Steve Tucker: plates 62, 124.

Credits for all other photographs appear below (numbers refer to page numbers):
Courtesy Mexican Museum, San Francisco: 32; Annie O'Neill: 6, 7, 8, 12, 16, 20, 24, 25, 59, 61, 65, 192, 195, 196, 197, 198, 199; Nelson A. Rockefeller: 15, 17, 18, 62; Courtesy Rockefeller Archive Center: 36, 49, 52, 53, 55; Charles Uht: 56, 57.